Global
Masculinities
and Manhood

Global Masculinities and Manhood

Edited by

RONALD L. JACKSON II

AND MURALI BALAJI

Foreword by

MOLEFI K. ASANTE

UNIVERSITY OF ILLINOIS PRESS

Urbana, Chicago, and Springfield

First Illinois paperback, 2013
© 2011 by the Board of Trustees
of the University of Illinois
All rights reserved
Manufactured in the United States of America
1 2 3 4 5 C P 5 4 3 2 1
∞ This book is printed on acid-free paper.

The Library of Congress cataloged the cloth edition as follows:
Global masculinities and manhood /
edited by Ronald L Jackson II and Murali Balaji ;
foreword by Molefi K. Asante.
p.   cm.
Includes bibliographical references and index.
ISBN 978-0-252-03651-4 (hardback)
ISBN 978-0-252-09355-5 (ebook)
1. Masculinity—Cross-cultural studies.
2. Masculinity.
I. Jackson, Ronald L., 1970–
II. Balaji, Murali, 1979–
BF692.5.G575 2011
155.3'32—dc23   2011044027
PAPERBACK ISBN 978-0-252-07965-8

To those who have taught us to be men
and to those courageous enough to stand up
and be men even when it seems impossible.

Contents

Acknowledgments

None of this is possible without God, who affords the possibility for any work I might accomplish. I give honor to him first. I dedicate this book to my father, Ronald L. Jackson Sr., for his spiritual and intellectual inspiration.

I am also blessed and thankful for my brother, Bruce Jackson, and his constant uplift and friendship. I would be remiss if I left out my mother, Sharon Prather, whose amazing fortitude, perseverance, diligence, and relentless pursuit of happiness almost single-handedly helped me become who I am today. Without her I am not sure I would truly know the relationship between love, respect, manhood, and masculinity.

Of course, I am ever grateful for the loving and unflinching support of my beautiful wife, Ricci Jackson, whom I have often called my "other rib." You have to know the Bible to get that one. She is truly my helpmeet and soul mate.

I owe many intellectual debts to those men who have directly or indirectly guided me in my thinking about culture, manhood, and masculinity. Those persons include my best friends Brad Hogue, Theo Coleman, Keith Wilson, Carlos Morrison, Ramone Ford, Wayne Gersie, and Torrence Sparkman. Other colleagues whose intellectual guidance has been a wellspring of inspiration are Henry Giroux, Richard Wright, Molefi Asante, Eric Abercrumbie, Ken Ghee, Michael Hecht, Eric Watts, Jamie Moshin, Mark McPhail, Reggie Brazzile, Wilton Blake, the late Jeffrey Lynn Woodyard, and my co-editor Murali Balaji. There are others, but too many to name. You too are appreciated.

Murali and I owe a special thanks to Joan Catapano at University of Illinois Press for her guidance of this project, and to all the copyeditors and staff at the press. Thanks again.

RJ

There are many people to thank, but I have limited space to share my full gratitude. I dedicate this book, along with everything I do in life, to my parents, my father Kodumudi and my mother Vijaya. My mother passed away before this book was published, but her spirit guides me every day.

I also couldn't exist without the support of Devi Ramkissoon and my siblings, my sister Lakshmi and brother Arvind.

I owe a lot of this book's creation to Ron, who has been my mentor and friend since I was a graduate student at Penn State. I also couldn't have gained the valuable intellectual perspectives I have now without the guidance of Matt McAllister, Marie Hardin, and Emory Woodard, to name just a few.

I also want to make this anthology a testament to all the men and women who have influenced my own masculinity. I think my conceptualization of manhood has changed dramatically in just the past five years, and I hope that I continue to learn more about what it means to be a man and what it is that encompasses my masculine identity.

MB

Foreword

MOLEFI K. ASANTE

Anytime someone says that we are living in a world of tremendous change we can readily say that such is the condition of human life. Yet in terms of intellectual critique, deconstruction, and critical inquiry we are truly undergoing monumental change in the discourse on masculinity. Ronald L. Jackson II and Murali Balaji have placed their new book, *Global Masculinities and Manhood*, at the center of this activity.

The election of President Barack Obama in November 2008 stretched the discourse about masculinity even more in American society. Indeed, Andrew Card, who had served in the administration of President George W. Bush, said in February 2009 that Obama was not dignifying the office of the presidency because he was photographed working in his shirt sleeves, that is, without his suit jacket. Clearly, Card had an idea of what he thought was the proper image of a president. The construction of white masculinity has certainly been a long process.

For more than five hundred years, the defining characteristics of masculinity have rested in the hands of European males, who essentially described masculinity in their own image. In tandem with the construction of a standard masculinity based on heterosexual white males was the disempowerment of African or Asian males in order to maintain control over the image and definition of the masculine. Through lack of discussion, omission, and distortion, this disempowerment made the masculinity of African and Asian men inaccessible.

Political and economic conquest creates the opportunity for the conqueror to define the conquered. There is an African proverb, "Until the lion is able to write its own history the hunter will always win." Definitions of masculinity by white males have dominated the interpretation of the discourse by referring to ideas of civility, protection, individuality, and assertiveness as characteristics of European society. While these men are just a small part of the human population, they have supplied the world's dominant image of masculinity.

In fact, the defining of white masculinity as the standard masculinity has cast other masculinities as erratic, off-center, or aberrations. The word had been given and all avenues for projecting symbols, meanings, and explanations were enlisted in the grand conspiracy to marginalize other forms of masculinity, while re-affirming white male masculinity as the definition of all masculinities. What was considered effeminate, undisciplined, or erotic had to be controlled by the established order.

What this book does is to seize some of the territory by enlisting new and different voices in a general assertion about the plurality and diversity of masculinities. I see the work of these authors as genuinely revolutionary in its implication for other disciplines, concepts, and constructed realities. While it is true that one book can only play a role in a much larger process to deconstruct the language of conquest, *Global Masculinities and Manhood* has staked out one of the most important aspects of an aggressive interpretation of progress and civilization and through a series of poignant chapters has opened up the discourse on masculinities in a profound manner.

It is cliché that American society is heterogeneous and multicultural, yet there remains a certain segment of our population, and indeed of the world, that has accepted as authoritative the European construction of reality as if that is the law. Thus, those who believe this doctrine have refused to engage in severe interrogations of comparative and distinct types of anything; they see any attempt to examine alternatives or other ways of seeing as disloyal, or maybe, anti-American. Obviously, in a world of nearly seven billion people there will be diverse interpretations and ways of *doing* masculinity based upon years of experiences and rituals of relationships; these will differ from region to region and from religion to religion. What the editors and authors of *Global Masculinities and Manhood* have shown us is that there are no static forms of masculinity, even in the Western world, where there has been an assertive strategy of imposing a model of masculinity. I do not hear anyone saying that this is only a Western way of approaching masculinity, because Muslims and other religious or cultural groups have their defining characteristics as well. It might be that because the West has been so successful in promoting its ideology of masculinity it is the most visible edge of the problem.

Clearly, the media and related institutions have advanced the Western idea of masculinity. Western masculinity has been dictated by the value system of rugged, confrontational individualism. The love affair with American western heroes and Australian outbackers has catapulted popular images of cowboys and lone adventurers as one end of masculinity. When we think of the fact that masculinity is a mediated construction, we can see all kinds of possibilities for rational discourse. Masculinity as an ideological tool to glorify conquest and imperialism was at the center of the disempowering of African masculinity. In fact, slavery itself institutionalized the idea of the scared, nervous, weak, rogue black man. Yet the contradiction was that the black male was also considered violent, oversexed (whatever that meant), and dangerous. Whites were apparently seeing the diversity of masculinities, but not the contradictions in their own view. These masculinities became contradictions for the whites because they saw how fluid these definitions of the blacks seemed to be when it came to whites dealing with their own prejudices and preconceived ideas about who black men were as enslaved people. We also saw the continuation of these ideas during the period of segregation when whites were uneasy about the fact that black males would be sitting in classrooms with their daughters. The image was of a fully matured black male sitting next to a young immature white girl. It was not an image of a black boy in school with a white girl. Fear of the black male, however, regardless of age, meant that even a young black male had to be seen as a threat to the constructions created by a racist society.

What I particularly like in this powerful book is the fact that the authors force open more widely the boundaries of the discourse on masculinities. Each author has discharged his or her responsibilities in this regard with diligence and deftness, leaving no stone unturned in their efforts to show the complexities of intersections between different forms of masculinity and race, culture, and religion. The homology between the nation and the masculinity of white males is explored and demonstrated to be one of the constructions that must be interrogated by a new cadre of intellectuals.

In the end, the authors are clear that to speak of the dysfunctionality of masculinity may be a critique of those constructing the reality. Are the Aboriginals of Australia portrayed as dysfunctional because of continuing colonial discourses in the media? What constitutes dysfunctionality for them? What are the masculine tendencies of the whites who took their lands? How do indigenous men, whose land and identity have been dispossessed, cope with their "loss" of manhood? How many people have lost an entire continent? What is the statement about white male masculinity in such episodes?

We find ourselves at a crossroads of history, when Western male triumpha-lism is being contested and exposed to competing notions that demonstrate how concepts of conquest, like imperialism, are no longer viable and sup-portable. Masculinities are now being constructed on the basis of global interactions and postcoloniality, although we are not quite there. This will open social spaces for other ways of discussing masculinity.

Global
Masculinities
and Manhood

Conceptualizing Current Discourses and Writing New Ones

RONALD L. JACKSON II

AND MURALI BALAJI

To the question about what masculinity and manhood really are, we humbly respond that they are cultural constructions. The velocity with which interdisciplinary researchers are willing to dismiss certain cultural masculinities from the ledger of appropriate, sustainable, normal, healthy, and progressive gendered identities is astounding. Those masculinities are then treated as unacceptable and rendered useless. The problem with this is not so much that ignoble, pernicious masculine behavior is instantly acceptable or compelling because of some relativist formula, but that these masculinities and these behaviors call for critical observation within their own global, historical, and cultural contexts. Persistent exclusion of selected masculine discourses leads to both marginalization and inaccessibility of those masculinities, thereby giving power to their volatility or simply leading to their invisibility. This has happened, in one way or another, to virtually every marginalized group masculinity throughout the globe.

In the early twentieth century, American journalist Katherine Mayo embarked on a personal crusade to report the "truth" about India and its colonized citizens (Sinha, 1995; Joseph & Kavoori, 2007). Mayo, who believed in the providence of Anglo imperialism, wrote pieces claiming to show the so-called barbarism and incivility of Indian society. She expanded her views of India into her well-known book, *Mother India*, which purported to represent the daily happenings of Indian life. Beyond making India a place where the odd, curious, and supposedly barbarous were routinely sanctioned and normalized, Mayo also emphatically argued that India needed the benevolent hand of the British man to guide the country into modern times. She did this often by noting the incapability of Indian men, whom she described as effeminate and impotent, to lead a country (Sinha, 1995; Joseph & Kavoori, 2007). Mayo derided Indian masculinity, writing that: "Given men who enter the world out of bankrupt stock, rear them through childhood in influences and practices that devour their vitality; launch them at the dawn of maturity on an unrestrained outpouring of their whole provision of creative energy in one single direction; find them, at an age when the Anglo-Saxon is just coming into full glory of manhood, broken-nerved, low-spirited, petulant ancients; and need you, while this remains unchanged, seek for other reasons why they are poor and sick and dying and why their hands are too weak, too fluttering, to seize or to hold the reins of government?" (Mayo, 1927, p. 32).

In her eyes, neither the Hindus nor the Muslims were capable of emulating the type of Anglo-Christian masculinity needed to civilize a vast nation-state (Mayo, 1927; Sinha, 1995). Through compatible discourses of this kind, Indian men became the Other, disempowered by Western subjectivities and prejudice and framed as the antithesis to how men and masculinity *should* be. This conceptualization of masculinity as both a biological and social construction, the latter assumed to be performed ideally by white men, served as justification for colonialism and the discourses that to this day shape representations of men and masculinities throughout the globe.

Mayo's depiction of Indian men was not uncommon at a time when white Americans and Europeans used exaggerated or false depictions of Other cultures as a way of justifying their colonial domination of nonwhite lands. Early social science justified the ideals of white European masculinity, while supposedly legitimating the inferiority of the peoples of Asia, Latin America, and Africa.

The "white standard" of masculinity, upon which manhood and masculinities were based in Western discourse, created notions of the Other. While early American scholarship on gender roles and practices lionized white masculinity, American and European popular culture reified these norms via distribution of racialized representations in stage plays, film, and radio beginning in the early to mid-1900s and continuing with the advent of television in the 1950s and beyond. The American film industry popularized images of white male protagonists and alternately vilified, caricatured, and marginalized men of other races and cultures. These images quickly became part of the global film landscape and were mimicked throughout the world in varying ways. Ultimately, these Others were vanquished by the ideals of white masculinity. Some scholars might maintain that race is a monolithic construction of the West that is only owned and perpetuated by the West; however, the marginalization and oppression of the racialized Other has been called by other names in other countries throughout the world, but remains as detrimental and debilitating as the Western construct of race. As Tierney (2006) argues, the historic representation of white (mostly male) protagonists and antithetical Others in U.S. media and beyond "helps to defend and perpetuate the conflation of White with human, to rationalize and camouflage cultural appropriation as a normal, harmless, natural behavior, and to promote a kind of supraethnic viability for Whites that is not equally represented for the Other" (p. 609). Ironically, these images of whiteness also shaped early masculinities studies, as the study of men became conflated with whiteness and heteronormativity. Perhaps these definitions of male and female, shaped by notions of Anglo-Saxon supremacy and Christian morality, were a prominent reason why male behavior and masculine identity was seen as rigid and fixed rather than as evolving and fluid. Though American behavioral scientist Alfred Kinsey sought to re-map human sexuality and articulate the fluidity of sex and gender roles in his research during the middle of the twentieth century, the conceptualizations of men and masculine identities continued to remain fixed upon notions of white heterosexuality. Popular culture representations glorified the alpha male, and the prevailing notions of masculinity became politicized in the West as a result of the discourse over the rights of women, minorities, and homosexuals (Butler, 1993, 2004; Rotundo, 1994). The dominant conceptualization of white masculinity as a civilizing force that prevailed in colonial, pre–civil rights discourse morphed into a reactive one that sought to suppress alternate forms of masculinity and manhood. As Ferber (2007) notes, the assertion of Anglo masculinity and manhood as the dominant form is a rhetorical and real response (through policy and violence) to the possibilities of different conceptualizations of men and masculinity. The threat of Othered masculinity and insistence to standardize maleness around whiteness led to numerous reactions in which Anglo manhood was seemingly threatened by nonwhite men. In India, Mayo's depictions of male behavior and her assumptions about the depravity of child marriage led to the British government passing the Child Marriage Restraint Act of 1929. In other countries, including the United States, interracial marriage was banned, citing both genetic and ideological justifications for racism. Even today, the historical structures that have continued to make white maleness and masculinity the ideal have led to reactionary policies grounded in Anglocentric supremacy. For instance, the conservative Australian government's decision to ban alcohol and pornography in Aboriginal territories was seen as an attack not only on Aboriginal sovereignty, but as an attempt to impose a colonial standard of masculinity among people who refused to adhere to Anglocentric notions of behavior.

Because of this turbulence, a fundamental shift took place in the scholarship of sex, sexuality, gender, and the study of the "-inities." Global masculinity studies emerged in the late 1980s and early 1990s with works like David Gilmore's (1990) *Manhood in the Making.* Additionally, publications like Robert Morrell's (2001) *Changing Men in Southern Africa* appeared. Morrell contends that the astronomical rates of violence and bloodshed in South Africa throughout the 1990s were a consequence of gender politics between factions that led to warfare. As part of London-based publisher Zed Publications' "Global Masculinities" series, in the same year Morrell's book was published, Bob Pease and Keith Pringle (2001) released *A Man's World? Changing Men's Practices in a Globalized World,* in which they challenged gender scholars to rethink how masculinity studies is explored. Rather than do comparative research using the West as an anchor, Pease and Pringle called for global masculinity research investigated within local contexts. While their book is still comparative, it explores men's practices within ten different countries, distinguishing masculinities constructed in First, Second, and Third World localities, with the West playing the role of minority among these multiple discursive formations.

Another progressive step toward explication of global masculinity perspectives emerged within the postcolonial discourse pioneered by Fanon (1965, 1967) and Said (2003 [1978]), which critiqued Western subjectivities. Thanks to the Foucauldian revolution and postmodernism, power relations and gender roles were no longer defined by the absolutism that had been legitimized and reified by years of heteronormativity (Woodward, 1996; Foucault, 2003). These critical interrogations helped separate manhood and masculinity, gender and gender roles, and sex and sexuality. The study of men and masculinity attempted to break away from essentialist definitions and into the realm of the postmodernist, feminist and postfeminist, postcolonial, and post-Fordist schools of analysis (Thomas, 1998; Whitehead, 2002). More importantly, critical scholars of masculinity have been able to question and debunk the so-called crisis in masculinity, a reaction by Anglocentric intellectuals to the rise of feminism and the new conceptualizations of manhood in the postcolonial era. As Edwards (2006) notes, "It would seem odd that the crisis of masculinity should at once be both so pervasive and yet so unsubstantiated. . . . Though there is some evidence to support the notion of demographically or geographically specific 'crisis tendencies' for some men, there is very little to endorse any overall masculinity in crisis thesis other than to say masculinity is perhaps partially constituted as crisis" (p. 24). The reconceptualization of masculinity in these terms, which correspond to Hall's invocation that identity is a production and a constant process, has greatly influenced feminist and queer theory. In contemporary cultural studies, definitions of men and masculinity have become more distinct and comparative, rather than homogeneous and absolute.

Yet while scholarship on masculinities over the past twenty years has helped to break down constructed walls of gender, sex, and sexuality and create new notions of gender as performative, one area remains largely problematic within the broad swath of masculinity studies: the pervasiveness of a Western-centric concept of men and masculinity. Global masculinity studies notwithstanding, there is still an insistence that global masculinity studies is nuanced and peculiar rather than ordinary and an accurate representation of how men live their lives in global, yet localized milieu. The Other, both as the constructed and performer of gender, still generally orbits around a standard of Western and/or colonialist normativity, which makes it challenging to break away from hegemonic constructions of masculinity in both mediated and inter-cultural discourse (Taister, 2000). To date, while there have been dozens of very important studies ranging from Taiwanese, Vietnamese, and Islamic masculinities to South African, Chilean, and Peruvian masculinities, there has not been enough scholarship in reframing manhood and masculinities across different cultural contexts to counterbalance the hundreds of studies, media images, and representations that concretized a white masculinity as the prototypical masculinity in the world. As a result, despite the important work exploring international or global conceptions of diverse masculinities, masculinity studies has generally become ghettoized by a Eurocentric paradigm of whiteness and its Others, the latter most closely associated with the representations and assumed practices of black masculinity (Fanon, 1965; Butler, 1993; hooks, 2003; Jackson, 2006; Ferber, 2007). The expansive gray area of how masculinity is communicated and practiced across cultures has yet to be fully interrogated and articulated in depth, showing that the radical changes in the study of masculinity and manhood in the West are merely the beginning of what should be a reconceptualization of what masculinity is in different cultural contexts and who men are (Gilmore, 1990).

Following the Foucauldian revolution in critical media studies, the study of masculinity has focused on the construction of manhood and its impact on gendered discourses. In the era of globalization, it has become easier to interrogate the images of masculinity on a global scale, from the mass-mediated representations of the "threatening" Arab to the "hypersexual" black man. Unfortunately, masculinity continues to be studied in a Western-centric context with an implicit focus on white American manhood as the standard by which masculinity is assessed. We realize these are contestable claims, merely contestable for no other reason than that they interrogate a privileged space.

Global Masculinities and Manhood aims to examine and deconstruct the history and politics of cultured masculinities within the contexts of the cultures from which they have developed. This anthology examines masculinity through the politics of identity, the cultural definitions of masculinity across the globe, and how masculinity is interpreted and practiced through discourse. The book follows three major themes: defining masculinity in the global sphere; mediated representations of masculinity; and the cultural practice of masculinity as both a local and global phenomenon. Drawing from diverse disciplines, the authors in this collection ask and attempt to answer the question: *What* makes a man *who* he is within his culture?

We start from the position that men and masculinity are, in many ways, mediated constructions that have created ideologies of power and division. To bring clarity to this argument, we must look at the historical framing of masculinity and manhood. Masculine identity was equated with strength, intelligence, and heterosexivity, and European writings on men and masculinity created an ideal type *man* and an ideal type *woman*. Men, through these mediated constructions, had to be masculine, while women had to be feminine. These binaries created by European philosophers and legitimized through images of the masculine—and through the ideological reinforcement of colonialism and the transatlantic slave trade—thus *made* men and women. As feminist scholars have repeatedly pointed out, the Enlightenment put gender roles in stasis, creating divisions that ignored the everyday realities of how gender was lived across the globe. Mediated representations of masculine identity and gender roles, whether valorized through the published word or mass distributed through art, photography, radio, television, film, and the Internet, have dictated how we see ourselves within our gender and with it. One can refer to Michelangelo's anatomically exaggerated image of David as the archetype of European masculinity; the chiseled body and the assertiveness of the sculpture indicate male conquest, an image re-created in mass-produced films and television shows and on the cover of hetero-sexualized magazines. Masculinity became an ideological tool that glorified the Crusader mentality of old Europe and the Manifest Destiny of the nineteenth-century American frontier. By the turn of the century, even as Europeans began to rethink masculinity, American white maleness became solidly entrenched in the absolutist definitions of manhood. Men were assumed to be aggressive and were therefore born to lead and conquer; passivity was unmanly and unmasculine. Even today, as we try to advance to solid representations and practices of masculinity across global contexts, there are traces of reversal of progress when we witness non-Western masculinities emulating the standards of white American maleness, a byproduct of both globalization and the increased effectiveness of women's rights movements in developing countries (Segal, 1990; Rotundo, 1994; Edwards, 2006).

Mediated representations have also become a framework for how we think about masculinity. The study of masculinity that grew from the cultural studies tradition remains grounded in the Americanist framework, making violence and hyper-heterosexuality ingrained in the expectations of how men should be (Kimmel, 1996; Taister, 2000; Katz, 2006). As Taister (2000) notes, cultural "masculinity studies" has become a code term for "heterosexual masculinity studies" (p. 275). Similarly, manhood, which has been problematized by the groundbreaking scholarship of scholars such as Butler, Woodward, and Thomas, is also a concept that cannot be easily explained by biology or gendered selves. The practices of manhood can be just as "gender bending" as the notions of masculinity and femininity, often localized to specific cultural contexts (Butler, 1993; Woodward, 1996). The discourses that have developed over the very ideas of a he/she dichotomy have influenced both the academic realm and the public sphere in the West, yet there has been very little attention given to how these discourses have formed in different cultural contexts. What we the editors and the authors seek to articulate is the different and contradictory domains in which masculinity is conceptualized, practiced, framed, and represented in diverse cultures. While we are reluctant to call our approach a cultural relativist one, we do emphasize relativity as key to interpreting masculinity in different cultural contexts.

The cross-cultural approach has been used before, especially in examining male sexuality and the performative aspects of gender (Gilmore, 1990; Butler, 1993). When we examine how ethnicity, class, gender, sexuality, and hegemony converge in localized domains, we begin to understand why the cultural production of masculinity and its cultural practice have been so difficult for masculinity scholars to articulate. One reason for this is that, as mentioned earlier, previous works examining masculinity within cultural domains struggled to negotiate with essentialist definitions of men and masculine identities. While these struggles have led to more expansive approaches of how we conceptualize manhood and masculinity, there seems to be a collective reluctance from cultural studies scholars to let go of the "traditional" notions (Kimmel, 1996; Thomas, 1998; Taister, 2000; Carrigan et al., 2002). This anthology interrogates the traditional, and through the representations of different cultural forms of men and masculinity, seeks to offer new paradigms of how we view gendered lives and identities in *specific cultural contexts*. We examine these interpretations of men and masculinity within their own domains, without the temptation of using the invisible standard that has made masculinity studies comparative and not contextual (Carrigan et al., 2002).

Looking at masculinities across cultures requires critical interrogations of the standards that we as scholars have relied upon in our own studies. Moreover, using different approaches, both theoretical and methodological, can help to better articulate the expansive and seemingly amorphous conceptualizations of masculinity throughout the world. Chapters in this volume seek to reframe masculinity studies to include global or what can be characterized as intercontinental perspectives that have rarely been included in current discourses. They do so by investigating masculinity firsthand, as it is practiced, or by stepping back and viewing it in more abstract terms. Hence, you will read essays that address African, Asian, European, Native American, South American, North American, and Australian masculinities and notions of manhood.

Overview of Chapters

The chapters are organized thematically. As you read through the book you will notice that the first half discusses how masculine identities become contested and negotiated spaces within the context of what can best be characterized as home, then even as this discussion progresses the theme gradually shifts in chapters 3 through 7 toward issues of power and agency. In other words, now that we have taken a glance into how masculinities can be displaced, disengaged, and disoriented, how do we make sense of what is happening? The reply in Mutluer's, Saona's, Nyawalo's, Roberts's, and Konishi's chapters is that we have to give critical attention to notions of power, politics, and agency. How is it possible to retrieve agency when the national politics combined with the cultural norms compete to define manhood in debilitating ways? Those five chapters address the query, and in the next two chapters (chapters 8 and 9) they are followed by a close examination of identity politics and agency within entertainment (in film and boxing). Each chapter offers sophisticated insights into how masculinity is conceived at a local level, and invites us to imagine the sociopolitical construction of those masculinities in situ.

This collection of original essays begins with an analysis of Jamaican masculinity. Maurice Hall's "Negotiating Jamaican Masculinities" begins by asserting that both gender and culture are largely intersecting discourses. Hall argues that the only way to make sense of Jamaican masculinity is to view it through the intersections of colonialism, race, and class. He locates U.S. male "leadership" models of masculinity within colonialist ideals that assume a universalized, idealized subject, and investigates sites of resistance among two iconic Jamaican figures, the late reggae artist Bob Marley and the late, former Jamaican prime minister, Michael Manley. Using these examples, Hall weaves together a deeply textured account of Jamaican life, and charts the construction of masculinity among three groups, the Rastas, rude boys, and mimics. Hall examines differential male and female socialization patterns, and like Mutluer's piece in this volume, argues that among the rude boys, masculinity is constructed through the use and control of public space; his discussion of the "yard" as a polysemic national marker is especially evocative in this regard. The essay ends with a discussion of the scholarly debate about the implications of the masculinities in present-day Jamaica.

Breaking the codes of "normal" meaning-making is the principal task of Bryant Keith Alexander's essay "Queer(y)ing Masculinities." Instead of simply discussing queer masculinities as those that diverge from so-called mainstream, conventional, accepted, or heterosexual masculinities, Alexander tests the limits of understanding what masculinity means or tries to mean. He insists that queer masculinities are those that are not only suspicious, resistant, or out of the ordinary, but are also those that elude while stabilizing meaning. In other words, at the moment we examine the *Rocky Horror Picture Show* or an online dating site we establish a set of assumptions regarding who people are; yet, we develop this interplay of subjectivities that presumptively iterates binaries without ever challenging how heterosexuality is nothing more than a construction of the masculine ideal. This chapter fits nicely at this point in the book because it lays the groundwork for later chapters. Alexander beckons us to not get too comfortable with our learned sense that we know what masculinity is. He turns our assumptions regarding masculinity topsy-turvy and forces us to recognize that whether you're a Rasta, rude boy, martial artist, womanizer, athlete, or soldier, masculinities are defined social constructions that vary across culture, context, and community.

Nil Mutluer's "Disposable Masculinities in Istanbul" is an ethnographic inquiry that examines the intersections of gender, ethnicity, nationalism, sexuality, and class interactions among Kurdish minorities who were victims of forced migration. These men and their families were relocated to the Tarlabaşı section in the center of contemporary Istanbul, Turkey. Mutluer not only carefully articulates the institutional forces that oppress this minority, but documents and analyzes, with the help of de Certeau, the counter discourses and tactics that the Kurdish minority use to subvert and resist Turkish nationalism. This is no small task, as these identities are formed and informed between these discursive frames: modern and traditional, urban and rural, and Kurdish and Turkish nationalist ideals. Using Mignolo's concept of "border thinking," Mutluer carefully lays out the various ways internally displaced Kurdish men negotiate their identities between these binaries. This is a gripping account of the ways in which masculinity is altered, fixed, transformed, and traversed in everyday life. Her analysis enables readers to comprehend the social structures that impinge on these men, while at the same time it keenly observes them as agents that contest and reshape traditional, national, and neoliberal formations.

Following this line of inquiry into national conceptions of masculinity, Margarita Saona in "Wounded Masculinity and Nationhood in Peru" offers a historical and literary analysis of the representation of masculinity in that country. Using a feminist psychoanalytic frame, Saona examines Peruvian literature to make sense of Peru's recent brutal past, which culminated in the confrontation between the Shining Path, the Tupac Amaru guerrillas, and the government-armed forces that resulted in 69,000 deaths. She posits that a homology exists between masculinity and the nation state. She reads the executions of indigenous Peruvian leaders by the Spanish as castration myths and traces these Peruvian castration myths to argue that they produce simultaneously a failed masculinity as well as a failed state. The failed nation and the failure of masculinity are rooted in the legacy of colonialism. She argues that resolving this oedipal dilemma would be a first step in resolving gender inequality and creating a more just nation.

Using a postcolonial framework in his essay "Postcolonial Masculinity and Commodity Culture in Kenya," Mich Nyawalo seeks to analyze the means through which tropes of masculinity and political power, which are manifested within the spectacle of commodity fetishism, operate within Kenya's contemporary neocolonial environment. He conducts a sociopolitical analysis of the different symbols of masculinity and power that have been implicitly and explicitly internalized within Kenyan society by asking the following questions: How have conceptions of masculinity and power been constructed in today's Kenyan society and how (or why) have they "evolved" from their traditional manifestations? What role does the Kenyan and Western media play in constructing new perceptions of manhood and power? And finally, how do these new perceptions reflect Kenya's economic and political position as a dependent "Third World" nation? Nyawalo addresses these issues by first focusing on the multiple facets and definitions of power (both at the macro and micro levels) that are manifested in neocolonial societies, before analyzing the ways in which they are represented in the Kenyan media and internalized by the society at large.

In an interesting follow-up on the idea of what is considered normal, native, and traditional about masculinity, Kathleen Glenister Roberts's essay "War, Masculinity, and Native Americans" draws on several years of ethnographic research on Native American ceremonials to examine the metaphor of the "warrior" in some Native American communities. This chapter discusses their views of "war," which are expressed both in military service and in other contexts within their communities (during powwow dance competitions, for example). Their perspective on war is at times an ancient one, and has impacted American history more than most non-Natives understand. Because this misunderstanding has through history often led to continued disrespect on the part of non-Natives, Roberts uses an ethnographic approach to explain the warrior ideal in the voices of those who fight to defend their homes and their cultural communities.

Much of what has been explored throughout this book looks at social practices that have shaped the norms around how masculinity gets defined and understood. In "Representing Aboriginal Masculinity in Howard's Australia," Shino Konishi maps the articulation of Aboriginal masculinity and its accompanying meanings within mainstream Australian culture during the last eleven years of Prime Minister John Howard's regime. Accessibly written, yet theoretically informed, the analysis is eerily resonant of the treatment of indigenous people in the Americas. Konishi demonstrates how anti-Aboriginal constructions of masculinity, informed by colonial discourses, cut across such varied institutions as journalism, politics, government, and the law. She argues that the trope of the dysfunctional Aboriginal man was deployed by the Howard government for its own political ends. Specifically, it functioned to justify the government's efforts to dismantle the rights of indigenous people, resist the global tide of decolonization, and elide wider social problems within the country. Starting from an anti-colonial frame, Konishi brings these discourses into a dialogue with masculinity studies in order to view indigenous masculinity alongside hegemonic white masculinity, a move that exposes how the social problems attributed to Aboriginal men extend to the whole of the country. Finally, she documents and interrogates how Aboriginal men respond to their demonization, and how they negotiate their own masculine identities in the face of a colonial culture that disparages them for their race and gender.

In contrast to Konishi's exploration of how Aboriginal masculinity is explicitly framed within national discourse, Murali Balaji critically interrogates the way the media implicitly frames Asian masculinities in his essay "Beyond Jackie Chan." Balaji sketches how the portrayals of Asian masculinity in Western media are informed by Eurocentric and Orientalist ideologies as well as the economics of identity. He shows how Western media producers frame Asian masculine Otherness as a means of enhancing the normativity of white European masculinity. Instead of industry producing culture, as Negus argues, industry produces caricature in order to uphold notions of Asian masculinity. The essay shows that creating alternative masculinities for Asian men in Western media has not been economically beneficial for media producers. Using the *Rush Hour* films as a case study, and guided by postcolonial and political economic frameworks, the chapter analyzes how images of Asian masculinity conform to or cultivate notions of Otherness. Clearly, the media is an entertainment utility much like sports. Both have broad popular appeal. Both enjoy the privilege of entertaining audiences while getting away with sliding signifiers.

Kath Woodward attempts to uncover some of these implicit and explicit signifiers and interrogates the socially constructed inequalities of racial masculinities as evidenced in sport. She argues, in her essay "Body Politics: Masculinities in Sport," that global sport remains largely dominated by the "men's game" in so many fields. However, the men's game does not necessarily invoke an unproblematic, hegemonic masculinity. The centrality of bodies and the measures of embodiment are part of the culture of sport, which offers such primacy to masculinities, but sporting masculinities are ambivalent and ambiguous too and are subject to the cultural transformations of other gendered identifications. Drawing on the works of Robert Connell, Michael Messner, and others, Woodward develops an argument around boxing as the embodiment of a normalized masculine activity that reifies a particular code of heterosexual gender identification.

In this volume we introduce the idea of masculinities in postcolonial and global contexts, trying to deliberately steer away from the definitions of gender identities and roles that have been largely shaped from a monocultural lens. The expansive gray area of how masculinity is communicated and practiced across cultures has yet to be interrogated and articulated in depth, showing that the radical changes in the study of masculinity and manhood in the West, or from any one cultural standpoint, are merely the beginning of what should be a reconceptualization of what masculinity is in different cultural contexts and who men are. Looking at masculinities across cultures requires critical interrogations of the standards that we as scholars have relied upon in our own studies. Moreover, using different approaches, both theoretical and methodological, can help to better articulate the expansive and seemingly amorphous conceptualizations of masculinity throughout the world. The essays in this volume seek to reframe masculinity studies to include global perspectives that have yet to be included in current discourses.

One of the most provocative aspects of this book is the way it vacillates between local and national conceptions of masculinity, as well as distinctions between masculinity and manhood. Moreover, while it takes an international look at masculinities, it is necessarily incomplete. No book can present every cultural perspective throughout the world, nor should it try to do so. Furthermore, there are multitudinous ways of defining "masculine" within any given culture, so naturally when we extend our focus to include multiple cultures there are going to be some voids. Nonetheless, we hope this book is a catalyst for additional research on cultural masculinities and manhood.

References

Butler, J. (1993). *Bodies That Matter: On the Discursive Limits of Sex*. New York: Routledge.

Butler, J. (2004). *Undoing Gender*. New York: Routledge.

Carrigan, T., Connell, B., and Lee, J. (2002). Toward a New Sociology of Masculinity. In R. Adams & D. Savran (Eds.), *The Masculinity Studies Reader* (pp. 99–118). New York: Routledge.

Edwards, T. (2006). *Cultures of Masculinity*. New York: Routledge.

Fanon, F. (1965). *The Wretched of the Earth*. New York: Grove.

Fanon, F. (1967). *Black Skin, White Masks*. New York: Grove.

Ferber, A. (2007). The Construction of Black Masculinity: White Supremacy Now and Then. *Journal of Sport & Social Issues, 31*(1), 11–24.

Gilmore, D. (1990). *Manhood in the Making: Cultural Concepts of Masculinity*. New Haven, Conn.: Yale University Press.

hooks, b. (2003). *We Real Cool: Black Men and Masculinity*. New York: Routledge.

Jackson, R. L. (2006). *Scripting the Black Masculine Body: Identity, Discourse, and Racial Politics in Popular Media*. Albany: State University of New York Press.

Joseph, C. A., & Kavoori, A. P. (2007). Colonial Discourse and the Writings of Katherine Mayo. *American Journalism, 24*(3), 55–84.

Katz, J. (2006). *The Macho Paradox: Why Some Men Hurt Women and How All Men Can Help.* Naperville, Ill.: Sourcebooks, Inc.

Kimmel, M. A. (1996). *Manhood in America: A Cultural History.* New York: Free Press.

Mayo, K. (1927). *Mother India.* New York: Harcourt Brace and Company.

Morrell, R. (Ed.). (2001). *Changing Men in Southern Africa.* London: Zed.

Pease, B., & Pringle, K. (2001). *A Man's World? Changing Men's Practices in a Globalized World.* London: Zed.

Rotundo, E. A. (1994). *American Manhood: Transformations in Masculinity from the Revolution to the Modern Era.* New York: Basic Books.

Said, E. (2003 [1978]). *Orientalism.* New York: Penguin.

Segal, L. (1990). *Slow Motion: Changing Masculinities, Changing Men.* New Brunswick, N.J.: Rutgers University Press.

Sinha, M. (1995). *Colonial Masculinity: The "Manly Englishman" and the "Effeminate Bengali" in the Late Nineteenth Century.* Manchester, U.K.: Manchester University Press.

Taister, B. (2000). Academic Viagra: The Rise of American Masculinity Studies. *American Quarterly,* 52 (2), 274–304.

Thomas, C. (1998). *Male Matters: Masculinity, Anxiety, and the Male Body on the Line.* Urbana: University of Illinois Press.

Tierney, S. (2006). Themes of Whiteness in *Bulletproof Monk, Kill Bill,* and *The Last Samurai. Journal of Communication,* 56(3), 607–24.

Whitehead, S. (2002). *Men and Masculinities: Key Themes and New Directions.* London: Polity.

Woodward, C. (1996). Lesbianism in Introductory Women's Studies Textbooks: Toward a Recognition of Difference? In B. Zimmerman and T. McNaron (Eds.), *The New Lesbian Studies: Into the Twenty-first Century* (pp. 134–44). New York: Feminist Press.

1

Negotiating Jamaican
Masculinities

MAURICE HALL

Old pirates yes they rob I, sold I to the merchant ships,
Minutes after they took I, from the bottomless pit.
Redemption Song, Robert Nestor Marley

Jamaican masculinity is a social construction that has everything to
do with the ways in which slavery, colonialism, and now globalization have
produced identity performances that are multiple and conflicted. There are
several current analyses that examine the history of the construction of masculinity in the Caribbean generally and Jamaica specifically (see, for example,
Lewis, 2003; Forbes, 2005; Lindsay, 2002; Reddock, 2004). These works approach analysis from interdisciplinary perspectives including history, literary
studies, and sociology. The concept of Caribbean masculinity is a subject of
significant debate between and among these scholars. In influential scholarly
volumes by authors such as Lewis (2003) and Reddock (2004), the debate
focuses on whether males in the Caribbean generally, and Jamaica specifically,
have been marginalized, with boys left to fend for themselves, or whether it
is in fact the privileging of males, rather than their marginalization, that has
led to an erosion of male status and authority in Caribbean societies.

It is not my intent to reproduce those analyses here; rather, this chapter will
focus on Jamaican masculinity using concepts drawn from the perspectives
of performativity and postcoloniality. I will argue that there are three major
performance stances that have come to characterize Jamaican performances
of masculinity: rude boys, Rastas, and mimics, performances that can largely
be understood in the context of Jamaica's postcolonial history. I will use two
well-known icons from Jamaica's history and culture, men who are seen as

leaders in their respective fields of endeavor, and I will argue that they are models for understanding the extent to which Jamaican masculinity has challenged Western notions of ideal manhood and reinvented and legitimized Africanized conceptions of manhood.

There are two important caveats in terms of how this discussion will unfold. First, I will embed the discussion and analysis of masculinity in broader discussions of culture, recognizing that gender and culture are largely intersecting discourses (Lewis, 2003). The mutual influence of these two discourses is at the heart of my thesis. Second, while there will be brief discussions of gender relations and issues pertaining to the status of women, this essay will focus on the construction of masculine identity. This is a choice made for reasons of space rather than a reflection or suggestion of a hierarchy of importance.

The concept of performance highlights the extent to which identity negotiation is a social construction. While performance scholars view a wide variety of rituals, media presentations, and literary/theatrical aesthetic creations as fitting under the rubric of performativity (Schechner, 2002), it is the concept of embodied performance as outlined by Conquergood (1991) that equates the body as a site of knowing. Judith Butler (1990) extended the concept of performativity to make the argument that gender is largely the product of repeated performances that, influenced by powerful social sanctions, produce an illusion of fixed identities linked to biological sex. From this perspective, masculinity, then, is an "acting out" of maleness, exteriorizing gendered behaviors through combinations of gestures, aggression, and gait (Lewis, 2004). The performances of the black male body in developing, previously colonized countries such as Jamaica have occurred in the context of European discourses that privilege the aesthetic and performance of the white, European, English body. Throughout the duration and aftermath of Jamaica's colonial history, there was a systematic effort to privilege white, British cultural identity discourses as normative and to marginalize cultural identity discourses of "Africanness" as inferior and unsophisticated. Jamaican sociologist Don Robotham (1998) argues: "White and Anglo-American/ European identities have established self-definitions more deeply driven by the historical experience of plantation slavery and the slave trade. These experiences have shaped the definition of whiteness and white hegemonies in deep contrast and contradiction to blackness and black subordination, as an entire hegemonic complex and structure" (p. 307).

One can conceptualize black subordination as the end product of enforced bodily performances that privileged white over black ways of being and behaving. The enslaved, black male body became a metonym for the savagery of Western European, specifically British, colonialism in the Caribbean. There has been a continuing struggle of the black male body to assert its own aesthetic and its own performance space in the context of dominant discourses that still regard it as periphery, strange, degraded, and marginal. The black male body's daily social performances have always occurred in the context of countervailing discourses that are always asserting that it should not perform like that and that it should not look like that. As a culture with a history of colonialism that has also had a sustained culture of patriarchy (Lewis, 2003), constructions of what Jamaican male identity means, then, in postcolonial Jamaica have everything to do with understanding the intersecting discourses of race, class, and gender, and the extent to which white maleness became the construct against which blackness was both constituted and defined.

Idealized White Masculinity

The colonial encounter and more recent discourses of cultural production associated with globalization have enshrined an idealized conception of masculinity that is largely Western and white, the election of U.S. President Barack Obama notwithstanding. For citizens of developing countries such as Jamaica, these idealized conceptions of masculinity are purveyed through influential narratives associated with literature, popular culture, and popular conceptions of leadership in the self-help and business literature.

High school students in postcolonial developing countries such as Jamaica are usually introduced through Western European literature to the concept of the hero. In Jamaica, Britain bequeathed its English-speaking colonies narratives in literature that merge conceptions of idealized masculinity with leadership and heroism. Many of these narratives revolve around the concept of the journey and the quest. Narratives such as *Beowulf* and *Sir Gawain* feature heroic figures with a noble cause whose journey, whether literal, metaphorical, or both results in the confrontation with and destruction of a literal and/or symbolic evil "Other" that threatens the community. The journey ends with the conquest of this evil and an often-triumphant return to home and safe harbor. In later narratives by authors such as Joseph Conrad, the evil "Other" subtly morphed into the nonwhite "Other," the symbol of savagery and destructiveness that had to be civilized, enslaved, or destroyed. These constructions of the heroic, idealized male as leader and as the hero invested with characteristics of nobility or bravery feature protagonists that are represented as universal, but are, in fact, male, white, and European, thereby implicating the nonwhite, non-Western male as deficient and "Other" (Nkomo, 2006).

Western popular culture, often created and marketed from the United States to the developing world, features compelling constructions of idealized masculinity, usually associated with white, male, American movie icons. These portrayals of masculinity often assume a rugged individualism, even heroism, which is synonymous with white American male ideals of masculinity. The view of the idealized white male as hero is a well-represented staple of media construction, from the cowboy heroes represented by American actor John Wayne to the male heroes represented by modern-day icons such as Harrison Ford and Bruce Willis. In the electoral politics of the United States, the strong male leader has also become a standardized trope in the aftermath of 9/11, with media attention often focused on who is strong enough to keep the country "safe." These portrayals of idealized white maleness are consistently represented as universal, with the motion-picture hero standing in as the modern everyman surviving against the odds.

In the popular and academic literature associated with business, the construct of leadership takes on strong associations of maleness. These conceptualizations of leadership and the link to constructions of maleness are important to consider, because the discourse of leadership, itself a deeply gendered discourse, is one of the most visible, prominent, concrete constructions of idealized masculinity that has influenced and continues to influence how we think about masculinity in terms of race, nationality, and class. Constructs of leadership, particularly North American leadership perspectives, tend to produce idealized, deeply gendered constructs of identity that have privileged maleness over femaleness, white identity over black, and Western over non-Western identity norms (Calas & Smircich, 1991; Fletcher, 2004; Parker, 2001). Embedded in constructions of leadership is an implication of idealized North American masculinity that is also presented as universal. Academic approaches to leadership, such as charismatic and visionary approaches, so-called heroic approaches to leadership (Fletcher, 2004), define leadership as an extraordinary phenomenon that is linked to the personally persuasive characteristics and charismatic behaviors of unique individuals. These heroic conceptions of leadership, such as transformational, visionary, and charismatic approaches (Nanus, 1992; Gardner & Cleavenger, 1998; Fairhurst, 2001), define leadership as a dynamic and interactive process in which the individual, usually male, leader has an exceptional ability to inspire and energize followers. Unfortunately, these approaches to leadership often assume the white, Western, usually male manager or CEO to be the leadership norm (Parker, 2001; Calas & Smircich, 1991).

Non-Western Masculinity as "Other"

These idealized constructions of white masculinity in literature, popular culture, and business literature gain their salience not just from innate positive characteristics associated with the constructions, but also from the contrast with that which is not white and male. There are few, if any, non-Western constructs of leadership or heroism representing an idealized form of masculinity (Nkomo, 2006). This deficit in representation helps lend credence to the suggestion that idealized forms of masculinity are exclusively invested in white male paragons of heroism. This is particularly true because the black male body has been inscribed with deficient characteristics that render the concept of black male leadership or heroism an oxymoron. Cultural scholar Ron Jackson, in his theory of black masculinity, reminds us that the black American male body is inscribed with racialized scripts that render it highly visible and yet peripheral. According to Jackson, the black masculine body is scripted as: 1) exotic and strange, 2) violent, 3) incompetent and uneducated, 4) sexual, 5) exploitable, and 6) innately incapacitated. Disturbingly, Jackson (2006) concludes, "race is about bodies that have been assigned social meanings" (p. 12). Jackson (2006) traces the history of the ideological and cultural scripting of the black body in the United States, particularly the black male body, from slavery through to current popular cultural expressions, arguing that "since the emergence of race as a social construct, black bodies have become surfaces of racial representation" (p. 12).

The scripting of the black male body in the context of the Caribbean, generally, and Jamaica specifically is equally as problematic. While Jamaica, and the Caribbean generally, have produced world leaders in the arenas of literature, the arts, and politics,[1] there are still enduring Western caricatures of the Caribbean male as breezily self-assertive, yet devoid of substance, exotic, and anti-intellectual. These caricatures are uncannily similar to the stereotypes attending images of the black American male (Allahar, 2001). These stereotypes of black Caribbean males can be traced back to white slave owners' characterization of enslaved black men as "Quashee" (Beckles, 2004). "Quashee" is the stereotype of the patient, submissive, happy-go-lucky slave who was also irresponsible, lazy, and childlike. In this construction of black maleness in the white imaginary, "Quashee" is reduced to significant dependence on the white master. This link between past and current stereotypes of black men in the Caribbean illustrates the extent to which understanding constructions of black male identity in Jamaica, in particular, calls for understanding the extent to which the history of the country has produced constructs of masculinity that are complex and contradictory.

Stephen Jay Gould (1996) argued for the ways in which race became a salient factor in negating the humanity of whole categories of human beings who were not white. These constructions of masculinity also have to be placed within the wider context of the colonial and neocolonial discourses, as described above, that have framed the black male identity as deficient.

Colonialism and the Subjugation of Black Jamaican Masculinity

Jamaica, an island of 2.5 million people, achieved its independence from Britain in 1962. Political independence did not mean economic independence, however, and the country has continued to struggle in the aftermath of the colonial enterprise. Complex intersections of history, politics, and culture have had a significant impact on how identity is negotiated there. The subjugation of the nonwhite male body is at the heart of the conflicted production of Jamaican male identity. Linden Lewis (2003) argues that colonialism in Jamaica was itself a system of patriarchy that "inscribed male domination into the culture" (p. 103); however, under this system of patriarchy, not all men were equal. Lewis (2003) asserts that African men in Jamaica were infantilized by the system of slavery to the extent that they were robbed of autonomy in every sphere of major life decisions. There was an internalization of the patriarchy that was inherent in the systems of slavery and, later, colonialism, and this internalization was played out in conflicted relationships with women in the aftermath of colonialism, as black men struggled to assert themselves in a social system that privileged white and brown men.

Black men were not just infantilized by the systems of slavery and colonialism; they were also gendered as feminine to the extent that they were reduced to dependence on the white slave and then colonial master. As a specific example of this, Lewis (2003) points out that while all men benefited from the system of patriarchy, in postcolonial Jamaica not all men controlled the means of production. Class and race, therefore, became predictors of political power. A white colonial elite controlled the means of production in the immediate aftermath of colonialism (Braithwaite, 1995), and the black middle and upper classes attained mobility through education: they did not control, but worked for those who controlled, the levers of power. Black masculinity in Jamaica had to fight to preserve its own cultural heritage and sovereignty in the face of colonial masters and the white local mercantile caste, which reinforced the message of the inferiority of blackness and Africanized cultural expression and the superiority of white British culture (Robotham, 1998). In fact, Robotham (1998) argues that the aftermath of slavery, and then colonial rule, created a deeply stratified society divided along lines of race, skin color, and class. White and brown people are generally the property owners, with a relatively small professional black and brown middle class and a significant black underclass (Robotham, 1998; Patterson, 1995). In modern Jamaica, the owners of property and the means of production have shifted location, but the positions are still the same: black bodies mark the peasant class, the workers, not the owners.

Since Jamaican male identity negotiation and performances, then, are largely products of these intersecting factors of class, race, history, and power, the impact on the sense of masculine identity has been catastrophic in some ways and redemptive in others. In an effort to negotiate and constitute blackness as a resistance to enforced white hegemonic cultural constructs, Jamaican men have had to invent indigenous performances of black masculinity. Cultural scholars Carolyn Cooper (1993) and Deborah Thomas (2004) provide detailed analyses of the consequent invention of a Jamaican identity that has become synonymous with urban expression, a reaction born out of frustration with the meager political and economic gains achieved in the aftermath of Jamaica's political independence. Cooper (1993), in particular, provides a detailed analysis of the extent to which the oral discourses that construct Jamaican identity are intrinsically linked to transgressive bodily performances: performances that are designed to bolster racial as well as cultural identity. Both researchers trace this identity to the polarized class structure in Jamaica, a legacy of colonialism. Thomas (2004) argues that by the late 1990s, most black lower-class Jamaicans saw the country's worsening economic crisis as a failure of the leadership of the black and brown middle class that had moved into positions of ascendancy in the aftermath of colonialism. Thomas (2004) argues that a black nationalist sentiment became pervasive in the politics and the culture of the island, culminating in the election of the late prime minister Michael Manley, who strategically conflated overt identity performances of Africanness with cultural progress.

Cooper (1993) links this development of a modern black identity with the country's oral culture and the tension of that orality with the written, "scribal" tradition that was imposed on the culture through colonial rule. Cooper (1993) argues that the legacy of the oral culture found its full expression in the Jamaican language, patois, religion, and music, such as dancehall[2] and reggae; but these expressions were those of lower-class, urban Jamaicans, designed to be a direct challenge to the sensibilities of the black and brown middle classes that still valorized aspects of white, British culture as the national norm. The combination of a ruling white elite, a disempowered black and brown middle class, a disenfranchised black underclass, and a patriarchy that differentiated between and among masculinities based on race and class produced complex performances of black masculinities.

These performances arose out of the anti-colonial struggle in Jamaica, and were manifested in the leadership behaviors of two prominent men who became leaders in their respective fields of endeavor, the late reggae artist Bob Marley and the late Jamaican prime minister Michael Manley. While there are many prominent Jamaican males who could have served as the focus of this analysis, these two men were chosen because they were significant and influential in the cultural, social, and political discourses that were salient in Jamaica's invention of a postcolonial identity. Their lives also capture some of the complexity of the impact of colonialism and slavery on the culture and national identity of Jamaicans. These two men serve as leaders and as heroic figures in the Jamaican narrative of anti-colonial struggle (Farred, 2003). In some ways, the Jamaican culture and how that identity is understood internationally is linked to broader perceptions of who these two men were, the time period in which they lived, and what their accomplishments have come to mean to people across the world who may be less than thoroughly familiar with Jamaica. The analysis of these two men as representative of the three performance stances discussed here, Rastas, rude boys, and mimics, is presented through a discussion that defines each of the performance stances, the historical and cultural issues that constituted these performances, and brief biographical information that frames these two men in the context of their lives in Jamaica as a developing democracy.

Black Jamaican Male Identity Performances

RUDE BOYS

One of the more compelling performances of masculinity in Jamaica is the rude boy. The focus on urban expression that had come to mark national identity in Jamaica found its most concrete expression in the performances of young males in the urban ghettoes of Kingston and in some rural areas of Jamaica. Since erudition, nuance, irony, and subtlety were highly valued in the discourses of British colonial identity performances as the markers of a cultivated, intellectual elite, many Jamaicans used the oral culture to transgress these unspoken norms. Some of the reasons that both reggae and dancehall music have achieved such popularity in the Jamaican cultural context is that they bypass the delicacies associated with Standard English expression and speak directly to the raw experience and emotion associated with living a life of disenfranchisement. Scholars such as Thomas (2004) and Farred (2003) discuss the fact that Jamaican male identity, in response to the harsh conditions afflicting the largely black, urban underclass, developed a swaggering, menacing presence that characterizes black underclass masculinity in Jamaica up to the current times. The "Rude Bwoy" phenomenon (literally, Rude Boys) as it was known then, was characterized by insolence, violence, and other transgressive social performances (Farred, 2003).

The "Rude Boy" phenomenon influenced the music and the cultural expression of Jamaican males in ways that impacted Jamaican reggae and dancehall music genres as well as the daily interactions individuals had with each other. The phenomenon was captured and documented in Jamaican movies from the era of the seventies and eighties, such as *Smile Orange* and *The Harder They Come*. Equally as important as the identity performances that characterized the behavior of these young urban males was the physical conditions that became characteristic of the life of the urban underclass. Scholars in the Caribbean have argued that the socialization, particularly of lower-class males, takes place largely in the streets (Chevannes, 2003). In Jamaica, while the concept of the street has equal salience, it can be argued that the physical conditions analogous to the concept of the street are best captured by the concept of "Yard."

It is, perhaps, no accident that Jamaicans living both in Jamaica and abroad use the term "yard" to speak affectionately of the country. "Yard" has multiple layers of meaning. Yard connotes home, whether one's house or one's homeland. Jamaicans abroad often refer to themselves as "Yardies." Yard is also a community space: there is the schoolyard or the playground for schoolchildren; the yard can also be the space around one's house. And a yard can be a space in which residents enact forced communal living, such as a "tenement yard." Bob Marley's plaintive "No Woman, No Cry" evokes the pain and the strange comfort of people being forced to live communally in Kingston's poorest urban areas.

Many rural homes in Jamaica are often built to share yard space. It is the middle classes who most often specifically demarcate territory with walls, fences, and "burglar bars." Because many Jamaicans must share communal space, a lot of life is lived communally, rather than within the confines of four walls and the nuclear family. A drive from the airport in Kingston will take one through communities where people are eating, cooking, chatting, playing dominoes, and otherwise interacting on the side of the street. These are not occasional interactions. These are glimpses of a lifestyle where much of life is lived in the open. High unemployment in poorer areas means that men spend many hours in these communal spaces rather than heading out to work on a daily basis (Chevannes, 2003). "Yard" then can be seen as a metaphor for communal living. "Yard" captures the propensity, indeed, the necessity, for many Jamaicans to live in such a way that their neighbors are privy to moments of joy and sorrow and even intimacy: there is always an audience.

It is in the context of communal living that the construct of masculinity as characterizing many of the Jamaican male underclass gains its salience. In the urban ghettoes of Kingston, many of the young men gained control of these communal spaces, which were the only spaces available to them (Farred, 2003). There they ruled with impunity, terrorizing the inhabitants and forbidding entrance to outsiders. It is in these communal spaces that young men learn from other men the kinds of performances of masculinity that are consistent with hyper-masculine behavior. Women are less influential in these spaces because the role of the girl is to be domesticated; hence, she spends most of her time inside the house. The boys, who are expected to be somewhat unruly, are therefore free to command the yard and the streets for their exploits in masculine derring-do (Chevannes, 2003).

RASTAFARIANS

An equally compelling performance of masculinity in Jamaica is the Rastafarian. Scholars such as Cooper (1993), Thomas (2001), and Farred (2003) discuss the Rastafarian as another visible performance of masculinity that was a manifestation of the struggle for survival by the rural and urban poor in the immediate aftermath of colonial domination. The Rastafarian ideology, which suffuses the lyrics of Bob Marley, captures the experience of black Africans through analogies to the Jewish experience. Drawn from the black nationalist ideology of Marcus Garvey, this movement captures the salience of an African sensibility, agency, self-determination, and black liberation ideology. The Rastafarian is significant to the analysis of male identity construction in Jamaica because it has been so influential on the negotiation of identity choices by many young Jamaican males. It is a deeply complex movement that features transgressive performances linked to the oral culture (Cooper, 1993). While it is liberatory in its politics and sensibilities, some expressions of the movement are deeply patriarchal and linked in complex ways to issues of class: Rastafarians are often seen as deeply offensive by members of the Jamaican middle class, who see the movement as an expression of the unsophisticated and the disenfranchised (Farred, 2003).

The value of the Rastafarian movement is that it provides a narrative for understanding the pain and alienation associated with slavery and its aftermath. All cultures create competing narratives that help explain the values and the value of the culture, and comparisons, while never definitive, can be useful. There was a reference earlier in this essay to European narratives of quest and journey. By contrast, one of the master narratives in Caribbean literature and the arts is that of exile[3] (Forbes, 2005). The tenor of this narrative is existential rather than heroic, fraught with feelings of anxiety, angst, and alienation. The ethos of this narrative of exile is captured in the often very existential lyrics of Bob Marley, himself a Rastafarian.

Certainly, one interpretation of the postcolonial history of the English-speaking Caribbean, generally, and Jamaica, specifically, as expressed in the music of Bob Marley (also the novels of Samuel Selvon and the poetry of Edward Kamu Braithwaite)[4] is that the African-descended inhabitants have been left in a continuing state of ambiguous tension: the history of slavery has so distorted, even truncated, the cultural history and the cultural memory that there is no clear sense of the history that occurred before these islands. Consequently, the enormous impact of slavery and colonialism has been to interrupt and distort black male identity negotiation in ways that have lasting impact in the culture today (Lewis, 2003). The Rastafarian movement provided inspiration for this deeply held and deeply felt anti-colonialist sentiment, as expressed in the music of Bob Marley. While the history books record that the ancestors of Jamaicans were captured and transported from Africa to the Caribbean and North America as slaves, black bodies as lucrative product in a vast industry of import and export, the facts do not fully capture the horror and humiliation deeply woven into the fabric of the collective cultural memory. In the lyrics to Bob Marley's "Redemption Song" there is a poignant allusion to the introduction to slavery framed through the experience of the Jewish patriarch Joseph of the Old Testament, who is himself betrayed by his brothers and sold into slavery. The song's lyrics acknowledge the sense of loss and the injustice. Bob Marley became an embodiment of the painful narrative expressed in his songs as well as the complex history and culture in Jamaica that produced rude boys and Rastas as performances of Jamaican masculine identity.

BOB MARLEY

Bob Marley was born in Jamaica in 1945 to a white Jamaican father and a black, teenaged mother in the parish of St. Ann in Jamaica—incidentally, the same parish in which Marcus Garvey was born (Farred, 2003). This was in the colonial period in Jamaica, so a union between a member of the white colonial class and a young black girl was, to say the least, met with significant disapproval. The birth of Bob Marley points up the intersection of class, race, and gender realities in Jamaica under colonialism (Toynbee, 2007). Marley's mother was literally a young, black peasant girl who found herself in an encounter with a member of the powerful white colonial class, and she had few options that would allow her to emerge from that encounter unscathed.

The patriarchal structure of the society certainly rendered her powerless as a female, and both her race and her class gave her little social standing in a colonial society. While it seems that Norval Marley (Bob Marley's father) wanted to marry young Cedella (Bob Marley's mother), his family completely disinherited him for his transgression of racial and class taboos. Their relationship was short-lived, and after providing some basic material arrangements for his family, Norval Marley largely abandoned Bob and Cedella to their own resources. Bob Marley grew up, for all intents and purposes, the son of a single mother (Toynbee, 2007; Farred, 2003).

While his father persuaded his mother to send him to the capital, Kingston, for educational purposes, he was in fact farmed out at age ten as hired help to an elderly white woman in the city. Bob Marley was, therefore, deprived of continuing his education. When Cedella Marley did eventually migrate from rural Jamaica to Kingston, her lack of formal education and skills led her to her only option of working as a casual laborer and living in a government shantytown, public housing for the poor. It is in this squalid shantytown that Bob Marley grew up. It provided the grist for the reference to the "government yard" in his song "No Woman, No Cry" and underscores the importance of "Yard," as discussed earlier. It is clear, too, that Marley's experience in public housing, and the nearby urban ghetto of Trenchtown, provided the material for the lyrics that later came to represent the very vivid sentiments in his music (Toynbee, 2007). Marley's sense of the suffering of the Third World poor was based on firsthand experience from his youthful years in inner-city Kingston (Farred, 2003). Marley took on the mannerism of the rude boys as he grew up in the Kingston inner city, finding friends who would also become lifelong collaborators. The inner city was also where Marley was exposed to Rastafarianism, which later became centrally identified with his music.

Bob Marley was literally born and lived at the intersections of class, racial, and gendered realities in colonial Jamaica that shaped the rest of his life, his experience of social reality and, eventually, his music. Nor is it accidental that the miscegenation that resulted in the birth of Bob Marley can be seen as a metaphor for the exploitation and oppressive circumstances that faced

poor and working-class black Jamaicans during and after the colonial experience in Jamaica. The stories of Bob and his mother were not unique, isolated
incidents. These stories represent the reality of the lives of many of Jamaica's
rural and urban poor during and after colonialism. The wave of strikes and
rebellions that swept Jamaica in the 1930s and 1940s, led by the trade union
movement, was the engine of the anti-colonialist movement that sought to
alleviate the suffering of the black majority (Toynbee, 2007; Thomas, 2001).
The call for freedom from colonialism and poverty found its expression in the
anti-colonial movement, as well as in the Rastafarian movement that became
central to Jamaica's sense of social identity in the aftermath of colonialism.

The story of Bob Marley also illustrates, briefly, the ways in which masculinity was shaped for the poor and working-class men by issues of race and
class that are directly linked to Jamaica's colonial history. His Rastafarianism
and the gritty persona that came to characterize the man are a direct result
of the initial struggles, both for survival and also for legitimacy as a black
male within the context of a white, European-dominated society and culture.
The intersecting male identity performances of the rude boy and the Rasta
in Bob Marley's life underscore the extent to which these performances of
masculinity are also linked to struggles for self-definition and freedom from
oppression that came to characterize masculine identity negotiation in the
waning years and the immediate aftermath of British colonialism in Jamaica.

One of the more devastating impacts of colonialism was the extent to which
there was an inculcation of mimicry of the white, British colonial master into
the black middle-class elite that rose to prominence in the aftermath of Jamaica's political independence. Caribbean novelist V. S. Naipaul captured the
essence of this phenomenon in his novel *Mimic Men*, a devastating critique
of the Caribbean political class in the aftermath of political independence.
He continued a similar theme in many of his short stories in the collection,
Miguel Street. Focusing largely on male identity negotiation, Naipaul painted
portraits of the Caribbean male as schooled in the mannerisms and performances of, first, the British colonial cultural system followed by the imitation of American popular cultural icons as the flood of American popular
culture seeped into the cultural expression of the Caribbean. The characters
in Naipaul's novels, then, become skillful imitators of the performances, but
not the essence, of British and American white male cultural expression.

Postcolonial scholar Homi Bhabha (1994) outlines in significant detail the
concept of mimicry as a trope of postcolonial theory. Bhabha (1994) argues
that mimicry is not an accidental aftermath of colonialism; rather, mimicry
was the product of a system of inculcation that ensured that white British

cultural expression would be seen as the cultural norm to which colonial inhabitants should aspire. According to Bhabha (1994), the discourse of colonialism mandated mimicry of the colonizer with the intent of fostering, not alleviating, dependence. Bhabha (1994) argues "Mimicry repeats rather than re-presents" (p. 88), producing "a subject of a difference that is almost the same, but not quite" (p. 86), or "almost the same but not white" (p. 89). Braithwaite (1995) picks up on a similar critique, arguing that this imitation of whiteness was the only kind of identity performance accepted by white slave holders, an empty imitation that persisted into the colonial era and found its continuing expression in the behavioral norms of the Jamaican black middle class. This mimicry of the colonizer was often seen for what it was by members of the working and urban underclass in Jamaica, and both Cooper (1993) and Thomas (2001) attribute the rise in the urban sensibility that came to characterize manifestations of Jamaican identity negotiation in the eighties, nineties, and currently as a backlash against the empty imitation of British cultural norms that was imposed as a requisite to economic advancement by the black middle class. It is within the context of this cultural reality in Jamaica that the late Michael Manley, former prime minister of Jamaica, assumes significance as both an icon of embodiment and transcendence. His brown body underscored the place of privilege accorded to those who were members of the descended European elite in Jamaica; however, his politics and his ideology interrupted and set out to dismantle the privilege of skin color, of which he had been a beneficiary.

MICHAEL MANLEY

Michael Manley was born to privilege as the son of a revered and well-known Jamaican leader and, later, prime minister, Norman Manley. His mother was a white English woman who was an artist. Manley grew up well educated and a son of an elite Jamaican family (Farred, 1993). His birth and upbringing represented the privileges that came with having a high-brown skin color that, in colonial Jamaica, meant, in some ways, you could pass for white. Manley attended the best schools and went overseas to the London School of Economics to complete his tertiary education. Manley was clearly born with a strong personality that led him to challenge many of the norms that were regarded as de rigueur by those of his class and social station (Meeks, 2001). That he was able to get away with challenges to the status quo, including incidents of youthful rebellion, also underscores the extent to which the privilege of his class and color protected him from the worst consequences of his actions in ways that would not have been an option for the young Bob Marley.

As a young man, Michael Manley immersed himself in the politics of the anti-colonial workers, organizing union workers and getting into high-profile scuffles with the management of a variety of Jamaican organizations (Meeks, 2001). Michael eventually succeeded his father as the head of the People's National Party (one of Jamaica's two national parties that is roughly analogous in philosophy and orientation to the Democratic Party in the United States or the Labor Party in England), and went on to create a mythic persona and a leadership style that has rarely been matched by any Jamaican politician before or since (Meeks, 2001). His nickname at the time, "Joshua," captures the extent to which the man was elevated to mythic status as politician draw-ing, in part, on the narratives of exile that were characteristic of the Jewish Old Testament.

Michael Manley was a noteworthy leader, and an interesting study when discussing the negotiation of masculinity, because he made a choice that was unusual for a high-brown son of the elite. He decided to consciously appropriate the language, culture, and sensibility of the black Jamaican ru-ral and urban poor and elevated these concerns to center stage on Jamaica's political landscape. Running on a platform that he dubbed "the politics of change," he focused on the inequities in Jamaican society and set out to make egalitarianism a central tenet of his administration (Farred, 2003). In order to do so, Manley immersed himself in Rastafarian social texts, drawing on the rhetoric, mythology, and music central to this nascent black nationalist movement. This move made him an enormously influential and very popu-list figure: it also brought him into a collaboration with Bob Marley that had a dramatic impact on the cultural and social fabric of Jamaica, and deeply influenced politics in Jamaica, an influence that is still being felt today.

Manley's Pan-Africanism and his hostility to what he saw as the prevalence of U.S. hegemony, transformed masculine identity negotiation in Jamaica. His appropriation of the cause of the black Jamaican majority moved the performance of blackness from a peripheral, marginal identity to a central feature of Jamaican national identity negotiation. This resulted in a challenge to the norms that sanctioned imitation and mimicry of the British colo-nial culture as an acceptable and even desirable performance of identity. In their respective scholarly work, both Deborah Thomas (2004) and Carolyn Cooper (1993) amply demonstrate that Manley's political stance resulted in legitimizing a black, Africanized ethos that was anti-colonial in its politics and expression and suspicious of U.S. market hegemony as represented in the exportation to Jamaica of U.S. consumer goods and other artifacts of its popular culture.

Heroic Postures: Inventing a Jamaican Idealized Masculinity

Farred (2003) suggests that because of the work of Michael Manley and Bob Marley in their respective fields of endeavor, Jamaica was significantly changed as a society. Both Manley and Marley's rise to prominence nationally and internationally put them on a similar trajectory in terms of time. Marley's role at the now infamous 1976 Peace Concert, in which he brought Michael Manley and Edward Seaga (then leader of the conservative opposition party, the Jamaica Labor Party, JLP) together and made them shake hands to signal an end to the devastating politically inspired violence that was ravaging Kingston in the wake of hotly contested election campaigns was a signature moment in the country's history. Both Michael Manley and Bob Marley were hailed as heroes for this accomplishment (Farred, 2003).

Both men also changed the politics of negotiating masculinity in a postcolonial society. Africanized thematics became central rather than marginal to negotiating masculine identity. But it is also important to note that in a society that was still significantly patriarchal, the reality of the contradiction of socially dominant but politically disempowered black men faced its first significant challenge. At least at the symbolic level, a black and a brown Jamaican male were transcending differences in class and asserting a defiance against ubiquitous structures of white power and white privilege as represented by the United States and Britain and their complicated political and cultural relationship with Jamaica. In his music, Marley challenged colonialism and white superiority, cloaking his provocation in lyrics that emphasized African nationalism and the moral imperative of black self-determination (Farred, 2003; Toynbee, 2007).

Drawing on the narratives of exile represented in the Old Testament, Bob Marley was able to evoke a powerful mythology of freedom for the disenfranchised that resonated worldwide. There was also the powerful spectacle of black maleness that challenged both the legitimacy and dominance of white, Western norms of male performance for black, Jamaican masculinity. Bob Marley wore his hair in dreadlocks, and in his speeches and interviews he regularly encapsulated the vernacular of the Rastafarian as well as the Jamaican oral tradition as represented by the Jamaican patois. For the black Jamaican middle class steeped in performances of mimicry of British culture, Bob Marley was a deeply controversial and even divisive figure (Farred, 2003) that challenged the normative representation of Africanized masculinity.

At the same time, Manley's appropriation of blackness as a political and cultural identity construct legitimized and resurrected performances of black masculinity that were distinctly African. This meant that the white and brown local mercantile class was forced to recognize the extent to which negotiating a modern Jamaican identity meant embracing rather than marginalizing an African ethos (Thomas, 2003). Scholars are careful to point out that this appropriation of blackness did not necessarily result in structural transformation in the Jamaican society of imbalances of power. But on a symbolic level, these invocations of blackness were incredibly powerful examples of leadership and idealized masculinity that transformed Jamaica's political, cultural, and social landscape (Cooper, 1993; Thomas, 2003).

Despite the assertion of a distinctly African ethos in the performances of masculinity represented by Manley and Marley, scholars such as Chevannes (2003) worry that the current generation of young men in Jamaica face serious and sometimes intractable issues. While the invention of a distinctly black, Jamaican identity has challenged the previous British or current North American concepts of idealized masculinity, this has not been reflected in structural changes in the distribution of wealth and power in the society. The black middle and lower classes still do not, largely, own the means of production in the society. Increased educational achievement has led to better opportunities for employment for them by those who do control the levers of power: the white and brown mercantile class.

In addition, Jamaica is still largely a patriarchal society. As noted by scholars such as Figueroa (2004), males in Jamaica have been historically privileged, having had access to a broader social space, control over a wide range of resources, and having had, generally, enjoyed greater prestige in the society than females; however, as Chevannes (2003) points out, patriarchy is not just the domination of women by men, but the domination of men by other powerful men; thus, all masculinities are not equal. In Jamaica, race and class have been markers of power in the society, and this has not changed significantly. The issues concerning male identity negotiation feature other layers of complexity, because while some scholars such as Miller (1986) have argued that black males in Jamaica are increasingly marginalized because of history and culture, scholars such as Figueroa (2004) challenge that contention by arguing that the male marginalization is an ironic byproduct of an opposite phenomenon: male privilege.

From this perspective, the fear of girls getting pregnant as teenagers has led to significant social scrutiny where their behavior is concerned, whereas for males, the central fear is that of being thought to be homosexual (Parry, 2004; Reddock, 2004). Drawing on statistical evidence in the research literature, Figueroa (2004) argues that this privileging is in many ways linked to the academic underperformance of Jamaican males. For example, more than 70 percent of the graduates from the region's flagship university, the University of the West Indies, are female. The figures are consistent for other higher education institutions in Jamaica.

Figueroa (2004) argues that the academic underperformance of males has its roots in gender socialization, where boys are expected and encouraged to be rambunctious, but girls are expected to be respectable and responsible in their behavioral choices at all times. There is very little latitude in the culture for a female who does not fit the stereotype of the "good girl." This continues, Figueroa (2004) argues, in the expectations for who will participate in and complete household chores; as the society has changed from a less agrarian, rural society to a more urban one, the decline in chores that are mostly male-oriented (largely outdoor, nondomestic chores) has resulted in less responsible participation by males in contributing to a household. In primary and secondary education, the expectations for self-discipline are lower for boys than for girls, resulting in an ever-increasing spiral of academic underperformance.

In terms, then, of current performances of masculinity, these scholars assert that the rampant fear that one may not be seen as a "real man" leads to the continuation of hyper-masculine performances that have destructive outcomes, including academic underachievement, homophobia, and various forms of violence. These hyper-masculine performances include the avoidance of participation in the domestic sphere, the avoidance of "nerdiness" associated with being a bookworm, and a hostility to school as a feminized space, an issue that has been exacerbated by the significant exodus of men from the teaching profession. Figueroa's (2004) central argument is that academic underperformance, far from being a symptom of male marginalization, is a symptom of the legitimizing of these performances of hyper-masculinity. Since educational achievement has been the ticket for most black Jamaicans into the middle class, the significant educational underperformance of Jamaican males is an issue of some concern.

Conclusion

Influential feminist Caribbean scholars such as those in the volume edited by Mohammed (2002) have made significant progress in discussing issues concerning patriarchy and gender in the Caribbean. Women are making significant progress in Jamaica and have influenced the discourse around the role and significance of men in the emerging twenty-first century (Chevannes, 2003). In fact, Figueroa (2004) argues that the outcry over the advancement of women in the society in terms of their educational performance is, in fact, a manifestation of the depth of the Jamaican patriarchal impulse, since the advancement of girls and women is met by cries of crisis and impending doom rather than celebration of the improving status of women. It certainly seems to be true that there is a need for the continued interrogation of Jamaican performances of masculinity.

It is encouraging that scholarly debates such as those referenced in this essay have been taking place in academic and cultural circles. Some of this scholarly debate has been the result of constructive scholarly discourse in the region around gender, and it is heartening that scholars such as Chevannes (2003) and Figueroa (2004) call for continued dialogue between the sexes as well as continued scholarly research as important means of moving towards dismantling the patriarchal underpinnings of the Jamaican society.

Notes

1. For example, Forbes Burnham, Michael Manley, Eric Williams in politics; Edward Kamu Braithwaite, V. S. Naipaul, Derek Walcott in literature; Bob Marley, "Mighty Sparrow," Peter Tosh in music.

2. Dancehall, an urban Jamaican music form, features rhyming performances, similar to rap music and hip-hop, that seek to capture the despair of urban poverty.

3. See, for example, Samuel Selvon's *Lonely Londoners, The Housing Lark*, and *Moses Ascending*.

4. Selvon and Braithwaite are celebrated Caribbean literary icons whose work has contributed to a significant canon of postcolonial literature in the English language.

References

Allahar, A. (2001). Charisma and Populism: Theoretical Reflections on Leadership and Legitimacy. In A. Allahar (Ed.), *Caribbean Charisma: Reflections on Leadership, Legitimacy, and Populist Politics* (pp. 192–211). Boulder, Colo.: Lynne Rienner.

Beckles, H. (2004). Black Masculinity in Caribbean Slavery. In R. Reddock (Ed.), *Interrogating Caribbean Masculinities: Theoretical and Empirical Analyses* (pp. 225–43). Kingston, Jamaica: University of the West Indies Press.

Bhabha, H. K. (1994). *The Location of Culture*. New York: Routledge.

Braithwaite, E. (1995). Creolization in Jamaica. In B. Ashcroft, G. Griffiths, & H. Tiffin (Eds.), *The Post-colonial Studies Reader* (202–5). New York: Routledge.

Butler, J. (1990). *Gender Trouble: Feminism and the Subversion of Identity*. New York: Routledge.

Calas, M. B., & Smircich, L. (1991). Voicing Seduction to Silence Leadership. *Organization Studies*, 12, 567–602.

Chevannes, B. (2003). The Role of the Street in the Socialization of Caribbean Males. In L. Lewis (Ed.), *The Culture of Gender and Sexuality in the Caribbean* (pp. 215–33). Gainesville: University of Florida Press.

Conquergood, D. (1991). Rethinking Ethnography: Towards a Critical Cultural Politics. *Communication Monographs*, 58, 179–94.

Cooper, C. (1993). *Noises in the Blood: Orality, Gender, and the "Vulgar" Body of Jamaican Popular Culture*. Durham, N.C.: Duke University Press.

Fairhurst, G. (2001). Dualisms in Leadership Research. In F. Jablin & L. Putnam (Eds.), *The New Handbook of Organizational Communication: Advances in Theory, Research, and Methods* (pp. 379–439). Thousand Oaks, Calif.: Sage.

Farred, G. (Ed.). (2003). *What's My Name? Black Vernacular Intellectuals*. Minneapolis: University of Minnesota Press.

Figueroa, M. (2004). Male Privileging and Male "Academic Underperformance" in Jamaica. In R. Reddock (Ed.), *Interrogating Caribbean Masculinities: Theoretical and Empirical Analyses* (pp. 137–66). Kingston, Jamaica: University of the West Indies Press.

Fletcher, J. K. (2004). The Paradox of Postheroic Leadership: An Essay on Gender, Power, and Transformational Change. *Leadership Quarterly*, 15, 647–61.

Forbes, C. (2005). *From Nation to Diaspora: Samuel Selvon, George Lamming, and the Cultural Performance of Gender*. Kingston, Jamaica: University of the West Indies Press.

Gardner, W. L., & Cleavenger, D. (1998). The Impression Management Strategies Associated with Transformational Leadership at the World-Class Level. *Management Communication Quarterly*, 12, 3–41.

Gould. S. (1996). *The Mismeasure of Man*. New York: Norton.

Jackson, R. L. (2006). *Scripting the Black Masculine Body: Identity, Discourse, and Racial Politics in Popular Media*. Albany: State University of New York Press.

Lewis, L. (2003). Caribbean Masculinity: Unpacking the Narrative. In L. Lewis (Ed.), *The Culture of Gender and Sexuality in the Caribbean* (pp. 94–125). Gainesville: University of Florida Press.

Lewis, L. (2004). Caribbean Masculinity at the Fin de Siècle. In R. Reddock (Ed.), *Interrogating Caribbean Masculinities: Theoretical and Empirical Analyses* (pp. 244–66). Kingston, Jamaica: University of the West Indies Press.

Lindsay, K. (2002). Is the Caribbean Male an Endangered Species? In P. Mohammed (Ed.), *Gendered Realities: Essays in Caribbean Feminist Thought*. Kingston, Jamaica: University of the West Indies Press.

Meeks, B. (2001). Jamaica's Michael Manley (1924–97): Crossing the Contours of Charisma. In A. Allahar (Ed.), *Caribbean Charisma: Reflections on Leadership, Legitimacy, and Populist Politics* (pp. 192–211). Boulder, Colo.: Lynne Rienner.

Miller, E. (1986). *The Marginalization of the Black Male: Insights from the Development of the Teaching Profession.* Kingston, Jamaica: Institute of Social and Economic Research.

Mohammed, P. (2002). *Gendered Realities: Essays in Caribbean Feminist Thought.* Kingston, Jamaica: University of the West Indies Press.

Nanus, B. (1992). *Visionary Leadership.* San Francisco: Jossey-Bass.

Nkomo, S. (2006). *Images of African Leadership and Management in Organizational Studies: Tensions, Contradictions, and Re-visions.* Unpublished manuscript.

Parker, P. (2001). African American Women Executives' Leadership Communication within Dominant Culture Organizations. *Management Communication Quarterly,* 15, 42–82.

Parry, O. (2004). Masculinities, Myths, and Educational Underachievement: Jamaica, Barbados, and St. Vincent and the Grenadines. In R. Reddock (Ed.), *Interrogating Caribbean Masculinities: Theoretical and Empirical Analyses* (pp. 167–84). Kingston, Jamaica: University of the West Indies Press.

Patterson, O. (1995). The Culture of Caution. *New Republic,* 213, 22–26.

Reddock, R. (2004). *Interrogating Caribbean Masculinities: Theoretical and Empirical Analyses.* Kingston, Jamaica: University of the West Indies Press.

Robotham, D. (1998). Transnationalism in the Caribbean: Formal and Informal. *American Ethnologist,* 25, 307–21.

Schechner, R. (2002). *Performance Studies: An Introduction.* New York: Routledge.

Thomas, D. (2004). *Modern Blackness: Nationalism, Globalization, and the Politics of Culture in Jamaica.* Durham, N.C.: Duke University Press.

Toynbee, J. (2007). *Bob Marley.* Malden, Mass.: Polity Press.

2

Queer(y)ing Masculinities

BRYANT KEITH ALEXANDER

Masculinity is performative. Not simply that it *is* a performance as in a doing; maybe masculinity is *performativity*; an assessment of the embodied thing done, the iteration and achievement of the expected (Butler, 1990b; Diamond, 1996; Pollock, 2006; Edwards, 2006). Yet the foundational logics and the vast body of literature on masculinity fall short of actually defining masculinity in concrete terms, outside of the referential social expectations of being a man or manly, in relation to its assumed opposite—within the social and cultural context of its assessment. Such referential discussions of masculinity just seem queer to me. *Queer*, not as the assumed liberatory construction in queer theory that *resists the regimes of the normal*, or queer in that all-encompassing alternative identity construction that conflates gender difference for some emancipatory otherness; and not even queer as in the assumed co-opted politically correct reference to being gay or homosexual (Alexander, 2008; Yep et al., 2003; Warner, 1993). Queer for me in this instance is the denotative reference to something as just being suspicious.

What I find queer is that masculinity, as a social interactional determination, is grounded not in principles of exactitude but principles of perceptional expectedness, perceptions that are fluid and limiting to the larger possibilities of performing gender and embodied presence, particularly when exclusively linked to the category of heterosexual man. Defining masculinity is slippery. Yet, as Judith Halberstam (1998) alludes, determinations of masculinity are held firm in the mind as an ideal imaginary. Halberstam continues, "As a society we have little trouble in recognizing [masculinity], and indeed we spend massive amounts of time and money ratifying it, and supporting the versions of masculinity that we enjoy and trust; many of these 'heroic masculinities' depend absolutely on the subordination of alternative masculinities" (p. 2). This is both a starting realization of most studies in/on masculinity and a clear point of intervention into the ways we think about and interrogate the social constructedness of masculinity (Whitehead, 2006).

In this chapter I explore the conflicted construct of masculinity through a queer lens that focuses on the definitional characteristics and assumed demeanor of "the masculine," which reductively suggest the equation between masculinity and heterosexuality. Hence promoting the heteronormative construction of "acting manly" that provides a suspect range of acceptable male expressions of being and desire and desire as being, in which case desire "is not primarily one of libido and sexuality, but rather production (of self)" (Whitehead, 2002, p. 211). In particular, the chapter engages a queer reading of selected moments, scenes, and literatures that invoke masculinity to show how certain articulations of male performativity describe, promote, and invoke particular responses that are relational. In the conclusion I also place the nature of the very specific examples used in the text into a larger context of global queer identities.

Why Discussions on Masculinity Still Matter

I recently participated in a symposium co-sponsored through the Center for the Study of Genders and Sexualities, and the Gender and Sexuality Resource Center at California State University, Los Angeles, addressing the question: "Why Discussions on Gender and Sexualities Still Matter?" I was asked to offer responses linked to the performance of masculinity. I want to offer the following responses as poetic framing logics that problematically define the nature and scope of masculinity studies in relation to the question posed.

> When the told and untold stories of violence against women and children at the hands of men performing a masculinity that is rooted in power, control, and domination continue and abound (Bowker, 1998: Boonzaier & de la Rey, 2003; Craib, 1987, 1998; Hearn, 1998; Gadd, 2002; Hanmer, 1990; Morgan, 1993)—discussions on gender and masculinity still matter.
>
> When the told and untold stories of gay bashings against those with a perceived gender variance from the reductively expected norm, happen everyday by men performing a hyper-masculinity that attempts to kill or maim difference (Linneman, 2000; Anderson, 2002)—discussions on gender and masculinity still matter.

When performances of masculinity are equated with heterosexuality and are defined relationally, against women and against gay men, instead of an internal impulse of personal integrity and social responsibility (O'Sullivan, 1998)—discussions on gender and masculinity still matter.

When acts of war (on a local, state, national, and international level) are perpetuated as a performance of bravado, machismo, and what bell hooks calls "a dick thing . . . masculinity" (Dudink et al., 2004; Goldstein, 2003; hooks, 1992; Morgan, 1994) *or a pissing contest between men that costs human lives*—discussions on gender and masculinity still matter.

When gay, lesbian, bisexual, and transgendered folks still feel that they need to live cloistered lives, as a form of self-protection from social ridicule, hatred, and violence—discussions on gender and masculinity still matter.

When on a state, national, and international level, in governments and in the realm of human social engagement, differential expectations, rights, and privileges are afforded to men over women, or heterosexuals over homosexuals, like the passing of California's Proposition 8 banning same-sex marriage—discussions on gender and masculinity still matter.

When acts of violence, "any relation, process, or condition by which an individual or group violates the physical, social, and/or psychological integrity of another person or group" are equated with the effects of performing masculinity (Bulhan, 1985, p. 53)—discussions on gender and masculinity still matter.

When staid notions of masculine performativity are keyed to heterosexuality and machismo, denying the plurality of masculinities that may temper the category of man and establish taxonomies of gender performances that might also liberate restrictive constructions of female performativities (Sinfield, 2002)—discussions on gender and masculinity still matter.

Rightfully or not, when women are still described as the "gentler sex," socially conscious and caring men must stand up and engage why—discussions on gender and masculinity still matter.

These reasons all serve as justifications for the importance of why discussions on masculinities still matter. But they also offer and reinforce the particular ways in which masculinity in everyday life and masculinity in academic discourse has focused its attention on the seemingly innate "aggressive, assertive, independent, competitive, insensitive" constructions of masculinity that easily make way for a destructive social dynamic in relation to its assumed opposite, women and gay men (Brittan, 1989, p. 4). Arthur Brittan offers a particular discussion of *masculinism* that is an important start to delineating assumptions about masculinism as a social construction of a performative identity that I could argue some women also perform, but is specifically attributed to masculinity and reductively to the category of man.

What is important in Brittan's analysis is that he gives a name to the ideology that constructs, if not empowers, the social expectation of a masculine subject imbued with a particular relational dynamic. In the process he delineates masculinism, the masculine ideology, from masculinity as the particularity of an embodied presentation of self. Such delineation opens a space of discussion, unshackling the particularity of actualized male performativity relative to each man from the social and cultural constructions of that desired sex or gender presentation. The delineation also makes vulnerable the social investment in male domination and a pernicious investment in heterosexuality. I believe that the delineation of masculinism from masculinity also provides space for a greater acknowledgment of a *masculinity without men* (Halberstam, 1998), one that altogether critiques a fundamental difference between men and women and the relational possibilities of negotiating a more fluid sense of embodiment, labor, power, and social influence.

Following Stephen Whitehead's (2002) analysis of Brittan, "masculinism becomes a dominant discourse rather than a dominant ideology" (p. 98). And while Whitehead offers a particular justification for the distinction, allow me to offer my own in these terms. If in its most rudimentary definition ideology is a system of meaningful cultural beliefs that attempt to make normative its perception of reality as socializing agent, discourse then serves as the articulating agent that translates thought and belief into action, enforcing the particularity of ideology in ways that have social and cultural consequences. I want to use Judith Lorber's (2003 [1994]) construction of gender as both exemplifier and battering ram to the ideology/discourse distinction being made here, particularly as it relates to a social construction of masculinism as social imaginary, and the relationship between the category of man and a particular performance of masculinity.

In her construction of gender, Lorber moves from gender located in individual self-definition or gender in the context of interpersonal negotiation, to "gender as an institution that establishes patterns of expectations for individuals, orders the social processes of everyday life, is built into the major social organizations of society, such as the economy, ideology, the family, and politics, and is also an entity in and of itself" (p. 3). In her arguments, Lorber reinforces Judith Butler's (1990a) logic that within the realm of gender politics "not biology, but culture, becomes destiny" (p. 8), noting that "gendered people emerge not from physiology or sexual orientation but from the exigencies of the social order" (Lorber, 2003, p. 22).

The masculine subject engaged in performing traditional notions of masculinity seated in power and domination—and particularly when that performance is embodied in a heterosexual man—over women as well as gendered others, cannot claim biological pressures as prime motivators in the particularity of performing masculinity; nor can he exclusively claim his acquiescence to the social expectedness of what it means to be a man (or what are acceptable performances of masculinity) as the dominating influence of his personal choices. The embodied performance of such a masculinity is the terrain of choice within the realm of social ideology; an enacted discourse as ideological manifestation is made palpable in a relational dynamic that asserts a will over another, seeking and gaining a social/cultural acceptance and advantage in that positional state of being and performing the assumed norm. Hence, the presumed opposite of the hetero-masculine endures the consequence of its subordinated position.

"In Just Seven Days" (I Can Make You a Man)

In the now cult classic science fiction film, *The Rocky Horror Picture Show*, released by 20 Century Fox (1975), the lead character, Frank 'n' Furter, a transsexual traveler from an unworldly Transylvania (with *trans* in the actual geographical locale now a specific reference to alternative sexual identity), challenges social constructions of sexual performativity—and the shifting, desirous directionality of masculinity. As a man who dresses in eroticized feminine garb, Frank 'n' Furter variously moves between female and male sex partners in ways that both develop the storyline of unworldly queerness and also trouble notions of heteronormative social propriety. And even though such seemingly salacious behavior is part and parcel of the allure of the film, the storyline also reinforces the social sanctions of heteronormativity, and maybe a particular performance of masculinity to which the film offers multiple *manly* models (e.g., Eddie, Brad, Dr. Scott), in opposition to the primary queer/queen that dominates and subverts the expected storyline of male performativity, contaminating most of the straight men in the film.

Most importantly to my discussion on masculinity is the literal creation of the character of "Rocky" from whom the film gets its name. This creation is described in song:

A weakling weighing ninety-eight pounds
Got sand in his face
When kicked to the ground
(His girl split on him and then)
And soon in the gym with a determined chin
The sweat from his pores as he works for his cause
Will make him glisten and gleam
And with massage, and just a little bit of steam
He'll be pink and quite clean
He'll be a strong man
Oh honey
But the wrong man . . .

Telling is the descriptively idealized masculinity of Rocky with whiteness in the line: "He'll be pink and quite clean." While this reference is to the particularity of Frank 'n' Furter's desire, the literature in masculinity studies is rife with examples in which masculinity, and the performance of man, is constructed in race-based ways, idealizing white masculinity and either feminizing, homosexualizing, infantilizing, or beastializing the male figure in nonwhite cultures, particularly black and nonwhite men (Alexander, 2006; Hall, 1993; Harper, 1996; Jackson, 2006; Wallace, 2002; Pinar, 2001, 2003). Historically, masculinity has been associated with white men, both as a description of desire and as celebration of power, and linked with issues of class (Dyer, 1997; Halberstam, 1998).

Playing off Mary Shelley's (1818) classic story of *Frankenstein*, the character of Frank 'n' Furter strives to build his ideal man/mate from borrowed male parts and essences. In the song lyrics of "In Just Seven Days," sung by Frank 'n' Furter both as anthem and incantation, he heralds the constructed man that defines masculinity based on physicality. Alternately referred to as "The Charles Atlas Song," the song offers the foundational logics and descriptives that undergird this particular construction of masculinity. The song (in various versions, from regional stage productions to the film soundtrack) actually narrates the now iconic Charles Atlas 1928 advertisement.

In the ad, in the promotional form of a comic strip, Mac, a thin preconception of Atlas himself, the ninety-pound weakling, is bullied and insulted on a public beach by a muscular and ostensibly more masculine man. This results not only in his personal humiliation but also the loss of his girlfriend, who is attracted to the more aggressive performance of masculinity. The simple plotline of this narrative immediately defines masculinity as both relational, man to woman in a heterosexual coupling, and masculinity as physical strength and competitiveness in relation to other men. Gene Kannenberg Jr. speculates that "the ad also plucks the emotional strings of adolescent males who are insecure in their masculinity and who see the Atlas method as a way to gain the confidence they lack—also, of course, a dominant theme of the superhero comics tradition." In defense and rescue of his own male subjectivity, Mac engages the Charles Atlas "Dynamic Tension" muscle building program and transforms his body and thus his masculinity—now equated not just with the pumped up physique but a particular level of aggression and defensiveness—making him less vulnerable to other aggressive males and empowering his ability to regain and defend femininity.

And maybe the Charles Atlas ad also signals and ignites a kernel component of male homosocial gendering: instilling an intentional comparative, competitive, and combative nature in men; bidding men against each other as a quintessential performance of masculinity with a presumed nonsexual desirous intent. In her essay "Back to the Boys? Temptations of the Good Gender Theorist," Lynne Segal (2001) writes: "Anxiety and insecurity have always shadowed men's assertions of virility. The search for affirmations of 'manhood' remains the cause of, not then the solution to, men's problems. Men have always been forced into proofs of 'manhood' to ward off the dangers of 'feminization': through obsessive self-control, defensive exclusion and fantasies of escape" (p.13).

Later in the song lyrics from the film, Frank 'n' Furter outlines and subverts Atlas's program of transformation for his own desirous intent. Rocky is both the aftereffect and intent of such desirous efforts. In many ways, Frank 'n' Furter's homily is really about his surgically imaginative technique of "making a man"—as well as a potentially salacious reference to having sex as a component part of activating a sexualized identity in man. The engaged seven-day regiment is only added flavor to a particular presentation of desirous physicality, but unlike the Charles Atlas campaign, which foregrounds heterosexuality, Frank 'n' Furter's desire is altogether queer.

Invoking the logics of David Morgan (1993) in his essay "You Too Can Have a Body Like Mine," the social construction of the ninety-pound weakling in the Charles Atlas ad brings an attention to the male body that has historically been on the female body; that being the body as a site of a particular construction of gendered identity that potentially reinforces what Morgan, signaling

Ortner (1974) and Sydie (1987), elucidates as "the women/men and nature/ culture" binaries, in which the bodies of women are examined as biological detours from being men, hence warranting a particular level of investigation and exploration; and the bodies of men are always and already known through the social construction of the body's own expectedness (p. 70, see also Ann Fausto-Sterling, 1995). The female in the Charles Atlas ad is presumably bio- logically predetermined to select the strongest possible male/mate, regard- less of any emotional ties. Mac, realizing the biological determination of this social encounter, willingly sacrifices what might have been his own physical determination for the more performative and power-laden engagement of a hegemonic masculinity, which he must engage as a means of rescuing both his own masculinity as well as his girlfriend (femininity). And following Richard Dyer's (1997) analysis on the representation of the white male body as desir- ous spectacle, "there is at least one aspect of muscleman construction that is generalizable and this is the way the hero figure both establishes white supe- riority and yet also transcends division. Indeed, it is perhaps the secret of all power that it both secures things in the interests of patriarchy, while passing itself off as above particularity" (p. 308).

In *The Rocky Horror Picture Show*, the introduction of Rocky's muscular and idealized white masculine body rescues and uplifts an assumed mas- culine ideal promoted in the film. This is in contradistinction to Frank n' Furter, the cross-dressing effeminate transsexual. In the juxtaposition of the two characters, each tied together by the animation one of the other—the viewer sees both what is presumed to be extreme opposites of masculine performativity and the ways in which the two are always and already con- nected to each other, but in a tensive struggle to individuate not as correlates of sameness (Bersani, 1995). While the song, "In Just Seven Days" references the sex-specific designation of man (male), the specified characteristics of Frank 'n' Furter's desire of a strong man are in alignment with the social construction of masculinism, which is counterintuitive to his own conflicted performance of masculinity. Like Shelley's confused and conflicted creature in *Frankenstein*, Rocky Horror is also seemingly born innocent. Yet the ho- moeroticism that undergirded and motivated his construction is resisted by the newly born Rocky—resisted, as if the category of man is equivocal to heterosexuality with an assumed and scripted masculine subjectivity in the very sinews of the male subjects from which Rocky was animated. In her essay, "How to Build a Man," Ann Fausto-Sterling (1995) might argue that while there are biological directives in gendered behavior, nurture might also play a larger role over nature.

In the film, Rocky eventually acquiesces to his master's nurturing will, yet later engages in a heterosexual encounter with Janet, who also successively nurtures and seduces him to her desirous will, suggestively fulfilling a more organic aspect of his masculine subjectivity. The viewer of the film is asked to see the fulfillment of this desire as normal (male-female coupling), in relation to the abnormal couplings of Frank 'n' Furter with the variously identified male characters in the film. Yet the fluidity of Rocky's sexual encounters may also realize the assumed biological determination of Frank 'n' Furter's faux-insemination that animated Rocky, and literally constructed his masculine subjectivity.

The project of theorizing masculine subjectivity is key to studies of the masculine subject (Gutterman, 1994; hooks, 1992; Jefferson, 1994; Whitehead, 2002). Such studies often try to tease at the internal tensions, impulses, and yearnings that guide the psychosocial dynamics of boys becoming men—the pull between the father and the son, and the assumed Freudian rejection of the mother as an extreme necessity to ensure masculinity, but also in an Adlerian sense, masculinity as the necessary compensation for a devalued feminine opposite (see Connell, 1994; Butler, 1995; Vance, 1995). These psychoanalytic and social dynamic models of the masculine subject all offer functional approaches between the male and female sex that find "the ideas that women and men function as socialized beings at some subliminal but essentially biological level for the wider benefit of an 'ordered society' is, for many, a compelling and seductive notion" (Whitehead, 2002, p. 18). And in many ways in the *Rocky Horror Picture Show* the queer and incestuous progeny of Frank 'n' Furter, Rocky, a man born of (created by) a transsexual father, rejects both the libidinal desires of the mother (in the father) and the queer performativity of the father (in the transsexual creator) for a performance of masculinity that is constructed in a social realism that is putatively normalized. *How queer is that?*

In the song lyrics, while Frank 'n' Furter celebrates his particular construction of an idealized masculine subject, he also acknowledges that this might be "the wrong man." When Frank 'n' Furter speaks of the wrong man, maybe he is also acknowledging that the social imaginary of the idealized muscle-bound white male lover is linked with a feminine desire that is heterosexually based. Hence, his homosexual desire for such a man, for a Rocky, would not be easily (or exclusively) reciprocated in such a construction by its assumed heterosexual nature, which may be part and parcel a component of his forbidden or resistant desire. In his essay, "Postmodernism and the Interrogation of Masculinity," David Gutterman (1994) plays off of Eve Sedgwick's

(1990) *Epistemology of the Closet*, developing a metaphor of cross-dressing to describe the ambiguity of profeminist men, who seek to destabilize notions of sexual and gender identity. While the character of Frank 'n' Furter in the *Rocky Horror Picture Show* may not have such lofty intentions, his presence, if only undermined by his versatile sexual exploits, offers the core of what Gutterman might call (drawing from Judith Butler, 1990a), an "incoherent and discontinuous gendered being" that challenges a stable notion of man and a consistent performance of masculinity (p. 231). Part of the storyline, and maybe the overall message of the film, the character of Frank 'n' Furter is a somewhat indiscriminate lover—seeking and achieving sexual couplings in ways that worry notions of what it means to be homosexual and/or heterosexual. Frank 'n' Furtur's performative sexuality veers into the terrain of bisexuality, but not in an easily determined specification that resists the strictures of codified taxonomies in sexual otherness.

Maybe Frank 'n' Furter is the filmic embodiment of what Judith Butler (1993) refers to as the failed *heterosexual logic of mutual exclusivity*: "if one identifies as a given gender, one must [exclusively] desire a different gender" (p. 239). This of course has always been a particularly heterosexist logic strongly mandated for the performance of masculinity, but held as a flexible and desirous variable for heterosexual men with their own *voyeuristic intention* (to quote the *Rocky Horror Picture Show*) of seeing same-sex activities between women.

At the end of the *Rocky Horror Picture Show*, the otherworldly science-fiction project of Frank 'n' Furter's mission is not really revealed, but his sexual exploits and maybe the *persistent instability* of his gendered identity might be the reason why his mission is described as *a failure*. And like Tony Jefferson's (1994) analysis of the poem "Looking Back at It" by Brian Patten (1967)—maybe the character of Frank 'n' Furter encounters the "chastening effect of experience on the unrealistic desire to live up to the ambitious ideals ('tremendous heights') of masculinity" (p. 10). And for this failure, the film ends with his murder. Thus the film engages in an act of queering masculinity in that it explores the constructedness of masculinity through a framework of queer sex-ploitation— Frank 'n' Furter creating and consuming, seducing and subjugating others to his desire. But maybe more importantly, most of the men in the film, presumably and committedly heterosexual, seemingly activate their own presumed feminine or queer performativity as displayed in acts of same-sex sex, and in their own cross-dressing performance of drag in the film. Such sexplotiation begs the question asked by John DeCecco and John Elia (1993) in their edited volume, *If You Seduce a Straight Person, Can You Make Them Gay?* In this volume, DeCecco and Elia question and explore issues in biological essentialism versus social constructionism in gay and lesbian identities. Such discussions always trouble the notion of a fixed masculine subjectivity.

The *Rocky Horror Picture Show* offers a particular consequence to the presumed opposite of hetero-masculine performativity: the subversive male protagonist is killed. Yet the film as a cult classic also authorizes in its still legend audience-participation showing at midnight theaters across the country, a cross-dressing fantasy opportunity that allows mixed audiences to explore the salaciousness of gender play, even as it also repeatedly reinforces the same tragic consequences of such queer exploration.

"Straight Acting Seeks the Same," or, Queer Masculinities

In the nomenclature of gay chat lines and dating sites, the description of desire is marketed both by positionality and performativity:

> Only real men.
> Top looking for bottom.
> Versatile top seeks versatile bottom.
> Straight acting seeks fem.
> Straight acting man seeks the same.

In this sense, positionality is not just political location but also a literal descriptive orientation in the performative act of sex. Such sites offer the potential for meaningful connections (a sort of queer interactive *eHarmony* type network), but also serve as a venue for immediate sexual encounters. The descriptive taglines serve as filtering devices both attracting the particularity of desire and signaling the incompatibility of others engaged in a search. The preceding epigrams reference such negotiations. And even though, as Scott Dillard (1997) points out, "we often, if not exclusively equate the masculine in men with heterosexuality and the feminine in men with homosexuality" (p. 1), these epigrams as marketing devices also demonstrate the ways in which the social constructions of the hetero-masculine or the dominating relational dynamic of the masculine-feminine binary seemingly *play or do not play out* in the context of a homosexual relational subjectivity and gay masculinities.

And noting in the quote from Dillard, there is not an easy correlate to the masculine in women and the feminine in women, that might suggest some other categorical distinctions of sexual identity. Maybe this is also what Halberstam (1998) refers to as a disavowal of female masculinity when she asks:

"Why is there no word for the opposite of 'emasculation'? Why is there no parallel concept to 'effeminacy'? . . . Why shouldn't a woman get in touch with her masculinity? . . . Gender, it seems, is reversible only in one direction, and this must surely have to do with the immense social power that accumulates around masculinity" (p. 269). And almost as in direct reference to Eve Sedgwick (1995), Halberstam offers one of a series of axioms of/on the relationship between masculinity and femininity that will appear in this chapter when she writes: "Masculinity and femininity are in many respects orthogonal to each other. Orthogonal: that is, instead of being opposite poles of the same axis, they are actually in different, perpendicular dimensions, and therefore are independently variable" (pp. 16–17).

In making the comparative reference to same-sex sex roles in a discussion on the queer play of masculinity in homosexual relations, I am not reducing homosexual performativity to the particularity or consistency of a singular identity, role, or sexual position. I am not relegating all same-sex couples or couplings in the reductive masculine-feminine binary evoking the presumed social power differentiation that plays out in those roles. Nor am I reifying that the particularity of desire in same-sex relationships can be reduced to a mirror of heterosexuality. For I clearly know, as David Halprin (2000) reminds, "homosexual object choice, in and of itself, is seen as marking a difference from heterosexual object choice. Homo and heterosexuality have become more or less mutually exclusive forms of human subjectivity, different kinds of human sexuality" (p. 112). I further acknowledge the important contribution of Halprin when he writes, "homosexual relations cease to be compulsorily structured by a polarization of identities and roles (active/passive, insertive/receptive, masculine/feminine, or man/boy)" (p. 112). Or even the versatility of partners not necessarily to switch assumed performative roles in the context of intimate same-sex, but to be flexible in their expression and embrace of same-sex desire.

Yet with that disclaimer and a clear understanding both in an intellectual-academic sense, and in a personal and practical sense as a gay man—the marketing of identity as expressed in the particular context from which the epigrams are drawn, gay chat lines, are real. They are presented as practical articulations of desire that neither diminish the meaningfulness of committed identity politics nor seek to pass as some subversive act of trying to be "a real man" while engaged in sexual negotiations and encounters with other men. *How queer is that?*

Yet of these particular constructions, in relation to a discussion on masculinity, I am most often intrigued by the phrase: "Straight acting seeks the same."

The subject of *straight acting* always begs the question of the performative na-ture of gender—whether such bodily enactments come naturally or whether they are put-on—as self-protection, deception, or passing, as in discussions on drag king performances (Halberstam, 1998; Volcano & Halberstam, 1999). *Straight acting* invokes what I have described elsewhere (Alexander, 2003) as *heterotropes*, reoccurring patterns of expected heterosexual behavior that become signifiers of masculine performativity—a public desirous display for women, the magnification of expected masculine performances and a vehe-ment rejection of an embodied performance of the other; restrictive emo-tionality, staid physicality, and so on. This in opposition to *homotropes*, those expected, stereotypical, or overly generalized characteristics that are associated with homosexuals that might reductively and problematically include lisps, sibilant *s*'s, limp wrists, oversensitivity, the use of double entendre, snapping, throwing shade, swishy walking, chants such as "we're here and we're queer," references to bull-daggers or queens, truck-driving dykes or hairdressing fags, flannel-wearing lesbians or flamboyantly fabulous gays, and so on. All of which are generated in and relative to culture, state, and nation.

The expectedness and evaluativeness of such performances of identity are spectacle enactments in need of an audience to assign particular interpreta-tion—regardless of the accuracy of assessment (Duranti, 1986). Further, in Judith Butler's (1995) terms—"there is no gender that is 'expressed' by action, gestures, speech, but that the performance of gender [is] precisely that which produced retroactively the illusion that there [is] an inner gender core. In-deed, the performance of gender might to be said retroactively to produce the effect of some true or abiding [masculine/] feminine essence or disposi-tion" that is socially assigned, reified, categorized, and interpreted in terms that are meant to delineate and dominate (p. 31).

The phrase "straight acting," when invoked by a gay man (in particular) as a self-reference or a desired performance, makes literal an acknowledged subversion or at least a knowledge of the expectedness of masculine hetero-sexual performativity in relation to its assumed opposite. It is an assessment of performance; it is performance as being. Acting is defined as an assump-tion of a character or demeanor that is presumably incongruent with the expectedness of a gay identity—otherwise why note its specification. And while such a description can be interpreted as a clear articulation of desire for a particular type of male performativity, the notion of being "straight" always invokes "the force of a compulsory heterosexuality" (Butler, 1995, p. 117), which becomes the standard on which the straight-acting identified queer bases the actuality of his performative self—outside of desiring men.

When in fact the *straight acting* gay man seeks a *feminine acting* gay man, in many ways "that investment in [a] hegemonic representation of masculinity is not only erotic . . . there is also a social chasm separating the two partners in this alliance," or even a weird subversive attempt to reconstruct the already power-laden relational dynamic of heterosexual relationships to which they become both resistant and complicit in sustaining (Bersani, 1995, p. 117).

In the instance of the *straight acting man seeking the same*, short of the particularity of desire, there is an undergirding investment in a queer masculine heteronormativity that shapes desire and publicizes a social positioning within a community of gays that has always and already been shaped by a heteronormative and relational standard. Borrowing from Lynne Segal (2001) for my own purposes, it is in these moments that gay men's "claims to identity, whether empowering or diminishing [to] us, and however necessary for uniting us in essential commonalities with others, also serve to obliterate different identifications we might have made, might still make" in renaming our masculinity in queer terms, and not in terms that further our own oppression (p. 10).

In the closing of his essay "Loving Men," Leo Bersani (1995) offers the following important logic: "In our societies, the power of representation of masculinity is such that it can perhaps be resisted only by a provisional withdrawal from relationality itself, and a redefinition of sociality" (p. 122). While Bersani's powerful charge is used to signal what he calls "a salutary devalorizing of difference that marks a move from homosexuality as castration toward a notion of difference not as a trauma to be overcome . . . but rather as a nonthreatening supplement of sameness," it also reinforces for me a series of complex notions about masculinity and homosexuality (pp. 122–23). First, masculinity has traditionally been determined in a relational disposition to femininity (each for the other), and male homosexual desire is perceived as a misplaced directionality in which the expected masculine becomes feminine. Second, using a heterosexist model of relational desire in same-sex male unions it is presumed that each male assumes a role that simulates the masculine and the feminine. And third, an intervention is needed in how same-sex male couples reorient themselves (ourselves) from relational dynamics that might reify a heteronormative parity, to establish a new social orientation to being in a same-sex relationship and the emergent possibilities in that relational dynamic that does not seek to simulate otherness but embrace sameness. I believe Bersani's primary construction can serve as a charge not just for gay men, but a broader societal perspective that would not demonize same-sex desire as deviant.

Queer Masculinities and Querying Masculinity: A Conclusion

I have engaged this project from two distinct yet overlapping perspectives. First, to *queer* masculinity is in many ways to challenge the constructedness of a masculine ideal that is heavily invested in hetero-male performativity, even when that performativity is homosocial in nature and reifies its potency in relation to a presumed opposite. Such a queering invited the illumination of alternative constructions of masculinity—queer masculinities and female masculinities—as locations of emerging expressions of masculinity within and outside of the category of man. And second, to *query* masculinity is to both question and doubt that there is substantive evidence of masculinity's essential quality outside of a social investment that defines masculinity as what it is not, which always places masculinity in a hierarchical position in relation to femininity and its embodied or performative presence even outside of the category of woman. Such a querying also invited reflections on the sometime destructive results of a hegemonic masculinity rooted in power and dominance, but also ways in which the heterosexual logic that is dominated by masculinity claims a particular authority over the social order and even penetrates the relational dynamics of queers.

In his essay "Are You a Man or a Mouse?" Homi Bhabha (1995) invokes the comparative relationship between a man and mouse in a way that harkens back to the Charles Atlas ad. The phrase is used to question masculinity itself, or the performative aspects of acting manly in relation to a diminutive opposite. In reviewing the challenge of defining masculinity, he offers the following:

> Attempts at defining the "subject" of masculinity unfailingly reveal what I have called its prosthetic process. My own masculinity is strangely separating from me, turning into my shadow, the space of my filiation and my fading. My attempt to conceptualize its conditionality becomes a compulsion to question it; my analytic sense that masculinity normalizes and naturalizes difference turns into a kind of neurotic "acting out" of its power and it powerlessness. It is the oscillation that has enabled the feminist and gay revision of masculinity—turning back, the re-turning, of the male gaze—to confront what historian Peter Middleton describes as the "blocked reflexivity" that marks masculine self-identification, masked by an appeal to universalism and rationality. (p. 58)

In what ways might my compulsive probing of the conditions of masculinity in this chapter (or even this book project) reveal itself not to be just another engagement of a *prosthetic process* of such efforts, a process of revealing yet again the artificial or performative qualities of an embodied performance, and not the undergirding formulations that anchor a social investment in masculinity—furthering our insights to both transform the social interrelatedness of gender possibilities working in relation? In what ways is the project of exploring masculinity a space of entrapment for men, both motivated to understand self in relation to other but with a blocked reflexivity that prevents the focused intensity that would reveal, unravel, or deconstruct our core investments of being?

In his edited volume *Gay Masculinities*, Peter Nardi (2000) states, "Gay men enact a multiplicity of ways of 'doing' masculinity that can be best described by the plural 'masculinities.' Some enact the strongest of masculine stereotypes through bodybuilding and sexual prowess, whereas others express a less dominant form through spirituality or female impersonation. Many simply blend the 'traditional' instrumental masculinity with the more 'emotional' masculinity that comes merely by living their everyday lives when they are hanging out with their friends and lovers, working out at the gym, or dealing with the oppressions related to their class and ethnic identities" (pp. 1–2). There are significant volumes to which this current volume significantly contributes that speak to the globalizing nature of queer and gay identity politics. Yet this volume also extends the ways in which place, space, and time as correlated with culture, race, and how ethnicities inform and shape the emergent performative nature of masculinities, and of my particular concern—queer masculinities.

Volumes such as Cruz-Malavé and Manalansan's (2002) *Queer Globalizations: Citizenships and the Afterlife of Colonialism*, Johnson and Henderson's (2005) *Black Queer Studies: A Critical Anthology*, and Hawley's (2001) *Post-Colonial Queer: Theoretical Intersections*, each take on not simply the caldron of culture that spawns and simmers queer identities but the progressive and counter-hegemonic rhetorical, political, activist, and pedagogical strategies used by queers of color to subvert, resist, and transform reductive conceptualizations of being, and expand progressive notions of raced and gendered identities—working and living within and outside restrictive gender categories.

Hence how do conceptions of queer vary across the globe? The answer is not a simplistic one. But what I purport, even in the very specific sites of my analysis in this project, is that the distance between the local and global, as it relates to queer identities, is mediated by the particularity of circumstance, the object of critique, or the audience to which such performances are directed. Queer is both an identity location and position in relation to the ways in which sexed identities are constructed within the context of cultural production and cultural expectations of the normal, even when the normal is queer. By suggesting that masculinity is performative, and or *performativity*, an assessment of the embodied thing done, the iteration and achievement of the expected, I have been outlining the evaluative sense of masculinity across borders of difference. Such references also focus on the performed knowledge, complicity, and subversion of the expected that gives rise to queer masculinities.

Here I offer several different examples of the subversion of masculinity and/or masculinism. In her essay "Stealth Bombers of Desires: The Globalization of 'Alterity' in Emerging Democracies," Cindy Patton (2002) outlines the case of young men in Taiwan in the early 1990s waiting to be psychiatrically declared homosexual, as a means of avoiding mandatory military service. While she frames this analysis as evidence of "emerging democracies that adopt apparently liberal stances on social issues as a means of demonstrating their modernness, or at least their distance from barbaric practices" (p. 195), I offer this reference as an example of queer masculine performativity in which the identified gays use a problematic social construction of queer (as pathology) as the grounds to subvert military service. In the edited volume, *Infamous Desire: Male Homosexuality in Colonial Latin America*, Pete Sigal (2003) outlines the complexity of homosexual desire; representations of masculinity, femininity, and power; and the more important understanding of the sometimes integrated practices of race, power, and sexuality as key components of cultural practice. Such analysis also reveals the ways that hierarchies of value, acceptance, and tolerance of sexual identities are also relative to cultural and historical definitional orientations to the nature of masculinity and masculine performativity. And in the work of Patton and Sánchez-Eppler (2000), *Queer Diasporas*, we encounter the important construct of *tactical queerness*, which invokes a strategy of performing a resistant queer identity. We see this in the case of *transmigrant* Filipino queers in New York who recreate and subvert a queer version of the Santacruzan Filipino religious ritual, as an act of subversion to restrictive cultural mandates on homosexuality in their homeland, creating an act of conversion and renewal, building an emergent and resistant spirituality within a queer Filipino community in diaspora.

I am suggesting that the social politics of *masculinism* are relative to culture and location, and grounded in a sensed expectation of gender performance, and a normalization of those identities both within the hegemonic tones of culture itself, as well as within communities of culture that might even subvert the larger social expectations, as in queer masculinities (plural not singular)

QUEER(Y)ING MASCULINITIES · 69

that seemingly pivot on the standards of the expected. And while the notion of queer is relative both to the politics of subversion that underlay or motivate queer politics, or the particularity of sexed desire or the multiplicity of non-normative identities in the construction of LBGTTQ, the essence of those identities emerge from a space of desire, and the performative enactment of that desire or desired way of being is evaluated against a social and culturally constructed template of the normal.

This book project as a whole has engaged a critical reflection on the cultural foundations of masculinities in particular contexts and the ways in which the cultural practices of masculinity are interpreted and practiced through discourse. In many ways, culture has been approached in a very traditional sense as *the knowledge, language, values, customs, and material objects that are passed from person to person and from one generation to the next in a human group or society*—used as a yardstick for social membership and evaluation. As such, culture—in the shifting contexts of racial and ethnic specificity, geographic locality, and socio-interactional networks—establishes cosmologies of knowing the world and one's place in that world. Place in this instance is not only location, it is a relational dynamic that circulates within and between embodied beings. Culture as *cosmology*, "that arises out of people's history . . . addresses issues of reality and creation, truth and value, meaning, process, and people's place with creation" penetrates the psyche of its citizens (Akoto & Akota, 2005).

So in this sense, "masculinity . . . is the 'taking up' of an enunciative position, the making up of a psychic complex, the assumption of a social gender, the supplementation of a historical sexuality, the apparatus of a cultural difference" (Bhabha, 1995, p. 58). This is never exclusively local—in the specified space of cultural practice with similarly informed beings—but becomes mobile in the migration of those cultured citizens in their social and historical dis/placement, and in their relations to other embodied beings. Thus, if culture is considered an animating process, a system of ideologies made manifest in practice and embodied presence, then our "capacity for communication with one another is based on [our] common ownership of culture [in time and place]. But if [we] own culture, culture also owns [us]. Proprietorship thus introduces the subject-object relation, in which either may become a thing in the hands of others. . . . [Culture] stands as a thing over and beyond [us]" (Strathern, 1988, p. 322).

In this regard, we also understand that culture is dynamic and shifting, if only as tectonic plates through the sheer force of competing energies and the will of time and desire. What if we were to take seriously the fact that we are not exclusively the products or victims of culture, but perceived ourselves— particularly in discussions of gender and masculinity—as those who *conceive culture,* and as such we are the composite representation of that conception, both woman and man; both masculine and feminine. Such a conception, as discussed in the work of Marilyn Strathern's (1988, p. 13) concepts of Melanesian epistemology and the ways in which Shelley Mallett (2003) engages that work in *Conceiving Culture: Reproducing People and Places on Nuakata, Papua New Guinea*—might further our concepts of the ways in which the cultural construction of identity is in fact held as sacrosanct, ways in which we both justify our "relational embodied experiences" and our helplessness in changing those experiences (p. 36).

Such a move might allow us to move from studies of masculinity and the attendant bodies on which particular expectations are affixed to looking at masculinity as not fixed and bodies as *contested landscapes,* emergent territories of possibilities (Bender & Winer, 2001). Referencing back to the work of Strathern, such a reconceptualization of gender would not judge masculinity by social or intimate engagements, or even performative enactments separate from the immediate procreatory needs of a species—in which case, the discussion shifts from gender performance as informed by communities of culture to mere biological functionalism.

It is only those gender rebels, the few and the brave who dare not only offer critical commentary in the sanctioned spaces of academic discourse to question such limited constructions of being (masculinity and femininity) but engage in embodied performances, who help to make emergent the expressiveness of being outside of the constraints of cultural categories of gender expectedness visible. Such performances thereby expand the interpretations and interpolations of culture to see itself anew. When I reference gender rebels, I am no longer exclusively referencing members of the lesbian, gay, bisexual, transsexual, transgendered, queer (LGBTTQ) community, those of us who follow an impulse of our own design and desire. In the case of masculinity, I am also including those "straight" men who engage in performances of masculinity that do not intentionally reify the social constructions and expectedness of that political position. Straight men, who acknowledge and practice a humanistic masculinity that is grounded in equality and care, in compromise and negotiation, in respectful and mindful coexistence with difference; men who don't measure their manliness on the principle of search and seizure, divide and concur, rape and murder; men who see the nature of their embodied experiences as relational and do not impose their sexed identity as a battering ram for social conformity. *How queer would that be?*

References

Akoto, K. A., & Akota, A. N. (2005). African Cosmology. In M. K. Asante and M. A. Mazama (Eds.), *Encyclopedia of Black Studies* (pp. 34–35). Thousand Oaks, Calif.: Sage.

Alexander, B. K. (2003). (Re)Visioning the Ethnographic Site: Interpretive Ethnography as a Method of Pedagogical Reflexivity and Scholarly Production. *Qualitative Inquiry*, 9(3), 416–41.

Alexander, B. K. (2006). *Performing Black Masculinity: Race, Culture, and Queer Identity*. Lanham, Md.: AltaMira Press.

Alexander, B. K. (2008). Queer(y)ing the Postcolonial through the West(ern). In N. K. Denzin, Y. S. Lincoln, & L. T. Smith (Eds.), *Handbook of Critical and Indigenous Methodologies* (pp. 101–33). Thousand Oaks, Calif.: Sage.

Anderson, E. (2002). Openly Gay Athletes: Contesting Hegemonic Masculinity in a Homophobic Environment. *Gender & Society*, 16(6), 860–77.

Bender, B., & Winer, M. (2001). *Contested Landscapes: Movement, Exile, and Place*. New York: Berg.

Berger, M., Wallis, B., & Watson, S. (Eds.). (1995). *Constructing Masculinity*. New York: Routledge.

Bersani, L. (1995). Loving Men. In M. Berger, B. Wallis, & S. Watson (Eds.), *Constructing Masculinity* (pp. 115–23). New York: Routledge.

Bhabha, H. H. (1995). Are You a Man or a Mouse? In M. Berger, B. Wallis, & S. Watson (Eds.), *Constructing Masculinity* (pp. 57–65). New York: Routledge.

Boonzaier, F., & de la Rey, C. (2003). "He's a Man, and I'm a Woman": Cultural Constructions of Masculinity and Femininity in South African Women's Narratives of Violence. *Violence Against Women*, 9(8), 1002–29.

Bowker, L. H. (Ed.). (1998). *Masculinities and Violence*. Thousand Oaks, Calif.: Sage.

Brittan, A. (1989). *Masculinity and Power*. Oxford: Basil Blackwell.

Brod, H., & Kaufman, M. (1994). *Theorizing Masculinities*. Thousand Oaks, Calif.: Sage.

Bulhan, H. A. (1985). *Frantz Fanon and the Psychology of Oppression*. New York: Plenum.

Butler, J. (1990a). *Gender Trouble: Feminism and the Subversion of Identity*. New York: Routledge.

Butler, J. (1990b). Performative Acts and Gender Constitution: An Essay in Phenomenology and Feminist Theory. In S. E. Case (Ed.), *Performing Feminisms: Feminist Critical Theory and Theater* (pp. 270–82). Baltimore: Johns Hopkins University Press.

Butler, J. (1993). *Bodies That Matter: The Discursive Limits of Sex*. New York: Routledge.

Butler, J. (1995). Melancholy Gender/Refuses Identification. In M. Berger, B. Wallis, & S. Watson (Eds.), *Constructing Masculinity* (pp. 21–36). New York: Routledge.

Connell, R. W. (1994). Psycholanalysis on Masculinity. In H. Brod & M. Kaufman (Eds.), *Theorizing Masculinities* (pp. 11–38). Thousand Oaks, Calif.: Sage.

Craib, I. (1987). Masculinity and Male Dominance. *Sociological Review*, 35(4), 721–43.

Craib, I. (1998). *Experiencing Identity*. Thousand Oaks, Calif.: Sage.

Cruz-Malavé, A., & Manalansan, M. (Eds.). (2002) *Queer Globalizations: Citizenship and the Afterlife of Colonialism*. New York: New York University.

DeCecco, J. P., & Elia, J. P. (Eds.). (1993). *If You Seduce a Straight Person, Can You Make Them Gay? Issues in Biological Essentialism versus Social Constructionism in Gay and Lesbian Identities*. New York: Harrington Park Press.

Diamond, E. (1996). *Performance and Cultural Politics*. New York: Routledge.

Dillard, S. (1997). *Pass, Passing, and Making Passes*. Paper presented at the meeting of the Central States Communication Association, St. Louis, Mo.

Dudink, S., Hagemann, K., & Tosh, J. (2004). *Masculinities in Politics and War: Gendering Modern History*. Manchester, U.K.: Manchester University Press.

Duranti, A. (1986). The Audience as Co-Authors: An Introduction. *Text*, 6(3), 239–47.

Dyer, R. (1997). The White Man's Muscles. In H. Stecopoulos & M. Uebel (Eds.), *Race and the Subject of Masculinities* (pp. 286–314). Durham, N.C.: Duke University Press.

Edwards, T. (2006). *Cultures of Masculinity*. New York: Routledge.

Gadd, D. (2002). Masculinities and Violence against Female Partners. *Social & Legal Studies*, 11(1), 61–81.

Goldstein, J. S. (2003). *War and Gender: How Gender Shapes the War System and Vice Versa*. Cambridge: Cambridge University Press.

Fanon, F. (1967). *Black Skin/White Masks*. New York: Grove.

Fausto-Sterling, A. (1995). How to Build a Man. In M. Berger, B. Wallis, & S. Watson (Eds.), *Constructing Masculinity* (pp. 127–34). New York: Routledge.

Gutterman, D. S. (1994). Postmodernism and the Interrogation of Masculinity. In H. Brod & M. Kaufman (Eds.), *Theorizing Masculinities* (pp. 219–38). Thousand Oaks, Calif.: Sage.

Halberstam, J. (1998). *Female Masculinity*. Durham, N.C.: Duke University Press.

Halprin, D. (2000). How to Do the History of Male Homosexuality. *GLQ*, 6, 87–124.

Hall, R. E. (1993). Clowns, Buffoons, and Gladiators: Media Portrayals of African American Men. *Journal of Men's Studies*, 1(3), 239–51.

Hanmer, J. (1990). Men, Power, and the Exploitation of Women. In J. Hearn & D. Morgans (Eds.), *Men, Masculinities, and Social Theory* (pp. 21–42). London: Routledge.

Harper, P. B. (1996). *Are We Not Men? Masculine Anxiety and the Problem of African American Identity*. New York: Oxford.

Hawley, J. C. (2001). *Post-Colonial Queer: Theoretical Intersections*. Albany: State University of New York Press.

Hearn, J. (1998). Definitions and Explanations of Men's Violence. In J. Hearn, *The Violence of Men* (pp. 14–39). London: Sage.

hooks, b. (1992). Reconstructing Black Masculinity. In *Black Looks: Race and Representation (pp. 87–113)*. Ontario: Between the Lines.

Jackson, R. L. (2006). *Scripting the Black Masculine Body: Identity, Discourse, and Racial Politics.* Albany: State University of New York Press.

Jefferson, T. (1994). Theorizing Masculine Subjectivity. In T. Newborn & E. A. Stanko (Eds.), *Just Boys Doing Business: Men, Masculinities, and Crime* (pp. 10–31). London: Routledge.

Johnson, E. P., & Henderson, M. G. (Eds.). (2005). *Black Queer Studies: A Critical Anthology.* Durham, N.C.: Duke University Press.

Kannenberg, G. (n.d.). The Ad That Made an Icon Out of Mac. Retrieved May 31, 2010, from: http://www.cagle.com/hogan/features/atlas.asp

Linneman, T. J. (2000). Risk and Masculinity in the Everyday Lives of Gay Men. In P. M. Nardi (Ed.), *Gay Masculinities* (pp. 83–100). Thousand Oaks, Calif.: Sage.

Lorber, J. (1994). *Paradoxes of Gender.* New Haven, Conn.: Yale University Press.

Lorber, J. (2003). Paradoxes of Gender. In M. Hussey (Ed.), *Masculinities: Interdisciplinary Readings* (pp. 3–24). Englewood Cliffs, N.J.: Prentice Hall.

Mallett, S. (2003). *Conceiving Cultures: Reproducing People and Places in Nuakata, Papua New Guinea.* Ann Arbor: University of Michigan Press.

Middleton, P. (1992). *The Inward Gaze: Masculinity and Subjectivity in Modern Culture.* New York: Routledge.

Morgan, D. (1993). You Too Can Have a Body Like Mine: Reflections on the Male Body and Masculinities. In S. Scott & D. Morgan (Eds.), *Body Matters: Essays on the Sociology of the Body* (pp. 69–88). London: Falmer Press.

Morgan, D. J. (1994). Theater of War: Combat, the Military, and Masculinities. In H. Brod & M. Kaufman (Eds.), *Theorizing Masculinities* (pp. 165–82). Thousand Oaks, Calif.: Sage.

Nardi, P. (Ed.). (2000). *Gay Masculinities.* Thousand Oaks, Calif.: Sage.

Newton, E. (1984). The Mythic Mannish Lesbian: Radclyffe Hall and the New Woman. *Signs,* 9(4), 557–75.

O'Sullivan, C. (1998). Ladykillers: Similarities and Divergences of Masculinities in Gang Rape and Wife Battery. In L. H. Bowker (Ed.), *Masculinities and Violence* (pp. 82–110). Thousand Oaks, Calif.: Sage.

Ortner, S. (1974). Is Female to Male as Nature Is to Culture? In M. Z. Rosaldo & L. Lamphire (Eds.), *Women, Culture, and Society* (pp. 67–88). Stanford: Stanford University Press.

Patten, B. (1967). Looking Back at It. In A. Henri, R. McGough, & B. Patten. *The Mersey Sound* (p. 151). London: Penguin Classics.

Patton, C. (2002). Stealth Bombers of Desire: The Globalization of "Alterity" in Emerging Democracies. In A. Cruz-Malavé & M. Manalansan (Eds.), *Queer Globalizations: Citizenship and the Afterlife of Colonialism* (pp. 195–218). New York: New York University.

Patton, C., & Sánchez-Eppler, B. (Eds.). (2000). *Queer Diasporas.* Durham, N.C.: Duke University Press.

Pinar, W. F. (2001). *The Gender of Racial Politics and Violence in America: Lynching, Prison Rape, and the Crisis of Masculinity*. New York: Peter Lang.

Pinar, W. F. (2003). "I Am a Man": The Queer Politics of Race. *Cultural Studies ↔ Critical Methodologies*, 3(3), 271–81.

Pollock, D. (2006). Performance Trouble. In D. S. Madison & J. Hamera (Eds.), *Handbook of Performance Studies* (pp. 1–8). Thousand Oaks, Calif.: Sage.

Sedgwick, E. K. (1990). *Epistemology of the Closet*. Berkeley: University of California Press.

Sedgwick, E. K. (1995). Gosh, Boy George, You Must Be Awfully Secure in Your Masculinity. In M. Berger, B. Wallis, & S. Watson (Eds.), *Constructing Masculinity* (pp. 11–20). New York: Routledge.

Segal, L. (2001). Back to the Boys? Temptations of the Good Gender Theorist. *Textual Practice*, 15(2), 231–50.

Sigal, P. (2003). *Infamous Desire: Male Homosexuality in Colonial Latin America*. Chicago: University of Chicago Press.

Sinfield, A. (2002). Lesbian and Gay Taxonomies. *Critical Inquiry*, 29, 120–38.

Strathern, M. (1988). *The Gender of the Gift*. Berkeley: University of California Press.

Sydie, R. A. (1987). *Natural Women/Cultured Men: A Feminist Perspective on Sociological Theory*. Milton Keynes, U.K.: Open University Press.

Vance, C. S. (1995). Social Construction Theory and Sexuality. In M. Berger, B. Wallis, & S. Watson (Eds.), *Constructing Masculinity* (pp. 37–48). New York: Routledge.

Volcano, D. L., & Halberstam, J. (1999). *The Drag King*. London: Serpent's Tail.

Wallace, M. O. (2002). *Constructing the Black Masculine: Identity and Ideality in African American Men's Literature and Culture*. Durham, N.C.: Duke University Press.

Warner, M. (1993) (Ed.). *Fear of a Queer Planet: Queer Politics and Social Theory*. Minneapolis: University of Minnesota Press.

Whitehead, S. M. (2002). Desires of the Masculine Subject. In S. M. Whitehead (Ed.), *Men and Masculinities: Key Themes and Directions* (pp. 205–21). London: Polity.

Whitehead, S. M. (2006) (Ed.). *Men and Masculinities: Critical Concepts in Sociology*. [Five volume set]. New York: Routledge.

Yep, G. A., Lovass, K. E., & Elia, J. P. (Eds.). (2003). *Queer Theory and Communication: From Disciplining Queers to Queering the Discipline(s)*. New York: Harrington Park Press.

3

Disposable Masculinities in Istanbul

NIL MUTLUER

At the peak of the armed conflict between the Turkish army and the PKK (*Partiya Karkeren Kurdistan*, the Kurdistan Worker's Party) in the late 1980s and early 1990s, Turkish state forces evacuated some Kurdish villages and hamlets in Southeastern Anatolia and displaced Kurdish inhabitants without offering them any other place to live. These internally displaced people (IDP) mostly settled in big cities like Istanbul. Here they have developed various tactics[1] to survive in their everyday life. Although a certain awareness of the issue of internal displacement has been raised with the contributions of some civil organizations and academic research in recent years, most studies focus on the macro-level analysis of state policies and legal issues (Kurban et al., 2006; Dinç, 2008; Joost, 2008). Micro-level discussions of the evacuation process have recently been studied and in them the gender dimensions of the issue have been addressed by placing women at the center of the study. Today there have been no studies about internally displaced men and the way their masculinities[2] have been shaped in their journey from homeland to the place they migrated to. By examining the everyday life practices of internally displaced men living in an inner semi-slum area of Istanbul, Tarlabaşı, this chapter aims to examine how the discrimination, which the internally displaced men living in Tarlabaşı face during the displacement and in city life, shape the formation of their masculinities as well as their sexualities.

This chapter is an attempt to shift the center of analysis to men in order to examine power relations from a different angle. By placing internally displaced Kurdish men at the center of the research, it examines the exercise of hegemony in relation to power relations based on gender, sexuality, nationalism, ethnicity, and class in daily urban life in Turkey. An analysis of policies and a deconstruction of discourses[3] of the state and political institutions on these internally displaced men and their masculinities, as well as an examination of the everyday tactics of these men in relation to those policies and discourses, reveals the dynamics of gendered local knowledge based on various power relations. Essentially, I endeavor to comprehend how macro policies and discourses of the Turkish state or the civil and political institutions, like the ones of the Kurdish movement, as well as the collective consciousness of family, community, traditional, national, and Islamic values are utilized, set, fixed, altered, redefined, transformed, and traversed in the everyday life of the internally displaced men living at the center of Istanbul, in the inner-slum of Tarlabaşı, and how the masculinities of internally displaced men are shaped in this tension.

In their everyday life in Tarlabaşı, internally displaced Kurdish men are in relation to various Kurdish and Turkish civil, economic, political, and state institutions as well as to individuals from various backgrounds in terms of class, ethnicity, profession, religion, and sexuality. The everyday discourses and tactics of these men who constitute one of the "underclass" (Yılmaz, 2006) groups in Istanbul are shaped in collision with the reifying and homogenizing strategies of the external identifiers (i.e., the Turkish state, the hegemonic social and political discourse of the society, etc.) that regard them as "bare lives" to which any kind of policy in the name of state of exception can be applied (Agamben, [1995] 1998), and in their encounters with Kurdish and non-Kurdish men and women. Internally displaced men's tactics in the formation of their masculinities reflect the gendered national, ethnic, class[4] hierarchies and power relations in the society. Their tactics reveal not only the institutional policies and distributive patterns (political, social, economic), but also the power-laden social relations. In this tension their masculinities are formed in a "disposable" way in which masculinity gushes out as an identification tactic in each everyday city-life encounter.

In this chapter, the formation of the everyday discourses and tactics of the internally displaced men are analyzed in areas such as the process of forced migration from the homeland and encounters with middle-class urban dwellers, as well as with the various institutions and the inhabitants of Tarlabaşı from differing backgrounds. The alterations in the meanings attributed to concepts and notions like rape, torture, and honor and the changes in gender structure within the Kurdish community are also examined. In this regard, after briefly explaining the methodological framework, the first part concentrates on state policies of displacement, the Kurdish nationalist movement, and power relations in the context of Tarlabaşı. In the second part, the focus is on the identification process of the internally displaced men in their everyday interactions with the institutions as well as the Kurdish and non-Kurdish communities.

Methodology

My study focuses on two generations of internally displaced Kurdish men from different classes, sexualities, and occupations. The first generation consists of Kurdish men who personally experienced the displacement, whereas the second generation consists of the ones who were very young (below the age of five) at the time of displacement or the ones who were born in the city. During the fieldwork, more than forty in-depth interviews were carried out with Kurdish and non-Kurdish men, as well as women from various occupations, classes, and sexualities in Tarlabaşı. The methodology is based on ethnographic methodology (in-depth interviews, participant observation, and life stories) and archival research (official state documents, non-governmental organizations' documents and publications, newspapers, and journals).

I locate researcher and research subjects in separate but interrelated subject positions in order to examine the responses of the research subject, including discourses, behaviors, and practices in social processes that are produced historically by mutual power relations on the one hand, and to analyze both the separate and the interrelated position of the researcher and the research subject on the other. The research draws on methodology of critical discourse analysis with a postcolonial and poststructuralist feminist point of view (Alvesson & Sköldberg, 2000), which enables me not only to understand the heterogeneity of Kurdish masculinity, but also to reveal more insight about me and my social stratification. Reflexivity is also crucial in carrying out my research, because it allows me to "assess the relationship between knowledge and the ways of doing knowledge" (Calas & Smircich 1992, in Alvesson & Sköldberg, 2000, p. 5), where I can self-reflexively examine my positioning from different perspectives as well. Critical discourse analysis enables me to situate the institutional, social, political, historical context and socially constructed meanings in my evaluation. On the other hand, the postcolonial and poststructuralist feminist point of view enables me to question both the gender categories and the terms such as men, women, male and female, and other categories based on power relations like ethnicity, class, and geography (Alvesson & Sköldberg, 2000).

SUBJECTS AND TERRITORIES UNDER
A "STATE OF EXCEPTION"

In order to examine the political background of the issue with a deeper analysis, I would like to introduce related concepts developed by Foucault and Agamben on the issues of power, the body, population, and life. Under the light of these theoreticians' conceptualizations, I discuss the sovereign state's power-based politics over its subjects and territories.

SUBJECTS: INTERNALLY DISPLACED PEOPLE   In modern Cartesian dualistic terms, mind and body are considered as separate notions functioning in binaries (Grosz, 1994). Bodies (populations) are regarded as an objectified, depersonalized and passive entity to be controlled and repressed by mind, the sovereign, which can be the collective consciousness of the family, community, or national and Islamic values (Helvacıoğlu, 2006). In Foucauldian terms, biopower fabricates and regulates bodies as a decision maker, making them docile, useful, and productive. Biopower refers to technologies that regulate personal behavior and all dimensions of life that are subjected to the exercise of power (Foucault, [1978] 1990). As Foucault argued, biopower includes disciplinary power that incorporates technologies of domination and technologies of self, as well as coercion and freedom. Technologies of self subsume both the subject's conformity and resistance to the prevailing disciplinary norms and rules. Biopower also reveals possibilities for the subject to generate new forms of power. Biopolitics, on the other hand, with the introduction of modern technology aims to regulate and administer the population—bodies and minds of masses. By introducing regulatory mechanisms that decide who to "make live and let die," biopolitics controls the area of life and sets and protects the borders of the normalizing society (Foucault, [1975] 1995). There is a mutual relationship between the exercise of power and the application of knowledge. The "normalizing" knowledge, which is regarded as "true," is reproduced by those who have the capacity to exercise power over others (Foucault, [1972] 1980, Young, 1990).

Agamben challenges Foucault's claim that modern biopolitics is characterized by a new form of politics that constitutes a decisive break from classical power relations. According to Agamben, biopolitics always functions in a "state of exception" whose rules and laws are set by the sovereign to impose its policies over their subjects and territory in its state mechanism ([1995] 1998). Yet through the declaration of rights, the modern state reveals the relationship between sovereignty and biopolitical body, just in a new way. Every subject is in a biopolitical relationship with the sovereign body. Its source is "bare life," which is a political form of life exposed to death, especially in the form of sovereign violence (Agamben, [1995] 1998, pp. 125–28). Bare life becomes part of the state structure by being inscribed as a citizen, a member of a nation state by birth. Thus, sovereignty resides in every citizen. Once the sovereign regards any "life devoid of value (or life unworthy of being lived)," bare life becomes "homo sacer," who may be killed without being sacrificed (Agamben, [1995] 1998, p. 139). Thus, when homo sacer is excluded by the sovereign, it becomes "explicitly and immediately political," and this, Agamben argues, is "precisely what characterizes the biopolitical turn of modernity ([1995] 1998, p. 153).

In respect to this theoretical discussion, the Turkish state functions in such a way that in its national and neoliberal decision-making processes, it acts as mind imposing its dominant knowledge as the "normal" knowledge and regards its citizens—population—as bodies who have to obey the founding principles and disciplinary norms and rules of the Turkish Republic. The "ideal" citizen of the state is supposed to devote her/himself to the national project through believing in progress, science, and professional achievement without questioning anything against rationality, and is supposed to be a complete stranger to her/his body (Helvacıoğlu, 2006). In addition, "ideal" Turkish citizens are expected to defend their land and the nation at the expense of their lives/bodies. The Turkish state as a sovereign sets the disciplinary roles and norms as well as states of exception. Others, who act against the Turkish state's norms, are regarded as *homo sacers*, "who may be killed but not sacrificed" (Agamben, [1995] 1998, p. 114).

The concept of nation plays a crucial role "in the unification of bourgeois with other fractional class interests in the securing of the bourgeoisie revolution" (Adamson, 1991, p. 34). Contrasting to this functional role of nation, in Kemalist nationalist discourse between 1930 and 1945 the Turkish nation was presented as a classless, unprivileged, "undivided, homogeneous, harmonious totality" (Çelik, 2000, p. 196).[5] Although this mythical discourse does not represent the reality, it is still in the collective memory of the Turkish society in everyday life.[6] As a matter of fact, the Turkish state considers "Turkishness" as an ethnic category based on kinship, on the one hand, and as a cultural identity that should be assimilated, on the other (Yeğen, 2006). The state organs in Turkey have kept on mentioning a possible "internal threat" to the national borders that would come from some of its citizens, whom they stigmatize or address as homo sacer. The stigmatized citizens constitute the ones who are not "Turkish" by ethnic origin or religion or who refuse to act according to the values of an "ideal" citizen or to the founding principles or the policies of the state. This stigmatization goes along with a code of devalued and stereotyped behaviors attributed to stigmatized ones by organs such as state institutions and the mainstream media. It also enables the state to exercise its regulatory mechanisms, which legitimize its security discourse, and to apply its national and neoliberal policies through declaring a "state of exception," by implementing restrictive measure in the regions it deems "dangerous."

The Turkish state declared a "state of exception" in Southeastern Anatolia as a result of the armed conflict between the state and the PKK, where there have been two antagonistic camps since the armed uprising of the latter in 1984. In the late 1980s, the internal displacement[7] policy of the Turkish state compelled Kurds living in the Southeastern Anatolian villages and hamlets to migrate to city centers such as Istanbul (Kirişçi & Winrow, [1997] 2004; Kurban et al., 2006). The goals of the internal displacement policy were to prevent possible Kurdish support to the PKK, which has been in armed conflict with the Turkish army since the beginning of the 1980s (Kirişçi & Winrow, [1997] 2004; Ayata & Yükseker, 2005) as well as to provide "security" in the region, which is the basic condition for neoliberal economic policies to be applied. The internal displacement policy of the state includes not only evacuating and burning villages and hamlets of the Kurdish people but also imposing various forms of discrimination and violence, including torture and rape, to the ones living in those territories. The internal displacement policy of the state on behalf of security allows the state to stigmatize those who lived in a particular geography or space as bare lives, to which every kind of disciplinary norm and rule can be applied under a state of exception. In other words, these stigmatized ones are "disposable" in the eyes of the sovereign.

As military forces destroyed Kurdish communities' settlements after evacuating them, most of the internally displaced persons' (henceforth IDP) relationship with their place of origin was extirpated (Ayata & Yükseker, 2005; Çelik, 2005; Kurban et al., 2006). In addition to the collapse of animal husbandry, agriculture, and the lack of security as a result of the ongoing armed conflict between the PKK and the state, one of the main reasons for the IDP to decide to go to cities instead of neighbor settlements in the region is the village guard system, which was introduced by the state in the mid-1980s (Kurban et al., 2006). With the introduction of the village guard system, the state urged the Kurds in the region to cooperate with the army against the PKK.[8] Whether or not one became a village guard was a matter of insecurity for the inhabitants of the region, since in either case there was pressure from both the state and the PKK. On the one hand, the state went on evacuating the villages whose populations refused to become village guards, and on the other hand, the PKK evacuated the villages whose inhabitants became village guard. As a result of the ensuing economic, political, and social problems, the IDP had to move to new cities such as Adana, Diyarbakır, Istanbul, and Mersin. Many of them did not have any relationships with the Kurds living in these new cities, and the state did not develop any policies to ease the integration process of internally displaced Kurds into the cities (Kurban et al., 2006). Furthermore, as many of the IDP's worked in agriculture and animal husbandry, practices that are almost impossible to do in the city, they started work as unskilled labor or as street vendors with virtually no employment or social securities. Thus, the IDP Kurds found themselves in a confined situation in the city, where most of them became members of the poorest group and were forced to struggle for a living (Erder, 1996 [2001]; Işık & Pınarcıoğlu, [2001] 2002; Ayata & Yükseker, 2005).

Before delving into the spatial dimension of the issue, it is worth mentioning that the gender dimension in Agamben's theorization is absent. Detailed analysis of this absence and its relation with the formation of masculinity is discussed below in the section "Disposable Masculinities in Urban Context."

TERRITORIES: TARLABAŞI AS "DIRTY INSIDE" Different than the other districts such as Sultanbeyli, Ümraniye, and Kanarya where IDP migrated to in Istanbul, Tarlabaşı, one of the inner-city slum areas, is at the very center of the city, with a heterogeneous composition of various ethnic and religious groups from different professions, sexual orientations, and so on. Nationalist policies of the state, on the one hand, and the neoliberal policies of the local governing bodies, on the other, share the same stigmatizing discourse that justifies any kind of state of exception on behalf of "security." As stated by Yılmaz, it is an area with multidimensional exclusion that includes economic, political, social, spatial, and discursive aspects (2006). There is criminality and compulsory sex work in the region, yet these facts are not new phenomena (Yılmaz, 2006). In addition, as argued by many interviewees, the state and the police regard Kurdish politics as the major crime compared to ordinary ones. Thus, the state authorities and the police connive in the crime and compulsory sex work, since they prefer to consider political activities of the Kurds as "crime" instead of the other types of crime. The discursive exclusion practiced by authorities such as the state and the mainstream media embeds crime and compulsory sex work with ethnic groups and/or the transgendered living in the region (Yılmaz, 2006). Therefore, the state and other authorities' policies are shaped around the discourse of "cleansing" the region. According to this ethnic stigmatization, Kurds are identified with terrorism, the Romani people as well as Kurds with criminality, and Africans with drug dealing. Although there is no officially declared state of emergency in the region and no official measures are in place for entering or leaving it, the mainstream "security" discourse functions in a way that shapes the imaginary borders of Tarlabaşı on urban dwellers' minds. These imaginary borders also stigmatize the bodies living within these borders, as if they were a single homogenized criminal community, and these imaginary borders function for excluding or disposing the "dirty inside" of the region from the "clean outside," in Massey's sense (1994).

The stigmatizing history of Tarlabaşı dates back to late 1940s, from the early years of the foundation of the Republic. During late 1940s, the main target of the policies applied to the region was to create a "national bourgeoisie." The measures involved in creating a national bourgeoisie included transferring the capital of minorities—Armenians, Jews, and Rums,[9] who mostly formed the composition of Tarlabaşı—to the state by expropriating their property. In 1942, non-Muslims were forced to pay high amounts of Wealth Tax, and on the sixth and seventh of September 1955, actions against non-Muslim minorities, which were furtively supported by the state, took place, mostly in the Beyoğlu area, which includes Tarlabaşı. Following these discriminatory policies, non-Muslim groups mostly left the region. This influenced the composition of not only Tarlabaşı but also Istanbul. Since the late 1980s, large numbers of Kurdish immigrants from the Southeastern part of Turkey either migrated into or were displaced to Tarlabaşı, where they encountered the Roma population. Nineteenth-century buildings were occupied and houses that were built for families were divided into smaller rooms and occupied, or if the owner was known, rented to immigrant families or single people, specifically men. After Kurdish migration, conflict between Roma and Kurdish communities rose due to economic pressures. More recently, Tarlabaşı has become the migration point of many immigrants, asylum seekers, and refugees from Africa and neighboring countries like Iraq. Tarlabaşı is known to be a place of transgender sex work as well, thus many transvestites and transsexuals who mostly work as sex workers live in the area.

The electoral tendency of the population in Tarlabaşı is basically divided into two. The ones who identify themselves with Turkish nationalism and religion mostly vote for the governing party AKP (Justice and Development Party), and the ones who identify themselves more with the Kurdish ethnic background and nationalism vote for the DTP (Democratic People's Party).

In the last elections, on June 22, 2007, the AKP won the majority of votes in the Beyoğlu region and in its Tarlabaşı district. It is also important to note that in the last elections the MHP (National Movement Party), the nationalist party, gained a remarkable share as well. Today, with the gentrification policies of the government, properties in Tarlabaşı that belong mostly to minority associations, Kurds, Romans, and other low-class groups are to be expropriated and sold to one of the private companies that has nepotistic relations with today's AKP government. The contractor of the gentrification project, GAP, is one of the companies of the Çalık Holding, whose owner is related to the prime minister by marriage. The inhabitants, who have not been allowed to restore their buildings by the Committee of Protection or who cannot afford the restoration of the buildings, are forced to leave their homes in Tarlabaşı and pass their dwellings over to the municipality and its subcontractor company. This will mean a second displacement for some of the inhabitants of the district, like Kurds.

DISPOSABLE MASCULINITIES IN URBAN CONTEXT:
CASES FROM TARLABAŞI

Cities are places where collective and individual identification is staked, belongings are negotiated, and rights are pursued (Secor, 2004). Everyday life in the city provides the opportunity to observe and analyze how individuals and collectivities ambivalently develop tactics (in de Certeau's sense, [1980] 1988) against the policies of macro structures on the one hand, while identifying themselves with these structures, on the other. The construction of individual and collective discourses occurs and subjectivities are shaped in each domain (i.e., urban life, streets, workplaces, and transports) where individuals and collectivities have their ingenious ways (tactics) in which "the weak make use of the strong" (de Certeau, [1980] 1988). This is the political dimension of everyday practices that are creative and dynamic. This approach to the city shows us the possibilities inscribed within the fabric of daily life against the effects of reification (Gardiner, 2000).

As a reaction to the oppressive policies of the sovereign, which include "exploitation, marginalization, powerlessness, cultural imperialism, and violence" (Young, 1990, pp. 39–65), stereotyped, and economically and socially segregated, groups develop a "double consciousness" (Du Bois, [1969] 1903, p. 45, in Young, 1990, p. 60). Double consciousness arises when the oppressed subject refuses to conform to the devalued, stereotyped projections of the dominant culture about her/himself (Du Bois, [1969] 1903, p. 45, in Young, 1990, pp. 60–61). The concept of double consciousness opens a path to unsettle conceptualizations of binary relations between the oppressor and the oppressed. Such a conceptualization neglects the bargaining power of the oppressed by her/his ingenious tactics and the value of the gap between the oppressor and the oppressed, which involves the opportunity for creating contrasting and different types of knowledge, "border thinking" in Mignolo's sense (2000). Alternatively, borderlands, in Anzaldúa's approach, are present physically when two or more cultures of different communities, races, and classes abut each other and live on the same territory in the sense that "the space between two individuals shrinks with intimacy" (1987). In this regard, such a conceptualization can be one of the alternative interpretations of the authorities' discourse.

Men's discourses and tactics are shaped in this discursive area where border thinking occurs. Men are a social category shaped by the gender order as well as collective and individual agents, often the dominant ones, of social practices (Hearn, 2004). The structural and interpersonal domination of men over women in various spheres of life can be regarded as historically differentiated patriarchies (Walby, 1990; Hearn, 2004). Hegemony exists in such an environment as a result of the interplay of coercion, persuasion, and consent (Connell, 1995; Hearn, 2004). Nevertheless, it is crucial to note that the bearers of the hegemony do not have to be the most powerful men in the society (Connell, 2001; Hearn, 2004). The differences among men as well as women in terms of age, class, ethnicity, profession, and other markers enable them to utilize the hegemonic, patriarchal values in different contexts. In the oppressive, colonial mind-set, the oppressed are regarded as body rather than mind (Shohat & Stam, 1994). There is also a direct relationship between masculinism and nationalism (Bhabha, 1995). Nation is represented through an ideal father figure who is the head of the nation as well as the carrier of the ideal masculinity. Such an approach naturalizes the way oppression and patriarchy is practiced through the men and women in the society who own the ideal masculinity discourses. In relation to such an approach, other men and women are more likely to be homo sacer, in Agamben's sense.

In their everyday interactions, internally displaced men become the subject and the object of hegemony and practice coercion, persuasion, and consent in various ways. Internally displaced men experience different power relations emerging from different interactions in the everyday life of the city from the relations in their place of origin. In their everyday identification, internally displaced men identify themselves with the codes and the values attributed to various types of masculinities of the specific locality. In the Kurd's place of origin, Kurdish nationalist institutions, Kurdish communities (having a relatively more similar living style), and the Turkish state were the main external identifiers for Kurdish men, whereas in the city, in addition to those, various social, cultural, economic, and political institutions, and both Kurdish and non-Kurdish individuals from various backgrounds, come into consideration. Therefore, there is a shift of power centers and the forms of oppression that influence the internal and external identification process of the internally displaced men. The internally displaced Kurdish men become relatively less reachable and there are times when they are almost invisible to the Turkish state institutions. In this case, the tactics developed by the internally displaced men not only become multiple but also more complex, leading Kurdish men to develop a discourse as a result of complex relations that are the subject of analysis of this study. The discourses and tactics of internally displaced men are shaped as a result of these practices in a discursive area of border thinking.

Internally displaced men make use of the strategies of the sovereign and develop various tactics in each of their encounters with the institutions as well as individuals in the urban space. In this tension their everyday practices are shaped in a positional way such that their masculinities are always in the process of being disposed and disposing in return. Thus, internally displaced men's masculinities are formed in a disposable way such that in each of their encounters in a specific power-based relationship setting they create a new form of masculine being. In the next section, how internally displaced men's disposable masculinities are shaped is discussed in various sites such as the bodily and the visual humiliation they experience, the supportive space that Kurdish nationalist institutions provide, and the changing gender relations they practice.

Shaving, Torturing, and Raping the "Other" Male Body

Contrary to the modern dualistic approach, which addresses the mind or state as the subject with controlling power and the body or citizens as the objects to be controlled, it is crucial to examine not only the state's hegemonic power but also bare lives' discourses and tactics in relation to the hegemonic power in order to have insight about power-laden everyday relations, and to examine how the dominant knowledge of the hegemony is interpreted and transferred differently in creating border thinking. The body, on which many policies have been developed, "must be regarded as a site of social, political, cultural, and geographical inscriptions, production, or constitution"

(Grosz, 1994, p. 23). Subjectivities developed by a person must be considered as the outcome of the self's individual and collective identification processes (Skeggs, 1997; Brubaker et al., 2000). The bodily behaviors of individuals can- not be extracted from their bodily practices (Bigwood, 1998). In this regard, men—as bodies—can also be regarded as sites for contestation where macro policies are applied and at the same time the resistances and conformities to these policies occur, even though the state regards them as a "threat" and declares a state of exception to regulate them. In other words, men can be regarded as sites to examine the border thinking developed in the formation of their subjectivities. The subjectivities of the internally displaced men are shaped in relation to "historically situated differences in social sensibility"; "cross-cultural differences in cognition, affect and action," as well as "the pe- culiarities of each individual" (Biehl et al., 2007, p. 3) in their everyday city life.

As discussed earlier, as a result of the economic and political tension in the Southeastern region, many of the IDP had no other choice but to go to the cities. On their way to as well as in the city, internally displaced men be- came homo sacers who passed through individual and collective humiliation, torture, and even rape under custody. There are various unknown murders in the villages and there are times when JİTEM,[10] the "unofficially" existing intelligence organization of gendarmes, organized raids on civilians' houses and took them under custody without any sufficient reason. As a result of these activities, many civilians were lost or murdered. In Tarlabaşı, when the military operations in Southeastern Anatolia are active, police have taken ex-guerrillas under custody for long periods of time, as long as six months without giving any sufficient explanation.

One of the practices of state institutions, mostly the army and JİTEM in the Southeastern Anatolian region, as argued by many of the internally displaced people, is to collect Kurdish people at the center of their villages and make men undress and stay naked in front of the rest of the community. They also beat men and shave their mustaches in front of their wives or in front of the community. Being beaten or being shaved by the state bodies in front of women and the rest of the society harms and almost crushes the virility of the men, whose masculinities are shaped by tradition and honor. As stated by Helvacıoğlu, having or not having a mustache and beard are signs of masculinity in various societies (2006). In regions such as the Mediterra- nean, Anatolia, and the Middle East, the mustache and beard become signs of masculinity as well as political affiliation. Secular men mostly prefer to shave their mustaches or beards as a sign of modernity, whereas some Muslim believers have them as a sign of their Islamic affiliation, or some guerrillas have them as a political sign. One of the interviewees, Hasan,[11] explains how he felt during the time when soldiers shaved him in front of the community:

> They shaved me in front of the community. At the beginning it was awful, but then I saw it as the beginning of my resistance, I almost stabilized myself. I was frozen. They tried to destroy me. I didn't look at anybody in the eyes. I just waited [for] them to finish. It's just the part of my body and I can devote it to my nation.

The idea of devoting his body and himself to his nation and national ideals enabled him to ease the humiliation that he passed through during the evacuation of his village. During the oppression, the presence of an alternative regulatory system comes onto the scene and the internally displaced man finds meaning for resistance by identifying himself with this new system. In order to protect his virility, he developed a subjectivity in which he regards this incident as a starting point of his resistance. Under the state's oppression, the identification with an alternative power such as the Kurdish nationalist movement enables him to sacrifice his body for a reason. In other words, his body becomes an entity to be sacrificed, not a bare life.

It is not easy for men to talk about this. Although one of the male interviewees explained his experience, most of the time it was women who explained in detail what had happened during the evacuations. Men were mostly silent about the humiliation, torture, and rape they passed through. Or they talked about these factors as other men's experiences. One way or another they developed tactics to explain what had happened without mentioning themselves. One of the interviewees who was subject to rape and serious sexual assault justifies their tactics as follows:

> Men cannot admit the rape which they experienced during the torture. Their male identity they want to defend leads to a serious depression.

Another interviewee, Cevat, states:

> He cannot admit it. Because if he is perceived as a raped man. His masculinity will have been degraded and his male honor will have been tainted. Therefore, he may admit torture but not rape!

"Degraded masculinity" and "tainted male honor" are the red lines where internally displaced men are willing to talk about torture, but resist talking about rape in order to protect their masculinity. Cevat also adds that,

> Torture starts by sticking a bottle into you. That is the basic reality and everybody knows, but no one can admit it in the prison.

Thus, on the one hand Cevat accepts the fact that there is a rape and he wants to explain and to show the inhumane treatments of the state, but he insists on explaining it as the experience that others passed through. In the Agambenian sense, this case reveals the fact that trespassing the bodily integrity of a man, which is a state of exception in everyday life, becomes a norm in the prison, something that everybody knows.

It is very recent and rare that interviewees start to talk about the rape that happened to them. Even if they start to talk about it, they prefer just to mention it very quickly and then go on justifying why they hide it or what should be done. As a "man," they feel the need to give reasons to explain such a traumatic incident. As stated by another internally displaced man, Mazlum:

> If it happened now, I would directly sue the state in the European Court of Human Rights. But it was harder for us. We couldn't do it during that time. You are the first person that I am telling this. But I should open it.

After this explanation we stayed silent for minutes in our interview. This explanation also shows how his discourses and tactics are in continuous change in relation to the Kurdish movement's strategies. Until the 1990s, the Kurdish movement regarded men as the main figures of their resistance (Caglayan, 2007), thus the responsibility of representing the movement prevented Mazlum from mentioning anything about rape "during that time." Like the reaction of Hasan being shaved in front of his community members, Mazlum's identification with the movement makes him feel that his body represents the movement and gives him a reason to sacrifice his body and his life. Thus, although his masculinity did not allow him to talk about the rape before, the changes in the discourses of the movement allow him to talk about it without harming his masculinity now. In both Hasan's and Mazlum's cases, they identify themselves with the Kurdish nationalist movement's regulatory mechanisms, or strategies in de Certeau's sense, instead of the state's ones.

During our interview Cevat also compares his position with women and argues:

> In the case of rape women seek for justice but men can't with the fear of losing their reputation as masculine. This is where they are weaker and more pathetic than women.

This statement reveals how in the minds of the internally displaced men the forced sexual intercourse is identified with women and femininity, while it is the fear that harms manhood and masculinity. Since "seeking for justice for rape," or in other words, rape itself, is normalized in this discourse, it is as if women can seek justice more easily. Women's bodily integrity and sexualities are considered as matters such that any kind of decision about them are decided by legislative, executive, and juridical forces, their integrity representing biopolitical borders of the sovereign (Miller, 2006). Sexuality, rape, abortion, and adultery are seen as the single crimes that only women are subject to (Graham, 2006). In the second part of the statement, Cevat regards men as weaker than women. Here he identifies himself more with modern urban values than traditional ones. The Kurdish movement's changing discourse about the roles and functions of men and women in Kurdish society also influences his discourse.

The torture, rape, and electric shocks that many of the internally displaced men experienced under custody hamper their psychology (in Kurban, 2006). Some of them stated that because they regarded the violence, including rape, that they experienced under custody as damaging to their virility, they needed to test their manhood. Thus, when they were released, some of them immediately went to brothels or married and had children, in order to test their sexuality and fertility. In some cases, some of them even tried homosexual intercourse to test their erectile function.

Many of the internally displaced men's bodily experiences in different power-laden relations are influential in their everyday identification process with the Kurdish movement, Turkish state bodies, their policies, city structures, and interactions with other city dwellers. Whatever the circumstances they encounter, one of the main factors that needs protection is their virility. Even in cases of encountering the most humiliating practices that have the high possibility of harming their masculinity, like shaving, torture, or rape, they immediately identify themselves with a strategic discourse—the Kurdish nationalist movement—that is worth devoting their body for, a cause that saves them from feeling that their lives are bare lives. Identifying themselves with such an "upper" ideal opens a space for them to protect their virility. Moreover, their discourses show that such a space provides them the possibility of proving their masculinity and manliness in front of an audience.

The Visibility of Internally Displaced Men

Internal displacement has influenced both the lifestyle and the gender roles of the Kurdish community (Şen, 2005). The IDP women and children have faced serious problems by becoming a cheap labor force for industries (e.g., the textile industry) in both formal and informal ways (Çelik, 2005; Kurban et al., 2006). At the same time, non-governmental organizations (e.g., TOHAV, MAZLUMDER, GÖÇ-DER, Başak Culture and Art Foundation, Tarlabaşı Community Center) have developed various projects in order to rehabilitate their poor conditions. Although these projects are not adequate enough to improve the Kurdish women and children's living standards at present, they have aroused a certain awareness in the society about the existence of this group. Moreover, the Kurdish women's movement has also become powerful in the cities and has supported internally displaced women and children.[12]

While Kurdish women were becoming more and more visible, internally displaced Kurdish men were not only ignored, but also stigmatized with such terms as "maganda," "hanzo," and "kıro"[13] by middle-class city dwellers at the end of 1980s. *Maganda* as a masculine figure emerged as a "derision who is totally oblivious to his own uncouth and offensive masculinity—thus 'interfering' with the moral discourses of the decade, to destabilize and debunk the authoritative codes of 'civility'" (Öncü, 2002, p. 174). The term *maganda*, which encapsulates the fact that the interconnectedness of contemporary consumption patterns and narratives of masculinity depend on place, setting, and context (Öncü, 2002), is not used in every context for every Kurdish man, but for the ones whose behaviors and manners are different than the ones regarded as "civilized" and "modern" by middle-class city dwellers. The media's interest in the issue of honor killings and the increase in crime rates in Istanbul also present Kurdish men as criminal and "uncivilized" figures. Therefore, internally displaced Kurdish men have found themselves in a position of both being *invisible* in the search for their economic and social rights and *visible* in debunking the authoritative civil codes of the city as "maganda" in the society, on the one hand, and both being *dominant* over less powerful women and men and *subordinated* by the patriarchal, dominant values of Turkish and Kurdish societies, on the other.

One of the interlocutors, Hasip's, words show this in-between position. He said that:

> They [people in Istanbul] call me kıro, *maganda*. Everyday in the television they laugh at the way I talk, I walk. They think I am ignorant, I don't know anything about their Istanbul. They say we have only one Istanbul. But they forget the fact that Istanbul is ours with its mosques. My father was an educated man, he was an *imam* [a leader of Muslim prayer]. If someone from our village went to Istanbul, my father told him to go to all the religious places. I know they want to humiliate me. But they couldn't. I am not ignorant as they think.

Education, but the secular education, is considered by the Turkish elite or middle-class city dwellers as one of the most crucial elements in shaping the modern, contemporary, and prosperous Turkish nation. While reproaching his self-representation in the minds of the middle-class city dwellers, Hasip uses education in his narration; however, he converts the content of the education from secular to religious. In this way, he shows both that he is aware of the "education" discourse of the Turkish state, on the one hand, and that he challenges this discourse through changing its content with another, "oppositional" knowledge of the founding principles of the Turkish one, a religious one, on the other. In his discourse, he also sets the hierarchy and the borders of this "oppositional" knowledge. By putting his father at the top of the hierarchy as *imam,* he presents his closest kin member as the authority, and by referring to the mosques in Istanbul he displays that his knowledge, as well as his authority through his father, goes beyond the borders of his hometown to include Istanbul.

Becoming a Kurd in Tarlabaşı: The Institutionalization of Political Embodiment

The Kurdish institutions like the DTP (Democratic Society Party) and MKM[14] (Mesopotamian Culture Center) in Tarlabaşı and İstiklal Street (very close to Tarlabaşı) play significant roles in the identification process of internally displaced Kurdish men in Tarlabaşı. While resisting the oppressive policies of the state or its bodies, these institutions become places with which internally displaced men identify.

The DTP, the pro-Kurdish political party with twenty seats in the parliament, is regarded as the successor of the DEHAP (Democratic People's Party), which was also the successor of several Kurdish parties that were banned by the Constitutional Court, which claimed that the party had connections with the outlawed PKK. The DTP and DEHAP are also regarded as the political wing of the PKK. Although the DTP does not officially declare whether it has links with the PKK or not, it does engage in symbolic gestures that refer to this link. For instance, in October 2007, the DTP sponsored a conference in which the jailed leader of the PKK, Abudullah Öcalan, was released.

The MKM, which was founded in 1991, also plays a significant role, especially in the young generation's everyday life, with its nineteen branches all over Turkey. The MKM is one of the crucial sights of the pro-Kurdish movement, since it is not only the first cultural center of the political movement, but also has a wide range of participation form Kurdish people. There is a mutual relation between the MKM and the PKK. Some of the activities, including political discussions and art projects, reflect the ideas of the leader of the movement, Abdullah Öcalan. The MKM plays a significant role in this identification process, since it provides the opportunity to Kurdish people for raising their voices in their own language and it provides the opportunity of education to the youngsters, especially those who have not had chance to complete their education.

As a matter of fact, as stated by many IDPs in Tarlabaşı, it is almost impossible for any pro-Kurdish party or institution not to have connections with the PKK, since family members or relatives of any Kurdish family are either murdered by the state or become "martyrs" as guerrillas in the PKK. Thus, in such an environment the PKK is regarded as the center of resistance to the state's discriminatory and anti-democratic policies by many of the IDPs in Tarlabaşı. Most Kurdish people need a central power that understands their pain, solves their problems, and with which they can identify.[15] Nevertheless, a paradoxical situation must also be taken into account in that some family members and relatives carry out their military service as citizens of the Turkish Republic. Therefore, there are cases where the same family has both guerrillas and soldiers at the same time. However, inside the houses, the photographs of the family member guerrillas on the wall are a sign of their dedication to the movement, whereas the photographs of the family member soldiers are kept in drawers as a sign of the obligation that they have to fulfill.

Like Turkish nationalism's mythical "classless, unprivileged society" discourse, Kurdish nationalism aims to create a "classless" equal society, and it openly declared this in its 1995 party program.[16] In light of this discourse, Kurdish nationalist institutions open a space to fulfill this agenda and to strengthen Kurdish nationalism among community members. As mentioned by the members of the DTP and MKM, both organizations constitute Kurdish people from various classes and educational backgrounds. "Classless society" discourse plays a significant role in the everyday identification processes of internally displaced men. As pointed out by a member of the MKM, "people, including construction workers or the ones with very poor conditions, for the first time in their life act and sing at the stage in their own language."

This construction-worker metaphor can also be seen in the discourse of Şeyhmus, another internally displaced construction worker, who is responsible for various office work of the DTP in the Tarlabaşı region. Holding such a responsibility gives Şeyhmus a confidence of being more than *amele*, which is a slang term used in everyday language instead of worker, and which he is used to hearing from middle-class city dwellers. Regarding the word *amele* and the DTP, one of the construction workers, Cafer, states that:

> It [*amele*] is not a bad word normally. But sometimes I realized that Turks used it to humiliate me. They look down on me. Of course not all of them, but some. But in DTP I am dealing with the office work from financial affairs to paper work. We had a congress last week. My audits were transparent. They reelected me for this duty. We Kurds are equal in the movement and in the organization.

While referring to his feelings about the DTP, Cafer is proud of himself and tries to show me, a non-Kurdish middle-class woman researcher whom he says he trusts and calls *heval, meaning friend in Kurdish*,[17] that the DTP manages what Turkish nationalism could not manage. This political capital provides him a social capital in which his status is not discussed, but justified. With this justification, he can show his capabilities in confidence. This confidence plays a crucial role in the formation of his subjectivity. On the one hand, he identifies himself with Kurdish nationalism, on the other hand, he challenges the power hierarchy by being the subject of the knowledge rather than the object of it in front of a Turkish woman. Challenging the stigmatization of internally displaced men in mainstream media and political discourse that presents them as potential criminals or thieves or as violent dangers both to Kurdish and to non-Kurdish women, internally displaced men's everyday discourses and tactics allow them to become part of the city where they shape and are shaped in.

Nevertheless, there is the other side of the coin as well. From the state bodies, like the police's point of view, having such memberships also means being close to the Kurdish movement. Such a closeness to the movement is regarded as a threat to "Turkish national unity" by the state bodies. In relation to this point, almost all of the interlocutors of this study argue that the state prefers to distract Kurdish IDPs' attention from political issues to criminal ones, since the state finds politics more "dangerous" than ordinary crime. Under these circumstances, the ways IDP men identify themselves with notions like nationalism, religion, and crime differ in various power-laden contexts.

These differences tell much about the political dynamics in the region. Many of my interviewees, both women and men from different ages and worldviews and so on, mention that police connive in creating the high crime rates in the region and accept bribes. While talking about the crime and security, some of my interviewees mention the fact when there is a decrease in the everyday crime they witness, they understand that "their criminals" could not afford the bribe. The criminals are said to be taken under custody only when they cannot afford to give a bribe to the police. Some even said that "the bribing time of the high police officials is Friday afternoons." Whether this is correct or not, it is a fact that crime and its relation with the state is normalized in the everyday discourses of the IDPs and becomes part of their collective memory.

In such an environment, where the police's relation to crime and the treatment of the political "criminals" becomes a collective knowledge, internally displaced Kurdish men develop various tactics in presenting their relation with nationalism, religion, and crime. For instance, one of the internally displaced men whose sons and daughters work, bringing money to the family, is more likely to identify with his own family than with Kurdish nationalism, since there are no other breadwinners in the family. As frankly stated by Fırat,

> I know they want us to become criminals, drug dealers, they even want our daughters to become prostitutes. They don't want us to deal with the politics. But, we as a family devote ourselves to our movement. My son and my daughter work for twelve hours to support the family. I spent ten years in prison, two of my brothers became martyrs in [the] guerrilla [movement].

The fact that Fırat can openly declare his affiliation with the movement and the guerrilla figure is significant in the formation of his masculinity.

On the other hand, Kamil, who has to work to support a family of nine, identifies himself more with religious values. Not wanting to risk identifying himself as a political figure and wishing to avoid attracting the attention of the police, he initially identifies himself with religion. But as the interview went on he asked me some questions about the people I know in Tarlabaşı, the DTP, MKM, some of my opinions about some political events, and then mentioned his loyalty to the Kurdish nationalist movement.

It is not easy for the community members of a society with strong and tight traditional ties based on notions such as honor and honesty to accept other members becoming sex workers or drug dealers. However, both the economic and political conditions of the IDP in Tarlabaşı leave no other space for them but to accept such things as normal factors. Nevertheless, on the other hand, instead of becoming victimized subjects repeating a victimized discourse, they prefer to alter the mainstream hierarchal order in the production of their subjectivities.

Changing Gender Relations

With its complex structure (Mitchell, 1971), gender organizes the social order in our everyday lives (Connell, 2001). Gender refers to the engagement of the relation between women and men, femininities and masculinities in different historical trajectories. It is also related to various power-laden relations based on the intersectionality of factors such as class, ethnicity, religion, and profession. It is directly related to bodies, sexuality, reproduction, and the subjectivities of women and men. Thus, examining gender relations between Kurdish men and women, Kurdish men and non-Kurdish women, enables us to analyze power-laden relations of various intersectionalities. It also enables us to question the equality discourse of both Turkish and Kurdish nationalisms. As mentioned earlier, gender relations in the city have changed enormously for both women and men. In addition, the changes in the discourse of the Kurdish nationalist institutions about gender structure, as well as the tension between these institutions and the state or governing bodies in Tarlabaşı, play significant roles in shaping gender relations. In this section, the main focus of analysis is upon the relationship between Kurdish men and women from various backgrounds.

The PKK's founder, Abdullah Öcalan, is the leading figure of the Kurdish nationalist movement. Although some Kurdish families are critical of the armed policies of the PKK, its founder Öcalan is regarded as untouchable, since Öcalan represents the PKK, which establishes a totalizing hegemonic identity upon Kurdishness. The PKK is the organ that aims to homogenize the multiplicity of the Kurdish identity in its discourses through creating a mythical history, the representation of "ideal" Kurdish men and women. Thus, Öcalan plays a significant role as an "ideal" masculine figure in the identification process of the internally displaced people. As mentioned before, changes in the discourse of Öcalan or the PKK have the capacity to reshape the gender structure in the Kurdish community. As stated by Çağlayan, until the 1990s, as women had not become the active members of the movement, the main focus was on men, and women were regarded as "weak people who cannot be trusted" (2007). However, as the involvement of women in the movement increased, the discourse of Öcalan as well as the PKK in general started to emphasize the role of women while criticizing the traditional, "feudal" virility of Kurdish men (Çağlayan, 2007). Nevertheless, this does not mean that the community is not patriarchal anymore; rather, the meaning attributed to various notions like honor has changed.

Honor is one of the crucial ways of controlling the gender and sexual relations among community members—specifically, the sexuality of women in patriarchal kinship societies (Sirman, 2004). With the influence of modernity, patriarchy is no longer based on the kinship system, yet fraternal relations form the base of the patriarchy (Pateman, 1988), and honor begins to be controlled by kinship relations or by modern nuclear family members (Sirman, 2004). The content and the definition of honor changes in the society as a result of a "patriarchal bargain" that is shaped by the possible existence of conflicting interest groups as well as the historical changes in gender regimes (Kandiyoti, 1988). Kandiyoti explains the "patriarchal bargain" as the male-dominated discursive space in which all social actors constantly negotiate, contest, and redefine gender relation.

Women who used to come to the city only when they needed a doctor begin to be the producers of the city after internal displacement. Due to economic reasons in particular, the young women of the IDP families who do not need to look after their children start to work. Changes as such are not new for men either, yet the meanings attributed to honor have to be changed. The meanings attributed to honor have also been changed by the movement. Honor used to refer directly to the woman's body and sexuality, whereas now it refers directly to territory of the country, but still indirectly to women's bodies and sexuality (Çağlayan, 2007). Although women who work in the city gain some "rights," as they argue, such as dressing in a modern way, shaping their eyebrows, or dyeing their hair, they cannot make their own decisions or act freely. As noted by one of the internally displaced women interviewees, Asya:

> My clothes and my hair style is different in Dargeçit [a district in the Southeast]. My brother was very conservative. He didn't allow me to take a seat with his friends or with the neighbors when they came [to] us as guests. He didn't allow me to go everywhere. But now, I can go to work. I have to because we need it. I can wear whatever I want to and can sit with the friends of my brother when they come. But I and my brother know that there are some limits. These limits are needed to protect our society. We Kurds know this.

The changes in the context and the need to survive also change the attitude of Asya's brother towards her. Her brother adapted himself to the new context, yet as Asya mentions, both know that "there are some limits" to be protected for the "society." The changing discourse of the movement in relation to the notion of honor enables Asya's brother to develop a border thinking that he can engage to utilize both knowledges. The patriarchal bargain that they share opens a space for them to act relatively free in the urban context while preserving the family's honor. He can allow his sister, whose behaviors and sexuality represent the family as well as the community, to do various things in the urban context while keeping the virility of his masculinity. On the other hand, it is worth mentioning that although Asya feels freer than before, her obedience to the discourse of "some limits" reveals the fact that there is a silent agreement between her and her brother about the new dynamics of the patriarchal relations.

In some cases, men mention the interaction between women's sexuality and men's masculinity. As Cemal frankly states, women's sexuality is one of the important factors that shapes men's masculinity:

> Although honor killings are exaggerated, women's sexuality must be kept under control . . . men are afraid of women. Sexuality is important for men and this is the only power they have got. Apart from this, women rule society. . . . I am telling this for the sake of society, otherwise I respect women's freedom for experiencing their sexuality.

This discourse embodies the conflict of urbanized Kurdish men: the conflict between traditional rural values and the modern values of the city. In this regard, Cemal's masculinity is "situational"[18] in Monterescu's terms. According to Monterescu, situational masculinity "praises the code of 'tradition' and seems to subscribe to it, but de facto it expresses a playful stance towards it and towards its own position" (2006, p. 134). Cemal's response is situational in the way that he advocates controlling the sexuality of women "for the sake of a peaceful society," which is a very traditional view on the one hand; while he wants to be perceived as a tolerant modern man regarding women's sexual rights, on the other hand, when he talks to me, a non-Kurdish, Turkish woman researcher, the "other" for him. Additionally, working on the feelings of the other and making her/him supportive of their causes is one of the tactics that IDP men employ in Tarlabaşı when dealing with more powerful figures.

According to Cevat, the main difference between women and men is their flexibility according to the circumstances. Cevat argues that "women are more flexible than men. Therefore, women change whereas men cannot change. This scares men." He argues that the real power is held by women, because they reproduce. According to him, men are aware of their weakness, and this weakness leads to a pursuit of security in a patriarchal society. This weakness and lack of confidence discourse is also utilized for legitimizing psychological or physical violence, especially towards women. This is the paradox where the power of manhood is exercised on the less powerful.

The importance of honor in internally displaced men's lives seems to emerge from their lack of confidence. This lack of confidence, which is influential in shaping male weakness and insecurity, has a relation to endogamous marriages as well, as argued by one of the interviewees, Hejan:

> How can my mother or father trust anybody outside the family? Both married their cousins. They couldn't even trust their cousins . . . we, Kurds, are all relatives. Therefore, everybody feels insecure and feels the right to control each other.

As Hejan states, endogamous marriages cause lack of confidence, since the taboo of sexuality could not even be controlled in such close relationships, which are supposed to be based on trust. Sexuality is a taboo that enables men to control women's behavior in both kinship-based and modern societies (Sirman, 2004).[19] Hence, everybody is responsible for her/his behavior. While sexuality is controlled by the members of society at various levels, the borders of freedoms and sanctions are altered in every context as well. This influences a person's relationships with other society members and also leads to the development of a double discourse towards women and the meaning attributed to sexuality. Internally displaced men develop different tactics in relation to Kurdish and non-Kurdish men and women from various backgrounds, and their masculinities are shaped in this tension. At the same time, although endogamous marriages are widespread and sexuality among family members is regarded as taboo, examining the meanings attributed to inter-family relations reveals their paradoxical approach.

Distinguishing traditional Kurdish women from urbanized and politicized ones, Kurdish men develop a double discourse towards Kurdish women as well. In the Kurdish nationalist movement, women are called *heval*—friends— who are regarded as being like siblings. Relationships with *hevals* are considered holy relationships, with sexual intercourse or any kind of private and intimate relation forbidden. This approach reveals the paradoxical discourse about endogamous marriages. It shows the limits of the sexual relations among community members: you can marry your cousin, but not your sister. *Hevals* are different from traditional women, who are mostly mothers. In their everyday life, internally displaced men position the mother figure in a more traditional place in which they argue they have "more" right to apply any kind of patriarchal treatment, from violence to strict control of their everyday practices. On the other hand, as *hevals* are considered political figures, they have the right to behave more freely. As it is in the case of Asya, *hevals* are supposed to internalize the patriarchal limits to protect their family name and community. In addition, internally displaced men show more respect to *hevals* and regard them as "equal" friends with urbanized or politicized values.

Some of the IDP men argue that the shift in the gender roles in the community and the interaction with women of the city becomes an ideological position for men. According to Cevat, "men have to prove themselves in various ways: as bread winners, as sexual partners, and as desired honorable men." This statement also represents the situational positioning of Kurdish masculinities: in-between traditional women, mothers, and siblings.

Conclusion

Being an internally displaced Kurdish man at the very "heart" of Istanbul, in Tarlabaşı, is an ambivalent state. It is a state of encountering various meanings of stigmatization, prejudices, and discrimination, on the one hand, and a state of encountering different relationships of opportunity, creativity, and freedom, on the other. It is a state of being visible and invisible as well as being dominant and subordinated at the same time. It is a state of redefining, interpreting, and practicing what hegemony defines and practices as the so-called mind of the population. It is a state of being regarded as a homo sacer by this "mind," and in turn being disposable in everyday practices. It is an ability to think from both and neither of the dominant and subordinated knowledge positions at the same time. For an urban dweller, it is a state of setting, fixing, altering, transforming, and traversing the borders of the city as well as the borders in minds.

Turkish state, government, and local governing and nationalist institutions regard Tarlabaşı as a dangerous place for living. They impose their nationalistic and neoliberal policies in Tarlabaşı, policies that have stigmatized the inhabitants of the area. The aim of the governing bodies is to discard and dispose of the inhabitants—homo sacers—of stigmatized Tarlabaşı. These policies have influenced the perception of city dwellers, leading them to exclude the region in their everyday life as if there existed a state of permanent exception. Yet, the everyday tactics of homo sacers show that they develop various ways of being.

In modern, dualistic, hegemonic settings, "Kurdishness" and "Turkishness," rural and urban, as well as men and women, are presented as fixed, opposing categories. In Turkey the dominant discourse regards "Turkishness" as the "original" aspect of citizenship and considers "Kurdishness" as its oppositional one. The middle-class urban dwellers, who identify themselves with this dominant discourse, consider themselves the "original" inhabitants of the city, defending its territory. Therefore, each encounter with the "other" is seen as a reaction. The tactics developed in everyday life reveal the fact that hegemonic discourse is utilized by both sides in various ways. Through examining the formation of the masculinities of the internally displaced men in Tarlabaşı, I have focused on how the discourse and the knowledge of the two sides are in the process of change in everyday life. Such an analysis enables us to comprehend the structured relationships powered by hegemonic discourse, on the one hand, and to evaluate the internally displaced men not as a passive, victimized category, but as agents that reshape the traditional, national, and neoliberal meanings attributed to city, masculinity, and nationalism, on the other.

In order to mediate between the Turkish state's assimilative and Kurdish institutions' nationalist "strategies," Kurdish men in the city develop "border thinking" (de Certeau, [1980] 1988; Mignolo, 2000) in their everyday interactions with other actors. Kurdish masculinities are interwoven "in between" (Bhabha, [1996] 2002) the traditional, nationalist, and neoliberal gendered discourses (both Turkish and Kurdish) and the everyday life realities of internally displaced men in the city. Kurdish men's resistance and tactics in the formation of their masculinities reflect the gendered national, ethnic, class hierarchy and power relations in the society. Kurdish men's resistance and tactics reveal not only the institutional policies and distributive patterns (political, social, economic), but also the power-laden social relations. In the formation of their everyday tactics, the internally displaced men become both the objects and the subjects of the hegemonic discourse. Nevertheless, each being, each position, is a new identification in the sense that even if they conform with hegemony, their interpretation of hegemonic values in their context is a new thing, different from hegemonic values.

Notes

1. Here the terms "tactic" and "strategy" are used as de Certeau uses them. According to de Certeau, strategy and tactic are complementary terms. Strategy is "the calculus of force-relationships, when a subject of will and power can be isolated from an environment," and assuming "a place that can be circumscribed as proper and serve as the basis for generating relations with an exterior distinct." Tactic is "a calculus which cannot count on a proper, nor thus on a borderline distinguishing the other as a visible totality," rather insinuating itself into "the other's place." A tactic depends on time and "must constantly manipulate events in order to turn them into opportunities" ([1980] 1988, pp. 34- 39). Various scholars like Kandiyoti (1997b) and Uğur (2003) use the term "survival strategy" in the way de Certeau uses the term "tactic."

2. I use the concept "masculinity" to refer to all the configurations of discourses such as behaviors, utterances, and wordings that have been attributed to male embodiment in specific times and spaces (Mutluer, 2009).

3. Here discourse is defined as "producing and organizing meaning within a social context" (Edgar & Sedgwick, 2005, p. 117). Discourse examines the various configurations of assumptions, categories, logics, claims, and modes of articulation, including knowledge, statements, propositions, institutions, and so on (Foucault, [1969] 2005). Structured by political, cultural, and institutional discourse, individuals and collectivities that have the capacity to exercise power in a specific historical moment normalize themselves, the images of themselves, "others," and world by accepting, preserving, categorizing, and transmitting knowledge that is constituted by discourse (Foucault, [1972] 1980; Young 1990).

4. I use the term "class" in Kalb's sense. According to Kalb, the expanded conceptualization of class searches for "the interconnections between relationships in (and of) production, narrowly conceived and social and cultural practices beyond the immediate point of production, albeit supportive of it, thus is really nothing new" (1997, p. 5).

5. According to Nur Betül Çelik, this mythical discourse was presented to establish a "set of equivalences, first between the Republic and the 'nature' of the Turkish nation; secondly, between the modern West and Turkishness; and finally, between the 'classless' nature of Turkish society and one-party rule" (2000, p. 196). Similar debate can be found in Paul Dumont's "The Origins of Kemalist Ideology" (in Landau, 1984, pp. 25–44).

6. Some examples of the everyday usage of this mythical discourse can be found in the following newspaper articles, columns, and so on: http://www.radikal.com.tr/haber .php?haberno=221053, http://yenisafak.com.tr/yazarlar/?i=5289&y=FehmiKoru, http://www.sokeekspres.com/Makale.aspx?MakaleID=1861, http://www .haberprogram.com/yz.php?yid=15&yyid=412, http://www.evrensel.net/haber .php?haber_id=7434. All sites accessed on February 8, 2011.

7. In the migration and international relations literature, internal displacement is used to refer to forcefully migrated communities.

8. Contrary to the general presentation showing that the opposing parties involved in the Kurdish issue are Turks and Kurds, the village guard system is a crucial example of revealing the fact that the conflict has various actors from at least both sides. Depending on the intersecting interests, or ongoing local hostilities, Kurds may relate to the issue on the side of the Turkish state as well.

9. Although the direct translation of *Rum* is "Greek," Rums living in Turkey prefer to be referred to not as Greeks, but as Rums.

10. Further details about JİTEM can be found in some interviews with ex-officers, confessors, and others: http://gaphaber.com/detay.php?id=14782, http://www.radikal .com.tr/haber.php?haberno=170609, http://www.navkurd.net/arsiv/jicapemeniye/ tanrikulu.htm. All sites accessed on February 8, 2011.

11. The names used in this study are the nicknames given by the interviewees.

12. One of the examples of the support of feminist Kurdish women is the speeches of these women in the Kurdish Conference, in which they criticize not only the policies of the Turkish state, but also the patriarchal system in the Kurdish community. The Kurdish Conference was held in Istanbul on March 10–11, 2006.

13. All of these terms, which are used interchangeably with the same meaning in the city, mean "yokel," "yahoo," "lout," or "hick" in English.

14. In Kurdish nationalist discourse Mesopotamia is regarded as the "holy" lands from which the Kurds originated. In this regard, it has a holy meaning in the myths of national discourse or in the discourse of the leaders of the PKK (e.g., Öcalan, 2004).

15. Similar discussion can be found in *Blood and Belief: The PKK and the Kurdish Fight for Independence,* by Aliza Marcus (New York: New York University Press, 2007).

16. The 1995 PKK Party Program was declared after the party congress held on January 24.

17. The word *heval* is discussed in the following section.

18. Here the terminology is inspired by Daniel Monterescu's *situational* masculinity model (2006, pp. 123–42). In his study about Palestinian-Arab men in Jaffa, Monterescu develops the model of situational masculinity to point to the discourses of masculinities that maneuver between the essentialist discourses of Islamic conservatism and liberal-secular masculinity (2006, pp. 133–37). While his research focuses more on the role of ideological formations in Jaffa in the construction of masculinities, my research focuses on how gendered nationalism is constructed in relation to everyday tactics of marginalized men in the city structures of Istanbul.

19. Although men's responsibilities in terms of controlling women's sexuality change, in both kinship-based and modern societies men are responsible for men's honor.

References

Adamson, D. (1991). *Class, Ideology, and the Nation*. Wales: Cardiff University of Wales.

Agamben, G. ([1995] 1998). *Homo Sacer: Sovereign Power and Bare Life*. Stanford, Calif.: Stanford University Press.

Alvesson, M., & Skoldberg, K. (2000). *Reflexive Methodology: New Vistas for Qualitative Research*. Thousand Oaks, Calif.: Sage.

Anzaldúa, G. (1987). *Borderlands/La Frontera: The New Mestiza*. San Francisco: Spinsters/Aunt Lute.

Ayata, B., & Yükseker, D. (2005). A Belated Awakening: National and International Responses to the Internal Displacement of Kurds in Turkey. *New Perspectives on Turkey, 32,* 5–42.

Bernauer, J. W., & Rasmussen, D. (1988). *The Final Foucault*. Cambridge: MIT Press.

Bhabha, H. (1995). Are You a Man or a Mouse? In M. Berger, B. Wallis, & S. Watson (Eds.), *Constructing Masculinity* (pp. 57–65). New York: Routledge.

Bhabha, H. ([1996] 2002) Culture's In-Between. In H. Stuart & P. du Gay (Eds.), *Questions of Cultural Identity* (pp. 53–60). London: Sage.

Biehl, J., Good, B., & Kleinman, A. (2007). *Subjectivity.* Berkeley: University of California Press.

Bigwood, C. (1998) *Renaturalizing the Body (With the help of Merleau-Ponty).* D. Welton (Ed.), *Body and Flesh: A Philosphical Reader* (pp. 99–114). Malden, Mass.: Blackwell.

Brubaker, R., & Cooper, F. (2000). Beyond Identity. *Theory and Society,* 29, 1–47.

Çağlayan, H. (2007). *Analar, Yoldaşlar, Tanrıçalar: Kürt Hareketinde Kadınlar ve Kadın Kimliğinin Oluşumu (Mothers, Companions, Goddesses: Women in the Kurdish Movement and the Formation of Women's Identity).* Istanbul: İletişim Yayınlari.

Çelik, A. B. (2005). "I Miss My Village": Forced Kurdish Migrants in Istanbul and Their Representation in Associations. *New Perspectives on Turkey,* 32, 137–63.

Çelik, N. B. (2000). The Constitution and Dissolution of Kemalist Imaginary. In D. R. Howart, A. J. Norvel, & Y. Stravtakaki (Eds.), *Discourse Theory and Political Analysis* (pp. 192–204). Manchester, U.K.: Manchester University Press.

Connell, R. W. ([1995] 2005). *Masculinities.* Cambridge: Polity Press.

Connell, R. W. (2001). The Social Organization of Masculinity. In S. M. Whitehead & F. J. Barret (Eds.), *The Masculinities Reader* (pp. 30–50). Cambridge: Polity Press.

de Certeau, M. ([1980] 1988). "Making Do": Uses and Tactics. *The Practice of Everyday Life* (pp. 29–42). Berkeley: University of California Press.

Edgar, A., & Sedgwick, P. ([1999] 2005). *Cultural Theory: The Key Concepts.* London: Routledge.

Erder, S. ([1996] 2001). *İstanbul'a Bir Kent Kondu: Ümraniye (Built Up City in Istanbul: Ümraniye).* Istanbul: İletişim.

Dinç, N. K. (2008). *Göç Hikayeleri (Migration Stories).* Istanbul: Göç-Der Publications.

Foucault, M. ([1969] 2005). *The Archeology of Knowledge.* London: Routledge.

Foucault, M. ([1972] 1980). Two Lectures. In C. Gordon (Ed.), *Power/ Knowledge: Selected Interviews and Other Writings 1972–1977* (pp. 78–100). New York: Pantheon Books.

Foucault, M. ([1975] 1995). *Discipline and Punish.* New York: Vintage Books.

Foucault, M. ([1978] 1990). *History of Sexuality: An Introduction, Volume 1.* New York: Vintage Books.

Gardiner, M. E. (2000). Introduction. In M. E. Gardiner, *Critiques of Everyday Life* (pp. 1–23). London: Routledge.

Graham, R. (2006). Male Rape and the Careful Construction of the Male Victim. *Social & Legal Studies,* 15(2), 187–208.

Grosz, E. (1994). *Volatile Bodies: Toward a Corporeal Feminism.* Bloomington: Indiana University Press.

Hearn, J. (2004). From Hegemonic Masculinity to the Hegemony of Men. *Feminist Theory*, 5(1), 49–72.

Helvacıoğlu, B. (2006).The Smile of Death and the Solemncholy of Masculinity. In L. Ouzgane (Ed.), *Islamic Masculinities* (pp. 35–56). New York: Zed.

Işık, O., & Pınarcıoğlu, M. M. ([2001] 2002). *Nöbetleşe Yoksulluk: Sultanbeyli Örneği (Shifting Poverties: The Example of Sultanbeyli)*. Istanbul: İletişim Yayınları.

Joost, J. (2008). *Türkiye'de İskan Sorunu ve Kürtler: Modernite, Savaş ve Mekan Politikaları Üzerine Bir Çözümleme (The Settlement Issues in Turkey and the Kurds: An Analysis of Spatial Policies)*. Istanbul: Vate.

Kalb, D. (1997). *Expanding Class: Power and Everyday Politics in Industrial Communities, the Netherlands, 1850–1950* (pp: 1–24). Durham, N.C.: Duke University Press.

Kandiyoti, D. (1988). Bargaining with Patriarchy. *Gender and Society*, 2(3), 274–90.

Kandiyoti, D. (1997a). Gendering the Modern: On Missing Dimensions in the Study of Turkish Modernity. In S. Bozdoğan and R. Kasaba (Eds.), *Rethinking Modernity and National Identity in Turkey* (pp. 113–33). Seattle: University of Washington Press.

Kandiyoti, D. (1997b). *Cariyeler, Bacılar, Yurttaşlar: Kimlikler ve Toplumsal Dönüşümler (Odalisques, Sisters, Citizens: Identities and Social Transformations)*. İstanbul: Metis Yayınları.

Kirişçi, K., & Winrow, G. M. ([1997] 2004). *The Kurdish Question and Turkey: An Example of a Trans-state Ethnic Conflict*. Oxon, U.K.: RoutlegeCurzon.

Kurban, D., Yükseker, D., Ünalan,T., Aker, T., & Çelik, A. B. (2006). *Zorunlu Göç ile Yüzleşmek: Türkiye'de Yerinden Edilme Sonrası Vatandaşlığın İnşası (Facing the Forced Migration: The Construction of Citizenship after the Internal Displacement in Turkey)*. İstanbul: Tesev.

Landau, J. M. (Ed.). (1984). *Atatürk and the Modernization of Turkey*. Boulder, Colo.: Westview Press.

Massey, D. (1994). *Space, Place, and Gender*. Minneapolis: University of Minnesota Press.

Mignolo, W. D. (2000). *Local Histories/Global Designs. Coloniality, Subaltern Knowledges, and Border Thinking*. Princeton, N.J.: Princeton University Press.

Miller, R (2006). *Limits of Bodily Integrity: Abortion, Adultery, and Rape Legislation in Comparative Perspective*. Surrey, U.K.: Ashgate.

Mitchell, J. (1971). *Woman's Estate*. Harmondsworth, U.K.: Penguin.

Monterescu, D. (2006). Stranger Masculinities: Gender and Politics in a Palestinian-Israeli "Third Space." In L. Ouzgane (Ed.), *Islamic Masculinities* (pp. 123–42). London: Zed.

Mutluer, N. (2009). The role of Transnational and National Institutions in Internally Displaced Men's Everyday Life in Tarlabası in Istanbul. In K. Harrison & J. Hearn (Eds.), GEXcel Work in Progress Report, Volume VI: Deconstructing the Hegemony of Men and Masculinities Conference, April 27–29, 2009 (pp. 91–108). Linköping, Sweden: Linköping University: Tema Genus Report Series.

Öcalan, A. (2004). *Bir Halkı Savunmak*. Istanbul: Berdan Matbaası.

Öncü, A. (1999). Istanbulites and Others: The Cultural Cosmology of Being Middle Class in the Era of Globalism. In Ç. Keyder (Ed.), *Istanbul: Between the Global and the Local* (pp. 95–119). Lanham, Md.: Rowman & Littlefield.

Pateman, C. (1988). Contracting In. C. Pateman, *The Sexual Contract (pp. 1–18)*. Cambridge: Polity Press..

Secor, A. (2004). There Is an Istanbul That Belongs to Me: Citizenship, Space, and Identity in the City. *Annals of the Association of American Geographers*, 94(2), 352–68.

Şen, L. (2005). Poverty Alleviation, Conflict, and Power in Poor Displaced Households: A Study of the Views of Women in Diyarbakır. *New Perspectives on Turkey*, 32, 113–36.

Shohat, E., & Stam, R. (1994). *Unthinking Eurocentrism: Multiculturalism and the Media*. London: Routledge.

Sirman, N. (2004). Kinship, Politics, and Love: Honour in Post-colonial Contexts— The Case of Turkey. In S. Mojab & N. Abdo (Eds.), *Violence in the Name of Honour: Theoretical and Political Challenges* (pp. 39–56). Istanbul: Istanbul Bilgi University Press.

Skeggs, B. (1997). *Formations of Class and Gender*. London: Sage.

Uğur, A. (2003). Notes from "Alterity and the Experience of Limits" seminar held at Boğaziçi University, December 12, 2003.

Walby, S. (1990). *Theorizing Patriarchy*. Oxford: Blackwell.

Whitehead, S. M., & Barret, F. J. (2001). The Sociology of Masculinity. In S. M. Whitehead & F. J. Barret (Eds.) *The Masculinities Reader* (pp. 1–26). Cambridge: Polity Press.

Yeğen, M. (2006). *Müstakbel Türk'ten Sözde Vatandaşa: Cumhuriyet ve Kürtler (From Future Turk to So-Called Citizen: The Republic and Kurds)*. İstanbul: İletişim Yayınları.

Yılmaz, B. (2006). Far Away, So Close: Social Exclusion and Spatial Relegation in an Inner-City Slum of Istanbul. In F. Adaman & C. Keyder (Eds.), *Poverty and Social Exclusion in the Slum Areas of Large Cities in Turkey* (pp. 26–40). Report for the European Commission: Employment, Social Affairs, and Equal Opportunities, Joint Inclusion Memorandum and Research Foundation of Bogazici University.

Yılmaz, B. (2008). *Türkiye'de Sınıf Altı: Nöbetleşe Yoksulluktan Müebbet Yoksulluğa. Birikim Yayınları. (Underclass in Turkey: From Poverty in Rotation to Permanent Poverty)*. Istanbul: Birikim Yayınları.

Young, I. M. (1990). *Justice and the Politics of Difference*. Princeton, N.J.: Princeton University Press.

4

Wounded Masculinity
and Nationhood in Peru

MARGARITA SAONA

Looking at the photographs in *Yuyanapaq*, the photo exhibit created by the Peruvian Truth and Reconciliation Commission (TRC), one is
overwhelmed by images of wounded men. There are also a few images of
men in power, but that power is mostly derived either from the guns they
carry or from a position of privilege acquired from a combination of factors
that include socio-economic status and, more often than not, the color of
one's skin. But even men in power look uncertain in those photographs. They
do not seem to be in control; they look scared or confused, inexpressive or
enraged. During the last twenty years of the twentieth century the violence
of centuries of social injustice erupted in the brutal confrontation between
the Shining Path, the Tupac Amaru guerrillas, and the government armed
forces. *Hatun Willakuy*, the abbreviated report of the TRC, consigns an es-
timate of 69,000 deaths as a result of this conflict. The great majority of the
victims were men between the ages of twenty and forty-nine[1] (Comisión de
la Verdad, 2004, p. 52).

The roots of this conflict are deep and complex, and no single perspective
can explain the unleashed violence that terrorized the country during the
last decades of the last century. However, an exploration of the representation of masculinity in Peru can illuminate structural faults in the patriarchal imaginary of the nation. These faults—a patriarchal model fraught with
contradictions in a system where most men are subordinated to other men,
and where authority is undermined by a cynicism that is rooted in the belief that there is an unbreachable gap between the law and reality—produce
simultaneously a failed image of men and of the imagined community.

Peruvian society combines an indigenous and a colonial heritage, African and Western influences, and populations attracted by diverse migratory waves. Men have to measure up to an ideal of manhood that does not reflect the experience of most Peruvians. It has always been assumed that Peruvian males would embody authority and power in their own society. However, they were subjected first to the Spanish crown, and then, from the onset of the republican period, to the external forces of international politics and market regulations. The indigenous majority did not conform to the ideas of modernity of the cultural elite, and the ruling classes often regarded Indians as a problem for the modern republic they wanted to establish. At the end of the nineteenth century, Peru lost part of its territory to Chile, and that event was often depicted as a form of emasculation. The internal war of the late twentieth century reenacts a history of failure in which the economical and political elites of the country are unable to build a modern, integrated, democratic nation (Manrique, 2002; Klarén, 2000). But one of the tragedies of Peruvian history is that it also fails to articulate an alternative project. The Shining Path does not provide an alternative.

According to historians such as Nelson Manrique and Peter Klarén, the crisis resurfaces over and over under different forms: indigenous rebellions during the late eighteenth century, the debacle of the Chilean war at the end of the nineteenth century, or the Shining Path at the end of the twentieth. However, these manifestations are always different forms of five basic problems: a crisis in representation, an economic crisis, a stunt modernization process, a failed republican system, and the unsolved legacy of colonialism (Manrique, 2002; Klarén, 2000).

The failure to establish a coherent picture of the nation in an imaginary that identifies manhood with authority and power, results in a series of images of inadequacy regarding the ideal, unattainable masculinity. The image of a wounded manhood has permeated literature and art in Peru, from representations of proud Incas that were defeated by Spaniards, to colonial rulers depicted either as ruthless and bloodthirsty or as weak epicureans with no real power, to men condemned to exile because they do not conform to the heterosexual norm, to ex-combatants who cannot find a role for themselves in civil society. To examine these images is to examine that against which they are measuring up. This demands an attempt to answer the question of what it means to be a man in Peru, and perhaps to imagine alternatives to these representations of manhood.

In this analysis it is imperative to acknowledge that Peru is a patriarchal society, a society in which authority and order are supposed to be embodied by strong men. Norma Fuller's study of masculinities in Peru establishes the existence of a traditional segregation of roles along gender lines (2001). According to Fuller, men clearly controlled politics and the economy in the public domain and exerted authority over women at home (2001, p. 38). Masculine domination was reinforced both by a patrilineal family system and by laws that supported men's authority and restricted women to the private sphere. The double moral standard in Peru used the family to consolidate class privilege, allowing even married men to maintain sexual intercourse with other women from lower classes and subordinated ethnic groups, while women from the upper classes were supposed to be chaste and faithful. This particular form of patriarchy can be traced to the times of the Spanish conquest.

Historian María Emma Mannarelli (2007) reports that relationships between Spanish men and native women took many different forms, from rape to alliances intended to give the Spanish access to local goods and support. In some cases, Indian nobles gave their women and daughters to the conquistadores in transactions in which women were "cogs in the machinery of power" (p. 8). However, those unions, or the children that resulted from them, were rarely legitimized. "Many Spaniards lived with whatever women they had at their disposal, principally those who served them" (p. 9). With the arrival of Spanish women, many men abandoned their native concubines to procure marriages that would give them better status in the colonies and access to favors from the crown (p. 15). Mannarelli summarizes the period of the Conquest in a way that sets up the development of gender roles in Peru:

> The conquest wars and contact with native women were new points of reference in the evolution of Spanish ideas of courtly morality. Spanish men chose cohabitation with women of various ethnic origins, especially with native servants and African slaves. In one sense, this was a continuation of the Iberian tradition of servitude. It replicated the patriarchal pattern between the masculine head of family and the network of servants, where powerful men took sexual favors from servants. It should be recalled here that the condition of servitude implied a relationship that was hierarchical and, most important, dependent. Likewise, because Andean women were from a variety of subjugated ethnic groups in the conquered territories, a new type of sexual relationship was created. In this new pattern, servants and lovers were closely identified. To this can be added the ethnic component that, in turn, also had an established hierarchy between masculinity and femininity. (p. 17)

Norma Fuller (2001) sees the effects of this pattern in the present. Traditional Peruvian society assumes that men (some men) have control over women of all social groups. It reproduces vertical relations between women and men of different ethnic and social groups (Fuller, 2001, p. 39). In the upper classes, women are supposed to be chaste and morally superior to men, and men are supposed to embody strength, virility, and responsibility. But sexual practices that give dominant men control over all women will establish a society in which the majority of the population cannot identify with a strong father figure. Peruvian patriarchy fails in part because the father—who is supposed to embody the law—perpetuates illegitimacy, and because the majority of men are subordinated to a minority that seems to have absolute power over men and women alike. It is my contention that Peruvian patriarchy's faults and inconsistencies are revealed in times of national crisis, and that those inconsistencies play an important part in the country's failure to establish a viable imagined community.

This does not mean that patriarchy is a desirable situation, or that there is not actual change happening in the ways gender is defined in contemporary Peru. Ideally, Peruvian society would create a more democratic and egalitarian image of itself with which every citizen, regardless of gender or ethnicity, could identify. And it is important to recognize that Peruvian women played a significant role in social movements throughout the twentieth century and their political participation has risen to unprecedented levels, particularly in the 1990s, with eight female ministers, and over twenty vice ministers (Blondet, 2004, p. 4). However, the imaginary of the nation still revolves around a masculine figure: as we will see in the works discussed below, Peruvian literature and culture return again and again to the topic of a conflicted masculine subjectivity, often burdened with a wounded body or a wounded psyche. While a "successful" patriarchy would articulate a strong, intact, male body, in Peru the image is that of a crippled, maimed, male body.

From a theoretical perspective, Kaja Silverman (1992) explores the way the idea of an "intact" male body informs—and is informed by—ideology. According to Silverman, the fact that male bodies have external sexual organs contributes to the idea that they are not castrated, that they are—unlike females—unimpaired (p. 42). But this fiction of the wholeness of the male subject also informs a view of reality in which society itself relies on this image of masculinity to incarnate the unity of the family and the structure of society. In Silverman's words: "Our dominant fiction calls upon the male subject to see himself, and the female subject to recognize and desire him, only through the mediation of images of an unimpaired masculinity. It urges both the male and the female subject, that is, to deny all knowledge of male castration by believing in the commensurability of the penis and phallus, actual and symbolic father" (p. 42).

Masculinities articulated on the margins of the dominant fiction, "those which not only acknowledge but embrace castration, alterity, and specularity," question the power structure that secures sexual difference and achieve some kind of reconciliation with femininity (p. 3). However, what I see as a fracture of the dominant fiction in the Peruvian case does not seem to produce an alternative to a gendered system. It only produces a failed gendered system. Once again: I am not saying that what Peru needs is a successful patriarchy. What I am saying is that the failure to produce a successful image of patriarchy permeates Peruvian culture with a sense of doom. Understanding the ways wounded manhood is portrayed in Peruvian culture and the fact that these images are still trying to measure up to an idea of wholeness might be a starting point for new understandings of gender and identity in Peru. It might even help to understand the need to search for a new understanding of the nation that does not rely on either gender, ethnicity, or the "manhood" of its citizens.

A succession of social traumas reverberates in Peruvian history. Particularly telling is the fact that one of the most influential books in Peruvian social sciences revolves around a messianic myth concerned with the integrity of the male body: Alberto Flores Galindo's *Buscando un inca: identidad y utopía en los Andes* (1986) explores the role of the *Inkarri* myth in Peru. According to the myth, when the Spaniards killed the last Inca, the king of the Andean empire, they severed his head and hid it. But the body of the Inca is growing under the earth and one day the body and the head will be reunited, the order of the world will be transformed once again, and the Inca will come back and rule the Andean territory (Flores Galindo, 1986, p. 18).

This decapitation amounts to symbolic castration. The body of the Inca is imagined as a previously whole entity, a virile body that stood for the grandeur of the empire. The Spanish conquest maims that body. In his book *Sex and Conquest: Gendered Violence, Political Order, and the European Conquest of the Americas* (1995), Richard C. Trexler gives evidence that "feminizing" the body of the defeated enemies has been a military practice that can be traced from antiquity to the times of the conquest, and that was also present among native societies. Male to male rape, castration, circumcision, and other forms of sexual violence are ways of "gendering" the enemy as less masculine.[2] Michael Hardin (2002) adds that the rape of native women—in a context in which they are treated as property—is also a way to exert power over defeated men (p. 6).[3] The well-known illustrations of the Indian chronicler Guamán Poma de Ayala add to this sense of emasculation in presenting the Inca in the horizontal position associated with the feminine, and penetrated by the swords of the Spaniards who, in an upright position, dominate his body.[4] The Inca killed by Pizarro's forces, Atahualpa, was not really decapitated, but garroted in 1533. Beyond historical accuracy, we are dealing with the construction of the imaginary. Guamán Poma's caption clearly reads: "Cortale la cavesa a Atagualpa Inga" *(Cut Atahualpa Inca's head)*.[5]

Almost forty years later, in 1572, Tupac Amaru I is decapitated in a public act (Flores Galindo, 1986). Considered a legitimate descendent of the Inca, his execution was the final blow of the conquest. Guamán Poma's drawing of this act is almost a copy, with slight variations, of Atahualpa's execution.[6] The Inca lies in a horizontal, passive, position, while the Spaniards armed with erect swords and hammer, are ready to penetrate the Inca's body, with the intention to separate the head from the torso. To this decapitation scene Guamán Poma adds an audience of weeping Indians that will reinforce the image of humiliated and feminized natives.

The feminization of the male body amounts to its subordination to a more powerful male and, as Trexler (1995) shows, has been a constant trait of masculine and military discourse in many cultures throughout history. He recounts a story in which Huascar, the rival brother of Atahualpa, enraged by the defeat of his troops, order his military leaders to dress as women and enter the capital of the empire, Cuzco, in female dress (p. 71). The Spanish Conquest is not only a military and cultural defeat for indigenous males, but also a source of humiliation, and loss of male pride. The collapse of their universe will be associated with the fragmentation of the once powerful body of the Inca. Flores Galindo sees in this body the incarnation of utopian thought in the Andes, and he traces the origins of the myth by concentrating on the traditions where the collapse of the Inca Empire becomes part of a cycle that promises the return of what was lost, the mystical reincorporation of the fragmented body. His thesis on messianism in Peru brings the Inkarri myth to the present of the 1980s: the bloody war of the Shining Path is a new attempt to transform Peruvian history in an apocalyptic move that draws from Marxist-Maoism, Andean traditions, and Christian syncretism (Flores Galindo, pp. 364–65).

If the conquest meant a kind of beheading of the state, colonial rule did not provide a space for a new order. Sociologist Gonzalo Portocarrero believes that transgression has become part of Peruvian criollo society as a legacy of its colonial past (Portocarrero, 2004). Although he does not focus specifically on gender, Portocarrero's essay "La transgresión como forma específica de goce del mundo criollo" reveals the dilemma men face in a postcolonial society in which power is always somewhere else: while Peruvian males were supposed to embody authority and power in their own society, they were always already subjected to external powers. While outside powers imposed some laws, those who represented those laws saw them as foreign to their experience of reality. The law ended up being manipulated by the same authorities that were supposed to enforce it. This resulted not in a counter-hegemonic attitude, but in a cracked hegemony, an ironic, distant, and skeptical perspective towards the moral ideals that give order and sense to a society (p. 191).

The word *criollo* in its original sense meant people of Spanish descent born in the Americas. According to Portocarrero, the *criollo* world of Peruvian colonial society was problematic for the Spanish crown: the criollo were seen as potentially treacherous to the crown and they competed for the surplus produced by Indian labor. Several stereotypes characterize them as overindulged by the abundant Indian servants at their disposal, and one of the negative views about the criollos assumes they were illegitimate children of Spain. In their desire for legitimacy and recognition, they tried to negate any ties to the indigenous world (Portocarrero, 2004, p. 209). This is part of a very racist component of Peruvian society.

According to Nelson Manrique (1993), ideas of "pure blood" are brought to America with the Spanish conquest, as a legacy of the persecution of Jews and Moors from Spain. Those ideas notwithstanding, *mestizaje*, the sometimes abhorred and sometimes praised "mixing of races," happened, as it had also happened for centuries in the Spanish Peninsula among peoples of different ethnic origins. In a more recent work, Manrique insists in reminding contemporary audiences that the much-celebrated racial diversity of Peru responds in part to acts of violence:

> La reproducción biológica no requiere en absoluto relaciones horizontales entre quienes intervienen en el acto sexual: dadas las condiciones biológicas adecuadas, éste será igualmente fértil tanto si hay amor de por medio cuanto si lo que acontece es una agresión sexual, una violación. Y es imposible entender la naturaleza de la discriminación racial si se la desvincula de la discriminación de género. (2002, p. 326)

> Biological reproduction does not require horizontal relationships between those involved in the sexual act: given the right biological conditions, the act will be equally fertile if it involves a loving relationship or if it is an act of sexual aggression, such as rape. It is impossible to understand the nature of racial discrimination if it is not viewed in the light of gender discrimination.

Manrique reminds his readers that from a gender perspective it is necessary to acknowledge that *mestizaje* was the product of force and of unilateral and asymmetric relationships from the beginning of the European presence in the Americas. The topic that links Latin American identity to the rape of indigenous women at the hands of the conquistadors has been widely explored throughout the continent, from Octavio Paz's "Children of la Malinche" (Paz, 1961) in Mexico, to Sonia Montecino's *Madres y huachos* (Montecino Aguirre, 1991) in Chile. The idea that the population of these nations is mainly the result of an original rape—that their fathers forced their mothers, or that their mothers betrayed their own race by willingly sleeping with the enemy—is perceived as marking their identity. The absence of those fathers and the difficulty of gaining a sense of belonging—either to the original culture of the mother or to the culture of the colonizers—is also a determining factor. Of course, these facts would affect both male and female children: both boys and girls would grow up without a father and be rejected by their culture. The rape of indigenous women as the rape of the land has been an important topic of feminist study in the Americas (Castillo, 1992; Kaminsky, 1994; Anzaldúa, 1987). However, it is interesting to note that the risk for the girls is being fixed in the destiny of their mothers. They might, like their mothers, be seen either as traitors or as the victims of violence. The destiny of the boys, their tainted identity, is less certain: in the great majority of cases they do not have access to the social status and power of their fathers and, at the same time, they might be rejected by the mother's family. The most renowned *mestizo* is probably Garcilaso de la Vega, el Inca, whose greatest work, *Los comentarios reales de los Incas*, demonstrates the difficulties of articulating the double legacy of a Spanish captain and a woman from the Inca nobility.[7] But most *mestizos* were not able to articulate their identities through literature or otherwise.

Alberto Flores Galindo describes the situation of *mestizos* in these terms:

> Children of the Conquest, youth who should have had a situation of privilege both because of their father and their mother, ended up being rejected when Spaniards decided to organize their families, end their concubinage, and replace their Indian women for Spanish ones; for their mothers, that first generation of mestizos was a reminder of the defeat and the shame of the alleged rape. Natural children, they did not have a trade, they could not have it . . . a colonial functionary called them "Men with torn lives." (Flores Galindo, 1986, pp. 53–54)

The situation of those considered "not white" does not improve with the emancipation of the country in the nineteenth century. After the Indian rebel movements in the late eighteenth century, the criollo elite lived in perpetual fear of all nonwhites, and the independence of the country meant mainly that the dominant criollo minority took over the colonial structures for their own benefit. The state they generated was profoundly segregationist, racist, and anti-indigenous. Peruvian society was divided into castes, and it was assumed that whites were biologically superior to Indians. This created a social fracture that continues in the present: in Peru, social conflicts do not only present a class character, pitting workers against the bourgeoisie, landowners against peasants. These conflicts are also fraught with ethnic and racial problems among whites, mestizos, Indians, blacks, Asians, and their offspring (Manrique, 2002, pp. 56–57). Manrique describes Peruvian segregation as a state in which a minority rules for a minority, excluding the majority from political power, and normalizing a situation in which the majority of the population is discriminated against as a minority (Manrique, 2002, pp. 57–58).

Men who belong to discriminated sectors of the population are, in effect, disempowered while still participating in the dominant fiction in which men embody authority and strength and provide for their families. José María Arguedas, considered the most important voice in Peruvian Indigenism, presented this dilemma in his early stories, where a first-person narrator, a boy of European descent raised by Indians, struggles to understand why Indian men would not rebel against the powerful landowners (Arguedas, 1954). In the story "Warma Kuyay" ("Child's Love") young Ernesto, who has a crush on an Indian called Justina, experiences a bitter awakening when he realizes that the white landowner has sexually abused her, and that Kutu, her Indian boyfriend, did not defend her. Kutu complains, "I'm an Indian, I can't do anything against the *patrón*" (Arguedas, 1954, p. 183), but Ernesto thinks he is a coward who would abuse animals, and pretends to be strong, but who in reality had "female blood" (p. 187). The insulting comparison to women appears also in "Agua," where a group of peasants cannot protest the abuses of the white men in town: "Sanjuanes were like women, they feared the rebellion" (p. 111). Indians are accused of not being "men enough," even when the author is trying to present the complicated web created by ethnicity, power, and manhood.

The currency of this discrimination is evident in the findings of the TRC. The majority of the victims came from rural areas, belonged to the poorest regions, and had Quechua or a different native language, not Spanish, as their first language (Comisión de la Verdad, 2004, p. 23). It is important to note that the TRC recognizes the right of the state to defend itself against terrorist attacks. What the commissioners do not condone and fervently denounce is that the armed forces were given impunity and that civil authorities disregarded thousands of reports of human rights violations. This was possible in part because these victims were "invisible" from the dominant sectors of Peruvian society: "These are the Peruvians our country is missing, the least visible, but not less real: the Quispes, the Huamans, the Mamanis, the Taypes, the Yupanquis, the Condoris, the Tintimanris, the Metzoquiaris" (Comisión de la Verdad, 2004, p. 27). The list of indigenous names stands for those victims ignored by the Peruvian elite.

The atrocities investigated by the TRC constitute what their report calls a "double scandal"—the fact that mass murder, kidnapping, and torture were not stopped, and the fact that the reaction to these atrocities was obliviousness, ineptitude, and indifference (Comisión de la Verdad, 2004, p. 9). To the crimes against humanity there is an added crime: the fact that those who were not directly affected by the violence preferred to ignore it. If we follow Portocarrero in assuming that a transgressive perspective with regards to the Law is ingrained in Peruvian society, these horrendous crimes and the lack of a massive outrage towards them are an example of the most perverse extreme in this tolerance of transgression. It is my contention that the pervasiveness of the normalization of transgression in Peruvian culture is a direct outcome of a fracture of the dominant fiction that did not produce any alternatives. The body of the Inca is supposed to incarnate the nation, but his head is nowhere to be found, and the Law is only a phantom of the Law.

Portocarrero's view on transgression centers on the colonial heritage, and the fact that criollo society historically came about from a gap between the legal system and a reality perceived to be far from it. Juan Carlos Ubilluz (2006) offers a different perspective on transgression in criollo society. For Ubilluz, the word *criollo* itself has lost its original meaning: it does not designate an ethnic origin, or Peruvians in general, or the populations from certain regions, but "a specific relationship with the Law" that Ubilluz has identified with a particular form of cynicism. Ubilluz considers Portocarrero's evaluation of Peruvian cynicism limited in circumscribing it to the colonial legacy. For Ubilluz, events in recent decades such as the failure of socialist initiatives and collective projects, along with the globalization of the market, have contributed to the transgressive impulse that, according to Portocarrero, was already a characteristic of the criollo. He considers that the exacerbated individualism of late-capitalism legitimated criollo transgression.

Ubilluz's analysis is particularly relevant for my work on masculinity since it links his view on Peruvian cynicism with the role of the Name of the Father in late capitalism. He brilliantly analyzes Mario Vargas Llosa's 1994 novel *Los cuadernos de Don Rigoberto* as an example of the postmodern transgressive father. Following Slavoj Žižek and Alenka Zupancic, Ubilluz believes that while modernity would question paternal prohibition by substituting it with a new symbolic order—let's say "Reason and Progress"—postmodern subjects have lost belief in the place of authority itself. When biological fathers have to be the Law, enforce repression, and at the same time they fail to incarnate an ideal image, the child simply questions paternal authority. But even as he questions authority, the child is able to imagine a different order. When paternal prohibition is no longer there, there is no authority, only narcissistic individualism.

Ubilluz's transgressive father would be the extreme opposite of Silverman's marginal masculinities: he rejects symbolic castration and believes in his individuality. Ubilluz shows how these individuals turn, not into subjects, but into objects subjected to consumerism, consumers at the mercy of the market, under the belief that every desire can be satisfied to achieve wholeness.

Los cuadernos de Don Rigoberto might be an extreme example of Vargas Llosa's neoliberal imagination (Don Rigoberto, the father, incites the affair between his underage son and his new wife, among other sexual practices that negate prohibition in favor of individual liberties). This suits Ubilluz's analysis, which focuses on a postmodern condition. However, the image of the transgressive father predates the kind of condition Ubilluz is presenting. The dissonance between the ideal father and the real father seems to be a constant trait of Peruvian cultural production, and in all cases this seems to debilitate the authority principle and the sense of order.

Peruvian narrative is populated by sons who live under the shadow of ailing, weak, or distant fathers. In Julio Ramón Ribeyro's "El ropero, los viejos y la muerte" (1994) the narrator's father, pale and thin, holds on to the only object he is proud of, a wardrobe he inherited from his grandfather, until its mirror is destroyed by a soccer ball shot by the son of a more successful friend. In "Con Jimmy en Paracas" by Alfredo Bryce Echenique (1979), the son suffers his father's humiliation in front of his rich boss. The reason why Arguedas's Ernesto, the protagonist of *Deep Rivers* (1978) and many other of his early stories, is raised by Indians is that his father is trying to make a living as a traveling lawyer and is unable to raise him by himself. Recent Peruvian poetry presents many examples of the voices of fathers who feel either incompetent or incapable of connecting to that role. In José Watanabe's "A proposito de los desajustes" (2000, pp. 31–32) the poetic voice expresses its confusion and disaffection towards the wife and the baby he is supposed to support, while he is struggling to say "the beautiful words (of an idiot)." In a heartbreaking collection of poems called *El mundo en una gota de rocío*, poet Abelardo Sánchez León (2000) mourns the death of his teenage son. Grief and guilt impregnate each line in which the father has outlived his son, and he "wails, secretly, gobbles up, drinks / in a human time that is not longer his" (p. 80). But probably the most conspicuous example of a controversial father figure comes out of the most famous of Vargas Llosa's novels, *Conversation in the Cathedral.*

Originally published in 1969, this highly experimental piece of fiction, full of interwoven stories, streams of consciousness, and internal monologues that link narrative levels in an almost hypertextual way, has been taken, even by historians, as one of the most important testimonies of the Odría dictatorship in the Peru of the 1950s. The consciousness that prevails in this narrative is the one of Zavalita, a young reporter who has renounced his bourgeois family to pursue studies in the politically oriented Universidad de San Marcos, and who has married a woman from a lower class. It is Za-valita who formulates the novel's mantra, "At what precise moment had Peru fucked itself up?" as he observes the decay of streets and buildings, and of the morale of his colleagues, and as he discovers the way the corruption of the government reaches every social strata. He also formulates possible answers in his mind "Perhaps then . . . perhaps then." However, there is a moment that stands out when he finally says: "It was then!" It is the moment when he discovers that his father leads a double life of homosexual encounters that link him to people involved in the corruption of the government and even to murder. The son's shock is understandable, because of the secrecy, and the betrayal of trust. A plot that connects the screwed state of the na-tion to the father's homosexuality reveals the deeply rooted homophobia of Peruvian society, but it also attempts to stress the general sense that reality itself collapses when the sins of the father are revealed.

A less renowned story, "El engendro," was written by Siu Kam Wen, a Chinese born author who lived in Peru from the early 1970s to 1985, when he migrated to Hawaii. Siu's marginality to the Peruvian literary establishment gives him an interesting perspective regarding certain symptoms of Peruvian society. The title, "El engendro" could be loosely translated as "The monster," but the Spanish word derives from *engendrar*: "to beget," "to father." The prob-lem is that the expression *el engendro* implies that whatever was begotten is somehow perverted and monstrous, and not a normal child. The story starts with an epigraph that recounts the horrors of the Chilean occupation of Peru during 1880, particularly the way women had been victims of the cruelest acts in the hands of Chilean soldiers. The Chilean-Peruvian war during the late nineteenth century left a traumatic mark on Peruvian consciousness. Essays published right after the war blamed the defeat on the weakness of Peruvian leaders. The loss of territory was experienced as a form of castration.

In Siu's story, Captain Ignacio la Barrera returns from the war only to find his wife five months pregnant. He takes her back, but abandons the child to the care of the baby's maternal grandfather. The boy, Horacio, grows up with the shame of being called "the bastard" or "the little Chilean." The grandfather tries to protect him by taking him out of the country, but when he returns as a man, he is determined to learn the truth from his mother. The final pages reveal little by little that even though Horacio had expected the worst, "there was an even larger horror" awaiting him. The last paragraph reveals, along with Horacio's suicide after killing his grandfather, that the trauma of war was only hiding another trauma. "El engendro" was not the result of the abuse of the Chilean troops, but the result of the more intimate horror: Horacio's grandfather was also his father.

Siu's story misleads the reader into imagining Captain la Barrera's honor tarnished by an external enemy, his manhood questioned by his wife's body carrying the foreign enemy's child. However, the perverse outcome reveals that the monster does not come from the outside, but from the aristocratic, patriarchal, structure that supposedly sustains the family's honor.

A very nineteenth-century story written during the last decades of the twentieth century, it reveals two threats to Peruvian manhood in the characters of Captain la Barrera and his son: one is to be humiliated in front of a foreign power, the other is to be begotten by internal corruption. Both undermine any belief in the dominant fiction of an intact masculinity and in the Law of the Father.

The intrinsic corruption of the ideals of the dominant fiction resurfaces in the new millennium. In the aftermath of the work of the TRC, Josué Méndez's film *Días de Santiago* (2004) deals with the lack of space for ex-combatants in civil society. While post-traumatic stress disorder is not a new topic in the United States, this is the first Peruvian film to deal directly with the issue, and to lay down questions of masculinity in a society that still has not confronted the serious wounds of recent and past history. This film tells the story of a twenty-three-year-old ex-combatant who, after participating in the war against the Shining Path and the border wars with Ecuador, finds himself unable to cope with civilian life. The first frame of the film—in a grainy black and white—shows a woman waiting for a bus in a dusty road in the outskirts of Lima. As she turns towards the camera we see bruises on her face. She stares defiantly, and then away. Only then do we see Santiago, presumably standing in front of her, looking down, as if ashamed. He also looks at the camera and then away a couple of times. Not a word is spoken, but it is evident that he has hit her, as he returns to an empty home. We can

read the bruises on the woman's face as the effects of a conflicted masculinity that only finds expression through violence. We will see in Santiago
many of the symptoms of post-traumatic stress disorder, from outbursts
of violence, to unresponsiveness, to disorientation, to paranoid delusions.
However, Santiago tries to hold on to his beliefs in a world where cynicism
reigns. He tries to hold on to a sense of honor. He is an ex-combatant, and
for him that means being an honorable man.

The cynicism Santiago is trying to resist seems to be the prevalent attitude
among Peruvian youth. Gonzalo Portocarrero (2004) found three different
responses to situations that would require moral judgment: morality, contestation, and cynicism. The first response tends to leave context out of the
question, and judge transgression in itself. Motivation or relevance of the
transgression is not important. It simply should not be done. The second
attitude corresponds to a contestatory view of the world. If a situation is
intrinsically unfair, transgression might be necessary. This position tends to
take into consideration the motivations for the act, and the consequences
of it. The last position will perceive transgression as a necessity. Everybody
needs to look out for his or her own interest. An unfair system is always assumed and there is a sense of complicity with the transgressive action that
is being judged. When cynicism prevails and society becomes a society of
accomplices, everybody pretends there is a Law, but nobody respects it (Portocarrero, 2004, p. 138).

If it is true that as a combatant Santiago had killed people, he believed
that what he did was in support of an order. War could suspend the Law. But
Santiago doesn't want to bring a "state of exception" (Agamben, 2005) to civil
society. He wants to be recognized as somebody who has served his country.
He wants to be able to reconstitute the dominant fiction: to have a job and
a family. To support his wife. To obey the law. When his ex-comrades try to
talk him into planning an armed robbery, because they cannot find a digni-
fied way of making a living, he is drawn back. He even lets out that he quit
the army for a reason. He does not explain the motives for this disenchant-
ment, but he hints at a reality that did not correspond to his ideal image of
the army. The dominant fiction had already revealed its cracks to Santiago,
but he was unable to process this. His comrades display a cynical attitude:
they have the means to perform the robbery and believe they can get away
with it, but Santiago refuses to participate.

Santiago's efforts to reestablish order enter the performative realm. As
soon as he receives a little money from his state pension, he acts and enun-
ciates the order of things: in a close shot we see him propose a daily sched-

ule, and explain, apparently to his wife, "This is this, the stove is the stove, the table is the table. . . . Everything has an order, everything has a reason, without order there is nothing. . . . I'm a man, you're a woman." When the shot widens to include the whole kitchen, we realize that he is by himself, rehearsing a speech for his wife. Seconds later she shows up, and he is unable to repeat his speech. As we can see, he cannot perform the dominant fiction even in front of his wife when she is the one who provides their meager meal. In his speech he makes us assume that she is a stay-at-home housewife, but later we find out that she has a job at a hospital. Many Latin American sociologists concerned with masculinity studies have noticed how women's entrance in the job force in the last decades has changed the balance of power in the home. However, while the effect of this shift could create a more egalitarian sharing of household chores and responsibilities in child rearing, it could also have the opposite effect. Some men feel emasculated and might compensate for their lack of power through violence (Cáceres et al., 2002, pp. 115–45).

Santiago struggles to achieve a precarious order, working as a taxi driver and signing up for some adult education classes, but this order soon starts crumbling around him. His wife abandons him, his brother's wife attempts to seduce him, he fantasizes about becoming friends with the careless young women who take classes with him, but it soon becomes evident that his way of coping with different situations has no connection with reality. The climax of the film occurs as Santiago storms into his family's house. A woman screams and he thinks he is going to save his sister-in-law from being killed by his brother. What he finds is even more horrifying: his own father raping Santiago's teenage sister. As spectators of this drama, we might feel that this is too extreme and out of place, a *deus ex machina*, since Santiago's father was a very secondary character up to this moment. However, incest as the ultimate taboo confronts us with the dissolution of the Law of the Father. If up to this moment Santiago had been an advocate of order in the form of the patriarchal system, if he had been trying to incarnate the dominant fiction, the revelation of incest forces the return of the repressed: Santiago's belief in the Law has been shattered, even though he struggled to hold on to an idea of order with all his might. He left the army for a reason, but he had been trying to uphold the legitimacy of the system. In the last sequence of the film Santiago, alone in his room, strokes his gun against different parts of his head. We see him shoot empty shots, three times.

The narrator of the Colombian novel *The Virgin of the Assassins* by Fernando Vallejos says, "In Colombia there are laws, but there is no Law." The same is true in the Peru that *Días de Santiago* represents, and that is the tragedy that Santiago incarnates. When transgression becomes the norm, the attempts to live the dominant fiction become futile. Violence, cynicism, and oblivion undermine belief in the system without providing an alternative. Historical trauma—in Silverman's terms—challenges phallic identification and exposes the abyss concealed under coherent male egos (121). The faults in the dominant fiction resurface in Peruvian literature through the images of decapitated Incas, of Indians who behave "like women," of absent or transgressive fathers. The challenge for the future would be to provide a new order in which gender roles could be reconstructed in more egalitarian terms. In Peru this task involves undoing centuries of discrimination and oppression. The Inca has lost his head forever and no other image has come to offer a future to Peruvians. Helping men face their own images, and their own lack, would be only a small step towards change.

Notes

1. The role of women as survivors of the conflict claiming justice for their relatives was acknowledged in the photo exhibit by a room specially devoted to the labor of the widows and mothers of the disappeared. The commission also introduced a gender perspective in their report by stressing the way rape had been used as a weapon targeting women during the conflict (Mantilla Falcón, 2007).

2. Eduardo Archetti's (1997) study of prevalent forms of insult among Argentinian soccer fans demonstrates that fantasies of sodomizing the enemy, emasculating him, and rendering him "female" are still current as discourses even if not necessarily as practices in Latin America.

3. Only in the last fifteen years have international organizations like the UN and the Red Cross started paying attention to sexual violence against women during a war as war crimes (Mantilla, 2007, pp. 14–18). The Peruvian Truth and Reconciliation Commission found that women tend not to report rape and that they had to do a thorough campaign to get women to testify on their own behalf (p. 28). Even if underreported, the rape of women continues to be used as a weapon to humiliate, paralyze, and traumatize the vanquished.

4. Drawing number 156 in Guamán Poma's manuscript can be seen at the *Guamán Poma Web site, A Digital Research Center of the Royal Library, Copenhagen, Denmark.*

5. Translations are mine, unless a translator is included in the references.

6. Drawing 182 in the manuscript.

7. The extensive corpus on the role of *mestizaje* in the construction of Garcilaso's identity both in his work, and in the interpretation of his work in Peruvian literary tradition, exceeds the limits of this essay. Antonio Cornejo Polar's chapter "Las suturas homogeneizadoras: Los discursos de la armonía imposible" in his *Escribir en el aire* (2003) will give the reader a sense of the crevices in an identity that at times

has been presented as the "harmonious" union of the Spanish and Inca heritage that informs the Peruvian nation.

References

Agamben, G. (2005). *State of Exception.* (Trans. K. Attell). Chicago: University of Chicago Press.

Anzaldúa, G. (1987). *Borderlands/La Frontera.* San Francisco: Spinsters/Aunt Lute.

Arguedas, J. M. (1954). *Diamantes y pedernales. Agua.* Lima: Juan Mejia Baca y P.L. Villanueva Editores.

Arguedas, J. M. (1978). *Deep Rivers.* (Trans. F. H. Barraclough). Austin: University of Texas Press.

Blondet, C. (2004). "Lecciones de la participación política de las mujeres." *Democracia, gobierno y derechos humanos. Documento del programa número 12.* Instituto de Investigación de las Naciones Unidas para el Desarrollo Social. Retrieved April 11, 2008, from: http://www.unrisd.org/80256B3C005BCCF9/(httpPublications) /96074418A9401BC7C1256BBA0029316B?OpenDocument

Bryce Echenique, A. (1979). *Todos los cuentos.* Lima: Mosca Azul.

Cáceres, C. F. et al. (2002). *Ser hombre en el Peru de hoy: Una mirada a la salud sexual desde la infidelidad, la violencia y la homofobia.* Lima: REDESS Jóvenes.

Castillo, Debra. (1992). *Talking Back: Toward a Latin American Feminist Literary Criticism.* Ithaca, N.Y.: Cornell University Press.

Comisión de la Verdad y Reconciliación, Peru. (2004). *Hatun Willakuy: Versión abreviada del informe final de la comisión de la verdad y reconciliación, Perú* (1st ed.). Lima, Peru: Comisión de la Verdad y Reconciliación.

Cornejo Polar, A. (2003). *Escribir en el aire: Ensayo sobre la heterogeneidad sociocultural en las literaturas andinas.* Lima: Centro de Estudios Literarios "Antonio Cornejo Polar": Latinoamericana Editores.

Flores Galindo, A. (1986). *Buscando un inca: Identidad y utopía en los andes.* La Habana: Casa de las Américas.

Fuller, N. (2001). *Masculinidades: Cambios y permanencias. Varones de Cuzco, Iquitos y Lima.* Lima: Pontificia Universidad Católica del Perú, Fondo Editorial.

Guamán Poma de Ayala, F. (1615). *Nueva corónica y buen gobierno. In Facsímil del manuscrito autógrafo, transcripción anotada, documentos y otros recursos digitales.* Retrieved April 15, 2008, from: http://www.kb.dk/permalink/2006/poma/info/es/frontpage.htm

Hardin, M. (2002). "Altering Masculinities: The Spanish Conquest and the Evolution of the Latin American *Machismo*." *International Journal of Sexuality and Gender Studies, 7*(1), 1–22.

Kaminsky, A. (1994). "Gender, Race, Raza." *Feminist Studies, 20*(1), 7–31.

Klarén, P. F. (2000). *Peru: Society and Nation in the Andes.* Oxford: Oxford University Press.

———. (2007). "'El tiempo del miedo' (1980–2000), la violencia moderna y la larga duracion en la historia peruana." *Historizar el pasado vivo en América Latina*. Retrieved March 31, 2008, from: http://www.historizarelpasadovivo.cl/es_contenido.php

Mannarelli, M. E. (2007). *Private Passions and Public Sins: Men and Women in Seventeenth-century Lima*. (Trans. S. Evans & M. D. Dodge). Albuquerque: University of New Mexico Press.

Manrique, N. (1993). *Vinieron los sarracenos: El universo mental de la conquista de América*. Lima: Desco.

Manrique, N. (2002). *El tiempo del miedo. La violencia politica en el Perú, 1980–1996*. Lima: Fondo Editorial del Congreso del Peru.

Mantilla Falcón, J. (2007). "Sin la verdad de las mujeres, la historia no estará completa." El reto de incorporar una perspectiva de género en la Comisión de la Verdad y Reconciliación del Perú. *Historizar el pasado vivo en América Latina*. Retrieved March 31, 2008, from: http://www.historizarelpasadovivo.cl/es_contenido.php

Méndez, J. (Director). (2004). *Días de Santiago*. [Motion picture on DVD].

Montecino Aguirre, S. (1991). *Madres y huachos: Alegorías del mestizaje chileno*. Santiago: Cuarto Propio-CEDEM.

Paz, Octavio. (1961). *The Labyrinth of Solitude: Life and Thought in Mexico*. (Trans. L. Kemp). New York: Grove Press.

Portocarrero Maisch, G. (2004). *Rostros criollos del mal: Cultura y transgresión en la sociedad peruana* (1st ed.). Lima: Red para el Desarrollo de las Ciencias Sociales en el Perú.

Ribeyro, J. R. (1994). *La palabra del mudo. Cuentos 1952/1993*. Lima: Jaime Campodónico Editor.

Sánchez León, A. (2000). *El mundo en una gota de rocío*. Lima: Peisa.

Silverman, Kaja. (1992). *Male Subjectivity at the Margins*. New York: Routledge.

Siu, K. W. (1988) "El engendro." In *La primera espada del Imperio*. Lima: Ediciones del Instituto Nacional de Cultura. Retrieved May 6, 2008 from: http://www.what-is-art.com/

Trexler, R. C. (1995). *Sex and Conquest: Gender Violence, Political Order, and the European Conquest of the Americas*. Ithaca, N.Y.: Cornell University Press.

Ubilluz, J. C. (2006). *Nuevos súbditos. Cinismo y perversión en la sociedad contemporánea*. Lima: IEP.

Vallejos, F. (2006). *La virgen de los sicarios*. Madrid: Punto de lectura.

Vargas Llosa, M. (1974). *Conversation in the Cathedral*. (Trans. Gregory Rabassa). New York: HarperCollins.

Vargas Llosa, M. (1994). *Los cuadernos de don Rigoberto*. Madrid: Alfaguara.

Watanabe, J. (2000). *El guardián del hielo*. Lima: Grupo Editorial Norma.

5

Postcolonial Masculinity
and Commodity Culture in Kenya

MICH NYAWALO

Introduction

In *The Wretched of the Earth*, Frantz Fanon (1961) describes the African social elite as a bourgeoisie without capital. This characteristic is attributed to Africa's "postcolonial" leaders, primarily because they are not endowed with the means and infrastructures of production through which their social status as a bourgeoisie can be validated. Conceptions of masculinity as embedded within political power structures have often been problematized within "postcolonial" discourse. African scholars, authors and filmmakers such as Ousmane Sembene (1974) have, for example, explored the theme of impotence as an embodiment of the African leader's sociopolitical condition. This chapter seeks to analyze the means through which tropes of masculinity and political power, which are manifested within the spectacle of commodity fetishism, operate in Kenya's contemporary neocolonial environment. The chapter conducts a sociopolitical analysis of the different symbols of masculinity and power that have been implicitly and explicitly internalized within Kenyan society by asking the following questions: How have conceptions of masculinity and power been constructed in today's Kenyan society and how (or why) have they "evolved" from their traditional manifestations? What role does the Kenyan and Western media play in constructing new perceptions of manhood and power? And finally, how do these new perceptions participate in the autopoietic economic world system to which Kenya belongs? I shall answer these questions by first focusing on the multiple facets and definitions of power (both at the macro and micro level) that are manifested in neocolonial societies, before analyzing the ways in which they are represented in the Kenyan media and internalized by the society at large.

Impotence as a common theme proliferates in a vast array of African postcolonial literary texts. In these texts impotence often manifests itself as an epiphenomenon of the clash between precolonial structures of power as embedded and signified within tropes of masculinity, and post-, or more appropriately, neo-, colonial embodiments of manhood and power. In *Xala* (1974), Sembene's protagonist El Hadji, a successful and wealthy businessman whose persona stands as a symbol for the emergent African bourgeoisie, has been struck by the curse of impotence, of which he struggles to rid himself throughout the story. In *Xala*, El Hadji's sexual impotence can only be cured through the debasement of his Western persona, the removal of his Western mask, which has to be shattered through humiliation and not just any kind of humiliation but one applied within the boundaries of traditional beliefs. One could argue that Ousmane Sembene therefore equates the forced alienation of one's "African" self, the exchange of identities in which the native is brainwashed into identifying with the oppressor, as a state of impotence. Impotence in this case means the inability to forge a future for one's community. Just as an impotent man is deprived of a future family legacy because he cannot have children, so is the westernized African bourgeoisie incapable of forging a future for his community.

In Ahmadou Kourouma's work *The Suns of Independence* (*Les Soleils Des Independences*, 1968), Fama, the main character, lacks the ability to impregnate his two wives; this symbolizes the postcolonial state of disempowerment experienced by the precolonial African ruling elite in an environment where structures of power have been reversed. Similarly in Chinua Achebe's *Things Fall Apart* (1958) and Wole Soyinka's play *The Lion and the Jewel* (1966) we find juxtapositions among traditional perceptions as well as performances of masculinity and power, and the colonial realities that threaten to destabilize them. The characters Obi Okonkwo and Baroka in *Things Fall Apart* and the *Lion and the Jewel*, respectively, personify embodiments of certain African traditional concepts of manhood and power. In *Things Fall Apart*, Okonkwo's suicide at the end of the novel signifies the protagonist's refusal to "effeminize" his cultural performance of manhood and sense of empowerment in the face of colonial realities. In *The Lion and the Jewel* the clash between Baroka the village chief and Lakunle the school teacher, both of whom desire Sidi the village beauty as the object of masculine empowerment, presents a dichotomy between traditional performances of manhood and contemporary applications of masculinity. Lakunle's emasculation at the end of the play problematizes the educated African male's projected internalization of Western manhood.

In many of the above texts, colonization and neocolonization present themselves as the negation of precolonial perceptions of African manhood. Furthermore, conceptions of manhood are not only negated by colonization but also restructured as a means to fit into the newly emerging colonial realities. In *Black Skin, White Masks*, Fanon (1967) contends that "the black man cannot take pleasure in his insularity. For him there is only one way out, and it leads into the white world. Whence his constant preoccupation with attracting the attention of the white man, his concern with being powerful like the white man, his determined effort to acquire protective qualities—that is, the proportion of an ego. It is from within that the Negro will seek admittance to the white sanctuary" (p. 51). The restructuring of power relations during colonization, where notions of authority and superiority are signified by "whiteness," creates ontological paradigms of power perceptions in which the native's sense of worth must always be performed in relation to the conqueror as an ideal. Fanon further argues that: "The black man has no ontological resistance in the eyes of the white man. Overnight the Negro has been given two frames of reference within which he has to place himself. His metaphysics or, less pretentiously, his customs and the source on which they were based, were wiped out because they were in conflict with a civilization that he did not know and that imposed itself on him. The black man in the twentieth century does not know at what moment his inferiority comes into being through the other" (p. 110). It is the moment of coming into being through the other that characterizes the manner in which the performance of masculinity as a signifier of power is altered and reframed in ways that differentiate themselves from precolonial African models. In the first section of this chapter I trace the social perceptions of masculinity and power in Luo society, by analyzing the ways in which they are embedded in Luo folklore, before outlining, in the remaining sections, the modes in which these percepts have been altered in contemporary Kenyan society.

Perceptions of Masculinity and Power in Precolonial Luo Society

Among the Luo, oral narratives had two purposes: they were told for entertainment and education. People normally told stories to each other in the evening around a warm fire. Under normal circumstances, adults did the telling while the children listened. On some occasions, however, children were the ones who told the stories while the adults corrected them whenever they left some detail out. In this way, the children could also learn the art of storytelling. The role of storytelling was mostly confined to elders in society, such as grandmothers. The relationship between an individual and his/ her grandchildren was a very special one. While children were expected to show respect towards their parents, grandchildren, on the other hand, often communicated with their grandparents on an equal level. Storytelling was therefore conducted in a most friendly and relaxed atmosphere. Young boys together with their sisters and grandmother usually slept in the *siwindhe*. The *siwindhe* was not just a place of residence, but a specified hut where Luo children received their education. It acted as an institution of learning where young boys and girls learned about social customs. It was also in this same place that the grandmother told narratives. Later on, however, when the boys reached puberty, custom required them to move into the *simba* (bachelor house). During this period of time they usually came together in the main men-only hut called the *duol*. It was in the *duol* that young teenagers listened to new kinds of narratives, which differed from the ones they used to hear in the *siwindhe*. These narratives mainly focused on heroic tales of war and bravery. I will briefly analyze the tale of Luanda Magere, an example of a narrative that was told in the *duol*, as a means to unearth Luo social percepts of masculinity and power.

Luanda Magere was a fierce and brave warrior who lived at the time when the Luo were engaged in a ferocious battle against the Kalenjin ethnic group. It was said that the skin of Luanda Magere was as tough as a rock, so that even the spears of the fierce Kalenjin tribesman could not pierce it. The only way to gain access to Luanda Magere's body and his life was through his shadow. But this was a very well-guarded secret, known only to him and his first wife. One day he decided to marry a new wife. This decision would have been a great cause for celebration but unfortunately it was against the advice of the elders (*jodongo*), whose disapproval of his new wife emanated from the fact that the lady he had fallen in love with came from the Kalenjin tribe. Little did Luanda Magere know that this woman had actually been sent as a spy by his enemies in the hope of discovering his Achilles tendon.

One day Luanda Magere became ill. His first wife was away and "thus the junior wife nursed Magere. Next day his illness was worse and in the late morning, when the sun reached its height and people in the garden had to leave their work to shelter from its heat, Magere told his young wife to bring a blade, cut his body with it, and then rub some potent ash into the wounds" (Ogutu, 1974, p. 144). Startled by this demand, his new wife replied:

> "Husband why do you demand the impossible? A thin blade cannot cut through the rock! And you're all rock." Then Magere pointed to his shadow. "Cut there," he ordered. Now, she went half-heartedly to Magere's shadow, and with the blade cut the part cast by his forehead. As she watched the blade sink into the shadow it seemed to her that it was sinking into the earth. She was astonished, therefore, to look up and see blood trickling from the "rock." She knew now that Magere's strength lay in his shadow, and not in his body. Her treacherous heart was warmed by it all. (Ogotu, 1974, p. 145)

His new Kalenjin wife had already learned his secret and one night while he was asleep she escaped at night to inform her people. During the next tribal war, Luanda Magere fought with his usual courage, in the process killing many Kalenjin tribesmen. However, his secret having been revealed to his enemies, one spear inevitably found its way into his shadow, killing him in the process.

One interpretation of this narrative would be that it might be dealing with the importance of kinship. Luanda Magere died because his Kalenjin wife, who was not a Luo, betrayed him. This in a way also implies that such an incident would not have happened had he married a Luo girl that his community approved of. Another interpretation would be that this narrative theorizes about the nature of man/woman relationships. The vulnerability of a man's life in the hands of a woman is portrayed in this relationship. In the story it is the wife who manages to destroy a man whose strength was legendary among his fellow men. The reference to the shadow is embedded in the Luo metaphysical concept of life as having a continuous flow from one form to another, with the shadow being its most potent form. But this tale also provides a worldview of gender relations in this community. It may be understood to imply that while men practice the art of warfare using raw force, women have perfected the art of treachery and sheer intellectual calculation, which as the story suggests, can be a more efficient, not to say a more destructive, tool. The story therefore warns the men against excessive chauvinism and the tendency to underestimate the intelligence of their female partners, which may not only jeopardize the destiny of an individual but also that of a whole community. In *Dismantling Black Manhood*, Daniel Black (1997) posits that, "During pre-colonial times in West Africa, manhood was primarily a socially-owned and operated construct. In other words, males did not consider themselves men, regardless of their age or perceived worth, only the community, that is, other men and women, possessed this right. In fact, males who boasted of their individual achievements of wealth, indirectly proclaiming the extent of their manhood, were usually shunned and cautioned that 'one man cannot build a town.' Individual achievements alone were not seen by most West African communities as evidence that a male understood what it meant to be a man. Indeed, proverbs and folktales suggest that manhood was inextricably linked to a male's ability to support others, whatever that entailed" (11).

The same phenomena can also be observed within the East African Luo community. Magere's status as a fallen hero is the result of an egotistic action—the decision to marry a new wife of his choice without any regard for the welfare of his community. Conceptions of manhood and masculinity were hence embedded within one's sense of communal responsibility.

In his book *Luo, Kitgi gi Timbegi* (*Luo, Culture and Behavior*), Ker Paul Mboya (1983) writes about the hierarchy of leadership in the Luo community. According to Mboya, power in the Luo community was not centralized around one individual. Even a chief had to take advice from the council of *Jodongo* (the elders of society). Everyone in society therefore had a responsibility to maintain order at various levels of the communal life. The combination of all these responsibilities glued society together. The individual was therefore defined by his or her society, whose needs preceded his/hers. The Luo, it seems, tried as much as possible to combine the needs of the individual and those of the community. In this sense, biopolitical realities were not only implicitly enacted in this social cohesion but also explicitly articulated in their folklore and tradition. We shall now examine how these perceptions of manhood were altered through the advent of colonization.

The Birth of the Kenyan Bourgeoisie and the Reformulation of Power

Kenya gained its "independence" from Britain in 1963, and the following year elected its first president, Jomo Kenyatta, who was a member of the Kikuyu ethnic group (one of the largest in Kenya). Although an oppositional party was briefly formed in 1964 by Jaramogi Oginga Odinga (a former vice president), the country was entangled in a single-party system that lasted until 1991, when that system was repealed by the Kenyan parliament as part of its constitutional reforms. In 1978, Vice President Daniel Arap Moi succeeded Kenyatta after his death and became the country's second president. Additional constitutional reforms further enabled the expansion of political parties from eleven to twenty-six in 1997. It was, however, only in 2002 that president Moi finally stepped down, leaving room for his former vice president, Mwai Kibaki, to take over after winning the national elections.

The birth and formation of the Kenyan bourgeoisie under the colonial regime can be demarcated as the starting points from which contemporary tropes and performances of masculinity and power were forged. During the colonial period, it was not only imperative for the colonizers to find a humane rhetoric that validated the inhumane practices of colonial exploitation, it was also similarly important that the colonized masses internalized the colonizer's logic and worldviews. In *Decolonising the Mind*, Ngugi wa Thiong'o (1981) exemplifies the different ways in which language as a communicative tool was used as a means to entrench foreign worldviews and conceptions into the native's psyche. Ngugi argues that European languages prevented the native from using cognitive tools within his or her own cultural repertoire that would enable one to disengage from the conditions of servitude that colonization had imposed. Instead, he argues European languages provided the native with a biased foreign gaze, through which he/she now viewed his or her immediate "realities." Familiar conceptions of social "reality" were hence rendered unfamiliar, perceptions of one's identity, which are often contingent on socio-linguistic dynamics, were reformulated within the framework of the colonial project. As native languages were thoughtlessly demoted to the status of dialects, the reading and writing of European languages such as English and French became the enabling tools through which social prosperity could be achieved.

Literacy as a communicative medium increasingly became an indispensable means that gave certain natives a limited access to power over their own people. Ideologies that supported the perpetuation of the colonial status quo were hence primed within one's pedagogic acquisition of literacy skills. Literacy became a medium that not only altered preexisting social structures but also sought to prevent the colonized masses from deviating from the norms of the newly imposed colonial order. In spite of the fact that the African populace outnumbered their colonial occupants, native rebellions were often squashed by colonially trained native forces that had been conditioned into operating within the boundaries of imperial "realities." The establishments of these social conditions were to set the tune for the political neocolonial climate of "post-independent" African nations, which were characterized by the emergence of an African bourgeoisie whose political agenda matched the interests of the former colonizers. According to Ngugi: "The biggest weapon wielded and actually daily unleashed by imperialism against collective defiance is the cultural bomb. The effect of that cultural bomb is to annihilate a people's belief in their names, in their languages, in their environment, in their heritage of struggle, in their unity, in their capacities and ultimately in themselves" (p. 3). The African bourgeoisie is formed out of a modus operandi of alienation through education. The "intellectualized" African is removed from his social and cultural surroundings and thrown into a foreign environment that will in time become his habitual repertoire of knowledge and self-definition. Through his training, the African is placed in a superior position of leadership in which he is made to acquire the taste of a limited sense of power over his own people. The collective identity of the "intellectualized" African and that of the peasant population is ultimately fractured and rendered more complex, as newly indigenous social class structures are formed under the colonial regime. Fanon (1967) posits that "colonialism almost never exploits the entire country. It is content with extracting natural resources and exporting them to the metropolitan industries thereby enabling a specific sector to grow relatively wealthy, while the rest of the colony continues, or rather sinks, into underdevelopment and poverty" (p. 106). Colonization is hence facilitated through the mediated help of the new African elite. In the neocolonial phase this status quo is sustained through the help of the African bourgeoisie.

In this respect, it is helpful to recall Baudrillard's (1985) concept of the simulacra as a phenomenon that "masks and denatures a profound reality, masks the *absence* of a profound reality," and may have "no relation to any reality whatsoever: it is its own pure simulacrum" (p. 456). In Kenya, the role of the political leader manifests itself as a pure simulacrum of a past that no longer exists, a past in which the agency of the masses was directly performed through their leaders, "chiefs" and communal elders. In today's Kenyan society, political leaders are socially and economically divorced from the masses who place their hopes in them. According to Fanon, African politicians increasingly turn their backs "on the interior, on the realities of a country gone to waste, and look toward the former metropolis and the foreign capitalists who secure [their] services. Since [they have] no intention of sharing [their] profits with the people or letting them enjoy the rewards paid by the major foreign companies, [they] discover the need for a popular leader whose dual role will be to stabilize the regime and perpetuate the domination of the bourgeoisie" (Fanon, 1967, p. 111).

It is in the face of new structures of power formed under a radically different sense of communal responsibility that contemporary manifestations of masculinity and power are performed. In the neocolonial era, the traditional social system that was embedded in moral structures that prioritized the well-being of society as a whole over that of the individual (although still somewhat present within immediate family structures), has on a larger scale been profoundly altered by the onslaught of colonization and neocolonization. This has also changed the performance of masculinity from the way it had been embedded in notions of communal responsibility. The moment of being through the projected image of the Western other has shifted precolonial percepts of masculinity and relocated them under the rubric of mass consumption and commodity fetishism. The African bourgeoisie psychologically "identifies with the Western bourgeoisie from which it has slurped every lesson. It mimics the Western bourgeoisie in its negative and decadent aspects without having accomplished the initial phase of exploration and invention that are the assets of this Western bourgeoisie whatever the circumstances" (Fanon, 1967, p. 101). It is hence not unreasonable to arrive at the conclusion that the contemporary performance of masculinity, as signified through tropes of commodity fetishism, is created out of an ontological process in which the native's sense of self and manhood is partly shaped in relation to the constructed image of the neocolonizer. The native's consumption of the colonizer's product can hence, in some cases, manifest itself as a subconscious desire for sameness and recognition. Fanon (1967) traces this phenomenon back to what he sees as a pathological inferiority complex. As he states, "The negroes' inferiority complex is particularly intensified among the most educated, who must struggle with it unceasingly. Their way of doing so is frequently naïve: The wearing of European clothes, whether rags or the most up-to-date style; using European furniture and European forms of social intercourse; adorning the native language with European expressions; using bombastic phrases in speaking or writing a European language; all these contribute to a feeling of equality with the European and his achievements" (p. 25). These percepts are further reproduced through the help of institutions such as schools, which are in themselves for the most part ideologically structured as residues of the old colonial system. Notions of power, masculinity, and success are hence institutionally maintained within a hegemonic ideological apparatus that propagates the already existing status quo. As Yvonne Jewkes notes, the concept of hegemonic masculinity can be comprehended as "a structural device which understands the production and reproduction of masculine attributes, attitudes and behaviors as outcomes of social processes and inequalities which are upheld at every level of society" (Jewkes, 2002, p. 41). Following this definition, it will be fruitful at this stage to analyze the socio-economic and political processes upon which the performances of masculinity are contingent within Kenyan society.

In the so-called postcolonial era, the simulacrum of "independence" sets the initial stage in which emerging local and global relations of power are to be formed. Mwaura (2005) contends that the gesture of granting independence to former colonies was not conceived out of a belief in the equality of all people (p. 6). Independence, according to him, emerged from "the realization that capitalism in the twentieth century no longer required colonialism to serve its purpose and that the political and military costs of maintaining colonialism were both high and unnecessary" (Mwaura, 2005, p. 6). These sentiments are also echoed by Debord (1967) when he posits that, "Even where the material base is still absent, modern society has already used the spectacle to invade the social surface of every continent. It sets the stage for the formation of indigenous ruling classes and frames their agendas. Just as it presents pseudogoods to be coveted, it offers false models of revolution to local revolutionaries" (p. 28). In other words, neocolonized nations maintain a political spectacle that masks the discursive patterns and tragic influences of global capitalism, by simulating local political oppositions under which the simulacra of choice and agency is maintained (Debord, p. 65). The radio and television media sustain the propagation of this simulacrum. As McLuhan (1964) stipulates, the affects of communicative media such as radio and television, "do not occur at the level of opinions or concepts, but alter sense ratios or patterns of perceptions steadily and without resistance" (p. 114).

In the global age of mass media, the Luo leader establishes a false intimate connection with his community. Through the media of radio and television, he infiltrates the living rooms and bedrooms of his constituents. While his presence is intimately felt, his audience is simultaneously alienated by his inaccessibility outside the presidential and parliamentary campaign cycles. While in the old days the masses could simply walk over and knock at their chief's door if the latter had behaved inappropriately, in contemporary Kenyan society the masses habitually mostly get to know their leaders via television, radio, and newspapers. What begins to matter is therefore the symbolic value of a leader to his community, as opposed to the pragmatic ways in which his deeds help the constituency that he represents. As Bourdieu (1996) explains, it appears that "ultimately television, which claims to record reality, creates it instead. We are getting closer and closer to the point where the social world is primarily described—and in a sense prescribed—by television" (p. 22).

In the context of Kenya, television and radio have come to dictate the kinds of relationships that the masses have with their leaders. The persona of the

Kenyan leader hence manifests itself as a fetishized commodity. In *Marxism and Media Studies*, Mike Wayne (2003) posits that commodity fetishism "represses, rubs away and dematerializes the social relations of an activity or commodity and just leaves us with its physical materiality, isolated or with its interdependence with everything else fading away" (p. 194). The Kenyan politician as a commodity, similar to the lifeless object, obfuscates relations of production by concealing the hierarchical social-class structures that are dominated by the national bourgeoisie. The relationship between the representation of the Kenyan politician as a commodity and the concept of hegemonic masculinity is solidified via the media. As Jewkes notes, "Hegemonic masculinity is very different from the notion of a biologically determined male sex role, and the ideal of masculinity most prized by a culture may not correspond to the actual personalities of the majority of men. Indeed, the winning of hegemony often involves the creation [of] models of masculinity which are—if not what powerful men are—nevertheless are what they are motivated to support in the interests of maintaining their power. These models are frequently fantasy figures, or real people whose image is intrinsically bound up in a somewhat exaggerated media persona; for example, footballers, pop stars and 'action movie heroes'" (Jewkes, 2002, p. 52).

The Kenyan political figure occupies a seemingly double but unified position as a commodity fetish as well as the masculine ideal of success and power. One only has to look at Kenya's current prime minister and member of the Luo ethnic group Raila Odinga, whose already immense popularity and media exposure was multiplied when he was seen cruising into parliament with his own brand-new Hummer, a car that has rarely ever been seen in Kenya and which, in the eyes of most Kenyan citizens, remains confined to the realm of Hollywood films. The objective here is not to examine Odinga's politics but merely to analyze the ways in which he is perceived by his community as the embodiment of political power and masculinity. In this context, Odinga's increased popularity among the Luo was a manifestation of his proximity to the Hollywood model of power and masculinity via his ownership of a Hummer. Also worth noting is the fact that Odinga has often characterized his new vehicle as a *nyundo* (the *Luo* word for hammer), with which he will destroy the rampant corruption that permeates the Kenyan government. As the embodiment of political power and hyper-masculinity, Odinga symbolically generates desire. In this context desire does not simply materialize out of a displacement or lack but is rather the very means of production around which society is organized (Deleuze & Guattari, 1984, p. 61). In other words, one's emulation of and identification with Odinga as an object of desire reifies and reproduces dominant social, economic and political structures.

On that note, we turn to an analysis of how the spectacle of commodity and the reality it generates through the cultural production of desire conceals and implicitly maintains dominant global and local forms of economic activity.

Unmasking the Reality Concealed by the Fetish

The reality that the spectacle of the commodity fetish seeks to conceal is nevertheless very much felt within the lives of the impoverished population. Kenyan exports have increasingly lost value over the years. Only six years after the country's independence, the export value of Kenyan products was down by 11 percent (Mwaura, 2005). Local Kenyan farmers have, over the years, had to produce twice as many goods to be exported to Western shores—for the same price. Meanwhile, imported goods have increased in value. A unionized body that would enable small-scale Kenyan farmers to set their own prices remains absent. As a result, they find themselves at the mercy of Western corporations, who are more than happy to buy more for less while increasing the value of their own finished products. Due to the low prices that small-scale Kenyan farmers have received for their goods, a growing opposition to farming these cash crops became so great that the Kenyan government was forced to enact a law that forbade peasants from uprooting, cutting, or in any way ceasing the farming of cash crops. The land was therefore not released to other crops, which would have increased their income as well as boosted local food production (Mwaura, 2005, p. 11).

According to Mwaura (2005), in Kenya "some 40 percent of peasants work for big landowners for very low wages. There is a gross mal-distribution of land labor. At one end of the spectrum, 30 percent of the cultivated land is splintered up to be shared by 70 percent of land-holders, and at the other end 70 percent of the land is shared among 30 percent of land owners that include local joint land-buying companies, foreign companies, the local rich and European settlers" (Mwaura, 2005, p. 11). Fanon (1967) contends that no sooner is independence proclaimed than the local bourgeoisie "demand the nationalization of the agricultural holdings. Through a number of schemes they manage to lay hands on the farms once owned by the colonists, thereby reinforcing their control over the region. But they make no attempt to diversify, increase production or integrate it in a genuinely national economy" (p. 102). Fanon further explains that: "The bourgeoisie cloaks local artisanship in a chauvinistic tenderness which not only ties in with the new national dignity, but also ensures them substantial profits. This cult for local products, this incapacity to invent new outlets, is likewise reflected in the entrenchment of the national bourgeoisie in the type of agricultural production typical of the colonial period. Independence does not bring a change of direction. The same old groundnut harvest, cocoa harvest, and olive harvest. Likewise the traffic of commodities go unchanged. No industry is established in the country. We continue to ship raw materials, we continue to grow produce for Europe and pass for specialists of unfinished products" (Fanon, 1967, p. 100).

In 1994, Kenya reportedly made an average of Kshs 25 billion ($417 million) from its tourist industry. Tourism is often cited as one of Kenya's leading national income venues. However only less than 20 percent of the revenue earned from tourism goes to the local populace; the remaining 80 percent is shared among Western companies, who own the hotels, lodgings, as well as the resorts and game parks in which tourists spend their money. Kenyans are, however, convinced that they are the ones who stand most to gain from tourism (Mwaura, 2005, p. 11).

The formation of the Commission for East African Cooperation (EAC) and the trade agreements that were espoused through its birth, momentarily threatened to destabilize the yoke of neocolonialism. According to Mwaura (2005), "The East African community attempted to integrate the East African region, which would have expanded markets for locally produced commodities" (p. 17). This caused a great degree of consternation among the wealthy Western states, who urged the World Bank and the International Monetary Fund to put pressure on local governments as a means to implement trade liberalization within the East African community. By complying with the policies of trade liberalization, "The markets that had been created and guaranteed by the cooperation between the East African states was lost. Kenyan-made products would have had a ready market in Uganda and Tanzania, and vice versa, but with trade liberalization the East African market is saturated with foreign products and so the main problem plaguing locally produced commodities—lack of a guaranteed market—persists, thus nullifying the most important aspects of the EAC" (Mwaura, 2005, p. 17).

The production of surplus capital and goods generates an impetus to domesticate foreign markets. The damping of these goods within the East African market is facilitated through trade liberalization. Trade liberalization restricts local East African governments from imposing any tariffs on imported Western goods. The heavily subsidized Western goods saturate the market and are sold at much cheaper rates than local commodities. This causes local businesses to fail, as more people lose their main sources of em-

ployment and income. Trade agreements such as the Trade Related Investment Measures (TRIM), which have been imposed on local governments,
sustain conditions of poverty in the region by disenabling African nations
from limiting the amount of imported Western goods as well as controlling
their prices. When processed Kenyan goods are exported to Western shores,
they are often charged with high tariffs of over 200 percent, making them
overly expensive and unable to compete with local Western goods.

The Kenyan consumer has also been conditioned to place a higher value
on Western imported goods as opposed to local ones. The fetishization of
Western luxury goods is ingrained into the psyche of the masses. An emphasis is placed on the consumption of imported luxury goods rather than
on local products. According to Mwaura, "It has been calculated that Kenya
loses up to 320 million shillings ($5.23 million) annually just through cin-
emas showing imported movies. Foreign musicians, too, make easy money
in Kenya. When the North American Barry White was in Kenya, he had
a special diet of non-African food and was accommodated in a foreign-
owned hotel. To see him perform, Africans were asked to cough up Kshs
2,500 ($42), or the equivalent of two weeks' wages of an ordinary worker,
and the hall was filled" (Mwaura, 2005, p. 14).

In *Some Thoughts on Theories of Fetishism in the Context of Contemporary
Culture*, Laura Mulvey explains that "a commodity's market success depends
on the erasure of the marks of production—any trace of indexicality, the
grime of the factory, the mass-molding of the machine, and, most of all, the
exploitation of the worker. It instead presents the market with a seductive
sheen, competing to be desired. While money appears as a sophisticated,
abstract, and symbolic means of exchange, capitalism resurrects the commodity as image" (Mulvey, 1993, p. 10). This phenomenon is exemplified in
Kenya by the fetishization of Western commodities, which masks the ways in
which their consumption as well as the manner in which they are preferred
to locally produced commodities, adversely affects the Kenyan economy and
consequentially the Kenyan consumer.

Kenyan politicians often like to highlight foreign investment as a positive factor that contributes to the development of the nation. In the Kenyan
budget of 1998, the minister of finance admitted that investors had "repa-
triated about Kshs 15,000,000,000 ($250 million) leading to a 20 percent
depreciation in the shilling" (Mwaura, 2005, p. x). Under the pressure of
the World Bank and the IMF, the Kenyan government was further made to
privatize some of its parastatal institutions, hence making them available for
purchase by foreign investors. These combined socio-economic causalities

have created large amounts of unemployment, as well as the collapse of many local factories. The country has fallen into so much debt that it now has to borrow more money in order to pay the accumulated interest on its loans. The solutions proposed by the local government often contribute to the perpetuation of the social conditions they seemingly attempt to eradicate. The politics of trade liberalization are hardly mentioned by Kenyan politicians in most political discourse. In 1996, the Kenyan minister of finance blamed the country's growing deficit on factors such as power supply shortages, bad roads, insecurity, and bad weather, as well as the suspension of IMF loans, which he claimed discouraged foreign investment (Mwaura, 2005, p. 33).

As a means to counter the national deficit, the Kenyan government decided to increase taxes, freeze salary increments, and retrench over "125,000 public servants, including 66,000 teachers" (Mwaura, 2005, p. 33). The causative elements that are responsible for these social conditions are masked through spectacles of commodities that either appear in the form of Western products or political figures that are consumed with the same willing eagerness. Foucauldian discourse on the nature of power contends that, "Power relations are rooted in the whole network of the social. This is not to say, however, that there is a primary and fundamental principle of power which dominates society down to the smallest detail; but, based on the possibility of action on the action of others that is coextensive with every social relationship, various kinds of individual disparity, of objectives, of the given application of power over ourselves or others, of more or less partial or universal institutionalization and more or less deliberate organization, will define different forms of power" (Foucault, 1976, p. 141).

In Kenya, relations of power are enacted at various social and institutional levels. The consumption of certain commodities such as imported vehicles (among many others), which have come to signify the ideal image of masculinity and power, therefore becomes the locus of value systems through which relations of power are performed at different levels. This desire to be like the other—the other being an empty signifier that encapsulates a shifting concatenation of both local and globalized images that create hegemonic perceptions of masculinity—produces and naturalizes existing social structures. In this sense, the very ways that people perceive themselves as well as their potential in the world, their manner of interacting and responding to the mediatized reality that surrounds them, reproduces the contours of the world system in which they reside. While these value systems are certainly not the only all-inclusive fundamental principles that characterize all relations of power within Kenyan society, they nevertheless remain some of the most dominant and perpetuated ones.

Conclusion

The evolution of social percepts of masculinity and power from precolonial, colonial, to "postcolonial" Kenyan society are contingent upon ideological structures and value systems that maintain the socio-economic and political status quo. In precolonial Luo society, the performance of masculinity and power was embedded within one's sense of communal responsibility, characterizing the way precolonial Luo society was structured. In the neocolonial era, however, masculinity and power have been conflated with contemporary spectacles of consumption that help maintain the present world system. This shift, it has been argued, was a result of the moment when the native came into being through the colonial other. The violence of colonization and neo-colonization sets up new frames of reference through which the native's sense of self and masculinity is constructed in relation to the dominant structures of power that permeate his reality. Unlike the precolonial period, the commodity fetish in the postcolonial era obfuscates local socio-economic and global power relations and places itself as the dominant and self-referential locus of meaning.

References

Achebe, C. ([1958] 2002). *Things Fall Apart*. New York: Chelsea House.
Baudrillard, J. ([1985] 2001). The Procession of Simulacra. In M. N. Durhamn (Ed.), *Media, and Cultural Studies* (pp. 453–81). Oxford: Blackwell.
Black, D. (1997). *Dismantling Black Manhood: An Historical and Literary Analysis of the Legacy of Slavery*. New York: Garland.
Bourdieu, P. (1996). *On Television*. New York: New York Press.
Debord, G. ([1967] 1995). *The Society of the Spectacle*. New York: Zone.
Deleuze, G., & Guattari, F. (1984). *Anti-Oedipus: Capitalism and Schizophrenia*. Minneapolis: University of Minnesota Press.
Fanon, F. ([1961] 2004). *The Wretched of the Earth*. New York: Grove Press.
Fanon, F. (1967). *Black Skin, White Masks*. New York: Grove Press.
Foucault, M. (2003). *The Essential Foucault*. New York: New Press.
Jewkes, Y. (2002). *Captive Audience: Media, Masculinity, and Power in Prison*. Cullumpton, Devon, U.K.: Willan.
Kourouma, A. (1968) *Les Soleils Des Independences*. Montréal: Les Pes De L'University De Montréal.

Mboya, P. K. ([1967] 1997). *Luo, Kitgi gi Timbegi*. E. Karachuonyo, Nairobi: Equatorial Publishers.

McLuhan, M. ([1964] 2001). *The Medium Is the Massage: An Inventory of Effects*. Corte Madera, Calif.: Gingko Press.

Mulvey, L. (1993). Some Thoughts on Theories of Fetishism in the Context of Contemporary Culture. *October*, 65, 3–20.

Mwaura, N. (2005). *Kenya Today: Breaking the Yoke of Colonialism in Africa*. New York: Algora.

Ngugi, W. Thiong'o. (1981). *Decolonising the Mind*. London: James Currey.

Ogutu, O. B. (1974). *Keep My Words: Luo Oral Literature*. Nairobi: East African House.

Ousmane, S. (1974). *Xala*. Chicago: Lawrence Hill Books.

Soyinka, W. ([1966] 1996). *The Lion and the Jewel*. Oxford: Oxford University Press.

Wayne, M. (2003). *Marxism and Media Studies*. Sterling, Va.: Pluto Press.

6

War, Masculinity, and Native Americans

KATHLEEN GLENISTER ROBERTS

Introduction

In many Native American communities, especially in the Western United States, one particular answer to the question "What makes a man who he is in this culture?" often surprises non-Natives. War veterans have a particularly honored place in these communities, and for as long as they have been American citizens, participation in the U.S. armed forces has been a highly significant source of pride for Native American individuals. It is commonly estimated that of all the racial and ethnic demographic groups who comprise the American military, Native Americans have the highest percentage of honorable discharges (Shoyo, 2005).

This chapter draws on several years of ethnographic research on Native American ceremonials to examine the metaphor of the "warrior" in some Native American communities. The term is used not stereotypically but emically. Non-Natives often assume that Native Americans would not want to participate in the institutions of a nation that has colonized, oppressed, marginalized, and even sought to eliminate their communities. But the cultural value of "defending one's home" is invoked repeatedly by these veterans as the driving force behind their choice to enlist in the armed forces. This chapter discusses their views of "war," which are expressed both in military service and in other contexts within their communities (during powwow dance competitions, for example). Their perspective on war is at times an ancient one, and has impacted American history more than most non-Natives understand.

This misunderstanding throughout history often has led to continued disrespect on the part of non-Natives. It is hoped that this chapter's method of ethnography will explain the warrior ideal in the voices of those who fight to defend their homes and their cultural communities. Their insights offer a glimpse into how masculinity is constructed in one particular way by some Native Americans.

Putting this one perspective into context is important. The chapter will first review some of the challenges inherent in the argument. As a non-Native, I want to pay special attention to an alternative side of war and participation in the armed forces. These alternatives have obvious negative consequences for Native Americans and their communities, many of which have been well documented. I review those in the first section, along with some caveats and cautions about the potentially "loaded" terms "masculinity," "war," and "Native American Studies." Following this section is an overview of the warrior ideal in a number of Native American communities, capped by an examination of several Native American voices on the topic of the warrior within multiple contexts: the literary, the civic, and the ceremonial.

Masculinity, War, and Native American Studies

The first caution commanding notice is that Native Americans cannot be generalized in any way, perhaps least of all in their constructions of masculinity. Hundreds of nations comprise the generic group "Native American," all of them unique. Some do not even prefer the term "Native American," although I use it for the purposes of academic discourse (the emic term for most Northern Plains groups, for example, is "Indian"). This is why I have stressed that this chapter will look at *one particular* construction of masculinity in *some* Native American communities.

It is also important to emphasize that the warrior ideal I describe here does not necessarily apply only to "masculinity," especially not in the twenty-first century. Native American women are strongly represented in the U.S. armed forces. In fact, the first woman to die in Iraq was Pfc. Lori Ann Piestewa (Indian name Qotsa-hon-mana, "White Bear Girl"), of the Hopi Indian Nation. Pfc. Piestewa was a member of the 507th Maintenance Company and was driving in a convoy near Nasiriyah on March 23, 2003, when her company came under attack. She was severely wounded and taken as a prisoner of war, dying in captivity shortly afterward (National Native American Veterans Association, 2008). She was the first Native American woman in history to die in a U.S. military action.

What is doubly tragic about Pfc. Piestewa's death is that it is so relatively obscure. Her passenger in the vehicle was Pfc. Jessica Lynch, an Anglo American woman who became a household name when she was rescued from captivity and brought back to the United States. *The Jessica Lynch Story* was broadcast on national television and her narrative commanded the nation's attention for weeks and even months after the incident, but few people have ever heard of Lori Ann Piestewa. Since both women were still alive when captured by Iraqi insurgents, it raises the question why one woman—the Anglo one—received far more attention than the other. Respect for any prisoner of war (regardless of race) notwithstanding, it is sadly typical of mainstream U.S. media production that the Anglo woman Jessica Lynch was the focus of coverage of an attack in which four of twenty U.S. soldiers were wounded, five were taken prisoner, and nine were killed—including a Hopi woman from Arizona who was friends with Jessica Lynch (National Native American Veterans Association, 2008) but whose name will never be known by the vast majority of Americans.

The second-class status Native American soldiers are sometimes afforded (as in the case just described) and the negative consequences of war do mitigate the rhetorical potencies within the cultural constructions of "warrior" that I explore in this essay. While Native Americans have more members per capita in the U.S. military than any other ethnic group (and they are the smallest in the U.S. overall), the U.S. military has not always honored them equally well. American military force is an intrusive presence on some reservations, where abandoned military bases or test sites leave dangerous unexploded ordinance (Hooks & Smith, 2004). One example is Pine Ridge, South Dakota, where about one-third of the reservation is uninhabitable and surrounded by barbed wire as a result of American active mines embedded in the soil. Veterans' experiences in past wars have been equally neglectful. Holm (1995) reports a number of compelling inequalities in Vietnam. First, prior to the war, Native Americans typically had less access to high-quality public education on the reservations, so their test scores were relatively low and ensured that they would have to participate in the war as infantry "grunts" and not in technical or elite forces. Some Anglo commanders retained old stereotypes about Native Americans: believing them to be good "trackers" or skilled in woodcraft, they were asked to serve reconnaissance or walk point more than soldiers from other ethnic groups. These and other factors led to severe levels of post-traumatic stress disorder, substance abuse, and suicide following the Vietnam conflict (Holm, 1995).

It is a common critique of American society that a disproportionate number of members of minority groups serve in the U.S. military because of inadequate economic opportunities in civilian life. On one level this may be a valid complaint, especially on some reservations where career aspirations may be high but opportunities and training are meager (Turner & Lapan, 2003; Hoffman, Jackson, & Smith, 2005). Yet the critique is also at least partly ignorant, because it effaces the diversity of cultural values and worldviews that might call young men and women to military service regardless of economic opportunity. I write this chapter both because of the inequalities and also in response to them as part illusion. Things have changed since the Vietnam conflict. In the words of the Manataka American Indian Council (2008): "The commitment of the Native American Peoples to the defense of the United States is unparalleled by any other population sector of the United States. As a people, we are the smallest ethnic group of the American population, and yet on a per capita basis we provide more members to the Armed Forces than any other population sector. The Native American People [also] provide more members to the elite force structure of the Armed Forces than any other population sector [in contrast to the Vietnam era]."

In their own voices, Native Americans acknowledge the negative consequences of war, yet also honor their veterans in ways that are unfamiliar to non-Natives. While Holm (1995) recounted the existence of post-traumatic stress disorder among Vietnam veterans, he also emphasized that a number of norms within their cultures encouraged better healing practices than Anglo norms could achieve. Positivity regarding participation in war, for a number of reasons, is built into some Native American cultures—even for participants in the Vietnam conflict (Holm, 1995). I discuss these cultural norms later in the essay, placing them in the context of United States and Native American history. While supporting the programs that serve the dire needs of returning soldiers, and acknowledging the reality of war's horrific consequences, I have been asked in this chapter to consider a particular construction of masculinity in some Native American communities. The warrior ideal in these cultures is unique, and deserving of focus and understanding—not the imposition of one's own political or emotional viewpoints. Thus, while the caveats I have explored in this section of the chapter are intended to show respect to the varying experiences of individuals, it is equally respectful to acknowledge and try to understand the cultural significance of the warrior for many Native Americans. The rest of the essay strives to do just that, beginning with a historical overview.

Historical Perspective

In the broader context of Native American studies, bringing the past into rigorous reflection can help to provide more ethical approaches to shared history. As Elmer Kelton writes, "A common misconception regarding America's Plains Indians is that their cultures had existed with little change for ages before the white man's intrusion" (Kelton, 1993, p. 50). Another common misconception is that indigenous peoples on the Plains lived in harmony with nature and with one another, with a relatively homogeneous culture. On the contrary, a historical survey of even a small part of Plains culture yields clear indications that not only were these groups quite different from one another, but also that the cultures themselves evolved in form. The Northern Plains, for instance, constituted a highly contested space before the reservation era, one with a very long history of trade, cultural adaptation, and both the clashing and blending of traditions (Harrod, 1995). The "clashing" certainly included intertribal warfare.

Written records of this period are nonexistent, but winter counts (pictorial representations of tribal histories) and oral traditions suggest the existence of a highly developed warrior ethic. War may be described for some societies, especially those on the Northern Plains, as a spiritual activity that included its own formal ceremonies. Dancing would have been part of these rituals. Significant to my purposes in this chapter, it is clear from historical documentation that the modern-day powwow has grown out of the tradition of war dancing on the Plains (Powers, 1990; Kracht, 1994; Ellis, 1999). Significantly, war dancing continued during the reservation period when the actual act of warfare was discontinued. The moving of Native Americans onto reservations (some as early as the 1820s, the last in the mid-1890s) definitively marked the end of the "Indian Wars" in America. Certainly, the desire of Native Americans to continue the ceremonies pertaining to war may have stemmed from a natural resentment toward their American enemies and a frustration at being confined to reservations without weapons or freedom. Some dances, such as the Ghost Dance on the Plains, were pure religious ceremonies designed to bring about victory over white Americans. Others, though, may have had a less direct rhetoric but were still intended to preserve the "warrior ethic" so intertwined with specific Native American cultures. Some government representatives on the Indian agencies and later reservations responded with paranoia toward this war dance heritage, interpreting "cultural revitalization as a political conspiracy" (Gump, 1997,

p. 35). But from the perspective of war dancers, giveaway donors, and other celebrants, attempts to suppress dancing and the giveaway were an attack on religious freedom (Williard, 1991).

Benjamin Kracht (1994) reports that war dancing became even more popular among Plains groups after World War I, when those returning from the fighting included a small number of young men from the reservations. The *embodiment* of the warrior tradition on the Plains was revitalized in their return and gained momentum once again (Kracht, 1994, p. 331). No doubt that the earlier "paranoia" about war dancing was directed more toward nineteenth-century cultural revival attempts such as the Ghost Dance, and by the end of World War I the potential for uprisings against the U.S. government was considered nonexistent in the minds of Indian agents. At this point though, Native American participation in the U.S. armed forces was underwhelming—because at the outbreak of World War I, most Native Americans were not yet American citizens.

The situation was much different by 1941, when the United States entered World War II. Native Americans now had full citizenship and responded to the Japanese attack on Pearl Harbor in ways remarkably parallel to Anglo Americans: they reported to recruiting stations and military offices in record numbers to volunteer for the war effort. Their willingness was quickly accepted. Curiously, while the armed forces were segregated during that time, Native Americans were integrated into white units—so that segregation applied only to African and Asian Americans. Recently, some Native Americans who fought in the war have been the focus of the attention they deserve. This is particularly true of the Navajo Code Talkers, although there were several other Native American cryptographers during the war whose contributions have remained relatively obscure (Walker, 1983).

As it did for so many young people of that generation, the experience of military service changed many Native Americans' lives forever. All told, 25,000 Native Americans served in the military by the end of World War II. Another 40,000 left the reservations to work in war industries. By order of the War Department, as noted above, the military recruits were integrated into white units, where they achieved a remarkable degree of acceptance and assimilation. Their drinking buddies called them "Chief"—which, in the specific bonding experiences of integrated military units during the war, signified respect rather than condescension. In recent years "Chief" has been exposed as a derogatory term, but the positive connotations of "Chief" in the context of the war are supported by historian Alison Bernstein (1991) (and also by Leslie Marmon Silko's novel *Ceremony*, which I discuss later in this essay).

It is reported that Native Americans were admired for their excellence at basic training. No doubt many Native Americans did excel at military activity, and their achievements of decorations and medals for bravery during the war bear out the assumption that they fought well. It is important to acknowledge that positive generalization or no, the warrior identity has continued as a stereotype imposed on Native Americans by non-Natives. Elsewhere (Roberts, 2007) I have discussed this warrior ideal in detail as a significant motif in the history of intercultural contact between Anglos and non-white "Others." Also, my invocation of the positive ideal is not intended to elide the ill treatment Native Americans (and other minority groups) suffered upon their return from the war. Indeed it problematizes it. Native Americans received "mixed signals" about their participation in World War II. Some described it as the best experience of their lives, when for the first time they were welcomed by non-Natives into Anglo American activities, social circles, and civic participation (Bernstein, 1991). But once the war was over, Native Americans, African Americans, and women were no longer needed for civic, industrial, or military efforts. In short, they were returned to "second-class status," or worse.

By many accounts, participation in World War II profoundly changed Native Americans. As Bureau of Indian Affairs Commissioner William Brophy noted in 1945, "The war caused the greatest disruption of Indian life since the beginning of the reservation era" (quoted in Bernstein, 1991, p. 131). The movement toward assimilation—or the desire for assimilation—that the war experience produced was highly disruptive to many communities. From the perspective of many Pueblos, for example, the impact of the war was the fulfillment of a prophecy (as told by Paul Johnson of Paguate): "It has been told that long ago my ancestors prophesied that from the East would come the white man who would conquer us in many ways—that we would eat his food, drink his drink, and after we drank his drink and ate his food we would no longer think as an Indian thinks, [of] beautiful things" (Dutton & Marmon, 1936, p. 21). From this perspective, assimilation is a very real danger. The war took most of the young men out of the reservations, for up to six years. It has been assumed that for those young people who left, ceremonial life virtually stopped. Non-Natives argue that they received "a heavy dose of American material, 'standard of living' values; they were pushed almost irresistibly toward the externalism of life" (Collier, 1949, p. 73).

Having considered a heteroglossia of voices pertaining to Native American participation in the armed forces, though, I would argue that these assumptions may be a bit hasty. Bernstein (1991) does recount the use of traditional rituals by young Native American soldiers during the war. Many of the Marines in the Navajo Code Talkers unit also recall placing pollen on their tongues—a traditional Navajo ritual—as a prayer that they would perform their duties well in battle. Collier's (1949) assumption that exposure to Anglo institutions and culture would automatically and irrevocably efface the ability of young Native American men to maintain their own traditions is well-meaning and sensitive, but also inaccurate and ultimately condescending. Today, his assumption is paralleled by the naïve idea that Native Americans only choose to participate in the military because of economic desperation and in spite of a tragic history with the U.S. government. These ideas could be considered equally inaccurate and condescending. At the very least, they represent a misunderstanding of intercultural communication in general, and Native American traditions in particular.

A few scholars have addressed these issues in productive ways. Holm (1995), while treating fairly the effects of post-traumatic stress disorder in Native American communities following the Vietnam era, offers a more balanced perspective. He points out that while PTSD has devastating effects for any individual, a number of cultural attributes in many Native American communities provide helpful ballast and even potential advantages in facing these problems. As he writes: "In most traditional tribal societies, warriorhood was not so much a social role as it was a relationship with the rest of the community. . . . By comparison, soldiers in modern western-style armies are servants of the state. . . . Those outside military service relate to soldiers as being the functionaries of a larger, very impersonal institution rather than as contributors to the contiguous community. Soldiering is playing a role; warriorhood is a relationship. [Today] Native Americans have more or less accepted the idea of becoming soldiers in the American armed forces. At the same time . . . many of their communities have continued to relate to them as tribal warriors and part of a very much older tradition" (Holm, 1995, p. 84).

A similar contrast between Native and non-Native traditions exists in the idea of dependency as a *value*, rather than as a problem, within a community. Because Native American societies are for the most part internally communal and interdependent (Gurian, 1977; DeMallie, 1994; Roberts, 2003), the warrior has a natural relationship of service and duty with the rest of the community. This is not to say that non-Native soldiers do not experience the same relationships and responsibilities with their own communities. However, one need only look to contemporary non-Native discourse against warfare in the United States to discern assumptions about the choice of military service that are grounded in highly individualistic worldviews. As Holm

(1995) mentions above, non-Natives outside of the military see soldiers as part of an impersonal and mechanistic institution and may map all kinds of (potentially fictional) intentions onto the choice to serve. The warrior tradition in Native societies offers a much clearer emic cultural picture of military service, regardless of how contradictory or unclear it may seem to non-Natives.

Because of the difference in worldviews, it is also possible to see a pattern of diversity in how warriors are received back into their communities after a tour of service is complete. Holm (1995) offers another important contribution in his point that non-Natives tend to see growing older as a negative attribute of personhood. Soldiers, especially young people, who return from service are often said to have prematurely aged. This is a valid concern for a culture in which aging is typically fought and resisted as much as possible. Native American communities often provide a contrast, since wisdom is a very significant goal of personhood and can only be achieved with experience and age. While Native Americans do not ignore the potentially horrific effects of battle, they are more likely to assist returning soldiers in reframing the experience as the acquisition of wisdom (Holm, 1995).

One of the ways in which Native American communities achieve this—and also combat other devastating consequences of warriorhood in the modern era—is by practicing traditional rituals with those who serve in the U.S. armed forces. The healing potential of these rituals for Vietnam veterans with PTSD has been effectively documented (Holm, 1995). This Native philosophy also forms the core of Leslie Marmon Silko's superb novel *Ceremony*. For the rest of this essay, I examine a few sets of Native American voices— first through literary analysis, then through ethnography—that meditate on the idea of the warrior in Native American cultures and the formation of masculine identities. I will briefly discuss the importance of community, interdependence, wisdom, and traditional rituals in *Ceremony*. Then I turn to a less orthodox vision of "war" by discussing the significance of pow-wow ceremonials and competition in the contemporary lives of some Native American men.

Native American Voices I: *Ceremony*

Leslie Marmon Silko's novel *Ceremony*, published in 1977, aptly captures the narrative trope of the acculturated warrior and his need to understand and more fully participate in communal relationships after he has served as a soldier in World War II. Silko's protagonist, Tayo, is a Pueblo from Laguna,

New Mexico. He represents the historical context of the war, as described above, even before military service, in his experiences on the reservation. However, in *Ceremony*, Silko responds both to these historical facts and also to the Western narrative motif of the assimilated "warrior Other." Tayo experiences all of the prejudices of Americans through military recruitment and service. Tayo's cousin Rocky wants to leave behind the old Pueblo ways and sees military service as a way out of reservation life. He and Tayo enlist with a white recruiter who says, "Anyone can fight for America, even you boys" (p. 64). It is quickly evident to Tayo that the rest of white society feels the same way. After basic training, Rocky and Tayo go to California to await transport to the Pacific, and, "The first day in Oakland he and Rocky walked down the street together and a big Chrysler stopped in the street and an old white woman rolled down the window and said, 'God bless you, God bless you,' but it was the uniform, not them, she blessed" (Silko, 1977, p. 41).

In the course of the war, Rocky is wounded. He and Tayo become prisoners of the Japanese and are taken on the Bataan "death march," where Rocky's wound becomes infected and he dies. Tayo, who already has a tenuous relationship with Rocky's mother (she is ashamed at her younger sister for having the "half-breed" illegitimate child Tayo in the first place), had promised that he would bring Rocky home safe. He begins to feel that he is an "accident" of time and space; that *he* was supposed to die, not Rocky. Worse, during the incessant rains at Bataan, he wishes and prays the rain clouds away and kills the flies around Rocky's wound. He ignores his Uncle Josiah's earlier admonishment never to kill flies, since they are bearers of rain.

Returning home, he finds that Laguna has been in drought since his prayer. He blames himself utterly for the drought and ultimately for all the suffering of his family. Tayo falls into despair, and the Anglo doctors who treat him think that his growing feeling of culpability for the drought is a mark of insanity. Compounding his despair is the realization that the experience of battle in World War II is completely foreign to the old men on the reservation. Ku'oosh tries to perform a healing ritual for Tayo, the same ritual traditionally done for warriors who had killed another human being. But when Ku'oosh asks Tayo if he killed anyone, Tayo replies that he is not sure. Ku'oosh has no comprehension of war as it is fought in modern times, when a warrior might not even be close enough to see one that he has killed.

Tayo cannot reconcile the things he has seen with the expectations of people at home. He does not recognize it at the time, but he, like the other young veterans who have returned from the war, is falling prey to witchery. Witchery is the evil that exists beyond all markers of race, culture, time, and space. Witchery is key to understanding the connections between characters in the novel and their responses to military service.

The prime example of witchery at work is Emo, another young Laguna veteran in the novel. Emo tries to lead the other veterans (Tayo, Harley, Leroy, and Pinkie) into falling prey to the witchery. With Emo, they spend their time getting drunk with the money from their army checks. During these episodes their dominant communication consists of storytelling wherein they attempt to relive the "glory days" of the war. While the others talk about the excitement of the cities and the details of their sexual exploits with white women, Emo consistently discusses his expertise in battle. "We were the best. U.S. Army. We butchered every Jap we found," Emo says. Emo even carries a sack containing teeth from each Japanese soldier he killed. Tayo soon notices the way "Emo grew from each killing" (Silko, 1977, p. 138), and realizes that Emo is a witch. The curative rituals Tayo undergoes will be meaningless unless he can "defeat" the witchery—yet the only way to do this is to avoid capitulation to evil. He cannot kill Emo or destroy witchery, but he can let it return to itself.

At the climax of this battle, Tayo finds himself fleeing from Emo. He hides in an abandoned mine while Emo tries to lure him out by torturing Harley. Here, Tayo realizes that he is halfway between two significant sites: Los Alamos (where the atomic bomb was created) and Trinity Site, White Sands (where the bomb was first detonated in a test). Silko (1977) writes, "He had arrived at the point of convergence where the fate of all living things, and even the Earth, had been laid" (p. 246). At last, Tayo understands the nature of witchery and the dangers of fooling with its magic. During the war and upon his initial return, he has been haunted by the mixing of Laguna and Japanese voices in his head, and he has been tortured by the vision he had in the Philippines of the dead Japanese soldier with his Uncle Josiah's face. Again, he blames himself for Rocky's death, for the drought, for everything. Initially, he attributes all this to madness, while the white officers and doctors call it battle fatigue. But now, arriving at the completion of his "ceremony": "He cried the relief he felt at finally seeing the pattern, the way all the stories fit together—the old stories, the war stories, their stories—to become the story that was being told. He was not crazy; he had never been crazy. He had only seen and heard the world as it always was: no boundaries, only transitions through all distances in time" (Silko, 1977, p. 246).

When Tayo first comes home from the war, he fits the stereotype of the warrior Other who has assimilated into the "mainstream" through military service. Once the public persona of the military is gone, his public identity is called into question. He also suffers from despair when he cannot explain what he saw in the war to anyone at home. In other words, Tayo is having a crisis of community. But the crux of his curative ceremony occurs when he finally sees the pattern: there is no difference between these two spheres of public/private or military/communal. His belief that he has prayed away the rain clouds in the Philippines yet impacted the weather in New Mexico is not crazy; it is true. Tayo's relief at understanding this is palpable and, better still, it allows him to overcome evil.

Silko's story of the post-war era in Laguna is far too complex to treat completely in a few pages. Yet *Ceremony* is a remarkable example of the warrior Other "talking back" to a very old narrative motif: assimilation through a fierce military public persona. In her "talking back," Silko announces a very particular, Laguna communal ethic. It is clear that Tayo succeeds at overcoming the gap between his life at home on the reservation and the experiences of war because he realizes himself as part of a collective. His initial despair, and physical and emotional sickness, results from his forgetting that he is part of everyone at Laguna and ultimately everyone in the world. Silko leads Tayo into a (perhaps uniquely Laguna) understanding that all people, places, and times are connected.

Silko's novel, although treated here only briefly, is remarkable in its clear statement that those who are "Othered" can and do tell their own stories. The same is true for contemporary ceremonial competition participants. In the final part of this essay, I explore the ways in which some Native American men describe their experiences as dancers in powwows on the Northern Plains. The definitions of war and masculinity become fluid and powerful in this context, as I explain.

Native American Voices II: Men and Powwows

Not only have Plains indigenous peoples had more regular contact with whites over the past half-century, but they have also participated more in dominant mainstream institutions. As explained above, there seems to be a direct correlation between Indian entry into the U.S. armed forces and the resurgence in tribal dance gatherings. The correlation exists in large part because powwow dances have their origins in the Plains war societies' dances of the past, and Native participation in the World Wars produced new generations of warriors for these societies (Ellis, 1999).

It is worth repeating, especially in light of powwow ceremonies, that indigenous peoples in the United States are justifiably proud of Native participation in the armed forces: of all the racial and ethnic groups (including whites) identified within the institution itself, Native Americans receive the highest percentage of honorable discharges (Shoyo, 2005). And this warrior identity has continued to permeate the powwow, as evidenced by the references made to the war in Iraq during princess greetings, at memorial giveaways, and throughout competitions and gift exchanges. These trends developed slowly at first, but based on my research in 1999 and 2005, they seem to have accelerated since the attacks on the World Trade Center and Pentagon in 2001. Before providing this evidence I will explain the powwow briefly.

After World War II, Native American dance and ritual forms spread quickly because of the sudden migration of indigenous peoples from reservations to urban areas. The powwow took on increased importance, replacing other forms of tribal gatherings on the Plains (Kracht, 1994). Today the powwow serves as a "homecoming" of sorts for urban Indians, and the chance to visit their reservation with optimum social density. Every reservation on the Northern Plains holds one "big" powwow per year, and there is a great deal of intertribal visiting. The powwows are marked by competitions with prize money, and multifaceted festival identities: there is food, vending, gambling, and general merriment (although drugs and alcohol are strictly forbidden at the powwow grounds in virtually all communities).

In powwows, individual selves become bound up in relationships of status and challenge as well as help and kinship. In this section, I examine the interplay of these dynamics not as dialectically opposed tendencies, but as unique performances of long-standing Plains traditions and their contemporary meanings for Native peoples in powwows. Some of these traditions include war, the negotiation of truce, the individual's search for a path in the context of community, and the development of skill as part of cultural identities.

The ethnographic data of this project suggests that there are many personal choices powwow participants can make about competition. Dancers in Plains reservation powwows seem to fall somewhere on a continuum between taking themselves out of the actual competition, and taking competition as the driving force behind their dancing. For example, one Lakota man named Ira is a traditional dancer and explicitly situates himself in the former category. He never wears an entry number on his regalia, and never dances for money or any other prizes. As he explained: "My uncle said to me, 'You have a good job [with Rapid City Cement], your wife has a good job. You don't need the money. Just dance to give something back. Maybe you did something bad once,' and I thought, 'That's true.' I used to be wild. So I just dance for the enjoyment, to show people that we are still traditional people" (personal communication, June 19, 1999). In this sense, although Ira is not a competitive "warrior" (as we will see a powwow fancy dancer describe himself below), he sees his dancing as part of his responsibility to his people. In an important way, he is constructing a particular view of masculine responsibility and communal relationship.

Further along the continuum of competition, though, are those dancers who do see the material rewards of contests as more of an incentive. The best dancers can enter competitions with rather beefy prize amounts—up to $1000 for an individual dancer, at a powwow like Crow Fair—and make more money on the weekends than they do at their regular job during the week. One former Blackfeet dancer speculates that these "professional" aspects of powwow are akin to the seasonal division of duties that has been present for a long time among Indian people on the Northern Plains. For example, the Blackfeet Nation is located in the space adjacent to Glacier Park, so some Blackfeet people work most during the summer months with the National Park Service and in the tourist industry. Still others are busy in the summer working as Montana Indian Forest Firefighters (as was the case with this individual, who worked for three summers as part of MIFF). The powwow, as he explains, is another option for summertime employment. In his assessment, the powwow circuit evokes the nomadic summers of buffalo days: it is a journey that sometimes only yields subsistence, but it is enjoyable nonetheless, and allows for the development of skills many people hold sacred (personal communication collected by C. Roberts, April 21, 1997).

The powwow does seem to fall in line with other seasonal, traveling jobs open to Native Americans on the Plains. Some powwows on the Plains are held in conjunction with Indian rodeo competitions, for example. Jim Nelson is a powwow grass dancer who used to ride broncs on the Indian rodeo circuit, and he sees the two events in parallel. Jim finds both highly enjoyable, and both also afford prize money that allows him to be financially independent. He no longer participates in the rodeo competition. A horse once injured him, although that alone does not prevent him from riding. In fact, he prefers the rodeo to the powwow because, as he says, there are "more adventures in the rodeo" (personal communication, June 19, 1999). While not explicit about those adventures, his rather mischievous smile and his comment that "those days were wild days" suggest that in his own opinion he is leading a much better life in the powwow. He says this is because the powwow demands that he draw on his mental skills as well as physical. He explained that there are at least twenty-seven different known versions of the grass dance, and he must master them all to be competitive. One needs to be sharp. There is no room for the kind of "wild" lifestyle he found prevalent on the Indian rodeo circuit, the competition is keen, and Jim is closer to the traditional way of life he has come to appreciate with maturity (personal communication, June 19, 1999). Like Ira, Jim seems to equate "being a man" in this culture with responsibility, even in the context of competition and celebration.

Other dancers take the competition even more seriously, but for very different reasons. The prize money is still welcome, but for these dancers, prowess is more a question of pride, honor, and tradition. Doug (Foote) Goodfeather is one such competitor. In 1999 he had been a top fancy dancer for several years already, but more significantly, he has been regarded as a pillar of the community—in and out of the powwow. Doug is a "whistle-carrier": that is, he has a whistle made of the bone of an eagle around his neck that he is allowed to sound during competition. Communities choose whistle carriers very carefully and bless them in an important ritual that calls them to a sacred role in Plains dancing (Ruml, 2000). While the whistle-carrier tradition does vary from tribe to tribe (for the Salish, for example, dancers from other tribes should not blow whistles at powwows), Doug is very important for the Lakota community in Kyle, South Dakota. For instance, the Oglala Lakota College MC John Around Him thanked Doug publicly in 1999 for sounding the whistle. Doug explains that whistle-bearers should not be misunderstood. He says, "I blow my eagle bone whistle when I'm having a good time, to show everyone how happy I am. It's not to show off. It's to show my community that I'm dancing for *them*" (personal communication, June 19, 1999). He continued to explain that "everything is connected when the whistle is blown; this connection among the earth and the people has a healing power, and it inspires the other dancers. These simple things are real. If you are praying and you see a butterfly, it is not just a butterfly happening by, but your prayer" (personal communication collected by A. Burgess, June 20, 1999).

These three men—Ira, Jim, and Doug—can be said to represent three different personal perspectives about competition, war, and masculinity in powwows. Ira respects competition in powwows, and participates in competitive powwows, but makes a personal choice not to enter the contests. Jim is drawn mainly to the spiritual aspects of dancing and also is grateful for the money he might win in competitions. Doug is at the apex of these two perspectives: he competes *because* of the communally spiritual rewards of dancing. He puts on paint before the finals of any competition, and describes himself significantly as *"a modern day warrior"* (personal communication, June 19, 1999).

In the context of the powwows themselves, there are larger, public decisions that are made about competition. Comparing traditional (noncompetitive) and competitive powwows, DesJarlait (1997) focuses on the role of the community and concludes that any powwow's *raison d'être* is the enrichment of the people participating—regardless of whether prize money is given. He does not perceive any radical difference between the two types of events.

DesJarlait's suggestions in this debate seem more effective because they can be placed within the context of other competitive traditions on the Plains. These background traditions constitute the third point about competition that emerges from the ethnographic data informing this chapter. Doug and other competitors see their dancing itself as a prayer, as something with healing power. But the inspiration to dance and even to set oneself against others has a tradition almost as long: it comes from the history of the warrior in Plains Indian culture. Modern powwow dance traces its ancestry directly to warrior society gatherings, and some included giveaways (elaborate gift-giving rituals) that are earlier variants of these rituals today. The popularity of powwow dancing increased after World War I, as noted above; overall, there is a direct correlation between increases in powwow gatherings and the reemergence of opportunities to fight for one's people (Powers, 1990; Kracht, 1994; Ellis, 1999).

Continuities between warrior societies, warrior traditions, and powwow competition are clear in the ethnographic data. For instance, as already noted, Doug wears face paint when he dances in the final round of a competition, evoking images of Plains battle preparations. Like the grass dance Jim Nelson discussed, the fancy feather dance has as many variations as there are individual dancers. Each dance tells a story, Doug says, and one must find his or her own. Jim's story was of a grass dancer flattening the grass for other participants. For Doug, the fancy feather dance imitates the steps of a charging horse. When making this distinction Doug again compared himself to other warriors in Lakota culture (personal communication, June 19, 1999).

Competition is thus the purest aspect of the event for dancers like Doug. Excelling at this modern activity is a way of giving honor to the past. But there is a certain situatedness about the skill he displays. Doug commands the attention and admiration of everyone around him, but from his perspective he fights *for the people*. He is embedded within the ethic of his community. As he says, "I'm not a spiritual leader, I'm no better or worse than anyone else. . . . It's the people I dance for. I dance for my community to show them my respect for the traditional ways. And sometimes people come up to me crying [because they are so moved by how well I have danced]" (personal communication, June 19, 1999). In that sense, powwow competition may be something of a paradox: competition is one of the powwow characteristics that *sustains* the community. Warfare has traditionally been described in the same manner.

A similar paradox constructs the fourth point supported by ethnographic data on the Northern Plains: it seems that, for many of these cultural groups, the idea of the individual is unique in relation to the community. Individuals are revered for their skills, "singled out" in a sense. But the worldviews of Plains Indian individuals are still highly communal. The ethic of community in most Northern Plains societies dictates that individuals do not achieve any prestige without the support and encouragement of the community. The relationship between the "individual" and the "collective" is highly potent in the fashioning of worldview for any given cultural group. Many scholars of culture try to place a given group on a continuum between "individual" and "collective." Typically, European cultures are considered highly individual on this scale, while most Asian cultures are collective. This is just one set of examples. But interestingly, on the Northern Plains, one could say that some cultural groups are not placed on a continuum between these two extremes. Instead there is a unique construal of "individual" vis a vis the collective.

On the Plains, the "individual" can only exist because of the community, the collective. In phenomenological terms, the individual competitor is called into existence by the supportive community. Again, there are cultural precedents for this ethic, and it directly correlates to Holm's (1995) assertion that the Native American soldier is praised, revered, prayed for, and cured because he or she is continually in relationship with his or her community. Young people, and especially warriors on the Northern Plains, were always encouraged to "find their path" and have always been appreciated for their unique qualities. A child born to a Plains society was special, unique, and revered: not merely a part of the group. But at the same time children were encouraged to find their own path, their discoveries always required interpretation and sanction from the community. Visions and dreams, for example, were considered a direct means of illumination about the individual self—but the individual would not be capable of interpreting the dreams or visions on their own. Spiritual leadership was required (Irwin, 1994).

This unique tension between individual and community was particularly evident during a research trip to the Plains in 2005, when I observed even more imagery and activity pertaining to war than in 1999. For instance, one of the warrior societies elected a "brave," the male equivalent of a powwow princess, to represent them in the Arlee Grand Entry. He was also asked to greet everyone at the powwow publicly along with the princesses, in the manner of powwow royalty. This is yet another step in the solidification of the enduring significance of warrior societies in many Native American communities. In 2005, in contrast to 1999, there were calls for "war mothers" to come forward and receive gifts from families. These women are mothers of those honorably discharged from military service—which applied to a mother of any veteran on this given reservation. The war in Iraq was an oft-referenced part of public discourse at all the events. Perhaps most poignantly, during the memorial service the night before the Arlee Fourth of July Celebration—when Flathead Nation residents process and carry items to commemorate those who have died in the past year—there were more items of war memorabilia than I had ever seen before. Families carried veterans' items to commemorate their loss during the previous year—uniforms, shields, flags, photographs—and let their tears flow freely.

Conclusion

Again, through these memorials the individual identity of a warrior was reified, but also restated as belonging to the community. Although military service is a complicated issue for all peoples and can be said to be paradoxical in its embodiment of both glory and tragedy, one should not make the mistake of imposing one given cultural worldview onto the idea of the warrior. In many Native American communities, the warrior ideal is a particular construction of masculinity. The unique history of Native Americans, especially on the Plains, provides a different context for military service than might be found in other co-cultures in the United States and around the world. There are compelling arguments for the significance of war as providing mature relationship, wisdom, protection, and healing for Native American communities. My attempt here has been to combine what scholars know about Native American worldviews with the voices of those who gather their lives around the warrior ideal as a means of communicating about masculinity in their communities. This communication of masculinity is done through the ethic of protecting one's home and community; of seeing all humanity as interconnected and interdependent; and through competing—even in powwow dances—not for the glory of individual self but for the rhetorical production of the public good of pride in tradition. Thus, the warrior ideal runs the gamut through both time and space, from the Ghost Dance through the fancy dance.

References

Bernstein, A. R. (1991). *American Indians and World War II: Toward a New Era in Indian Affairs*. Norman: University of Oklahoma Press.

Collier, J. (1949). *Patterns and Ceremonials of the Indians of the Southwest*. New York: Dover.

DeMallie, R. J. (1994). Kinship and Biology in Sioux Culture. In R. J. DeMallie & A. Ortiz (Eds.), *North American Indian Anthropology* (pp. 125–46). Norman: University of Oklahoma Press.

DesJarlait, Robert. (1997). The Contest Powwow versus the Traditional Powwow and the Role of the Native American Community. *Wicazo Sa Review*, 12(1), 115–27.

Dutton, B. P., & Marmon, M. A. (1936). *The Laguna Calendar*. Albuquerque: University of New Mexico Press.

Ellis, C. (1999). "We Don't Want Your Rations, We Want This Dance": The Changing Use of Song and Dance on the Southern Plains. *Western Historical Quarterly*, 30(2), 133–54.

Gump, J. O. (1997). A Spirit of Resistance: Sioux, Xhosa, and Maori Responses to Western Dominance, 1840–1920. *Pacific Historical Review*, 66(1), 21–52.

Gurian, J. (1977). The Importance of Dependency in Native American–White Contact. *American Indian Quarterly*, 3(1), 16–36.

Harrod, H. L. (1995). *Becoming and Remaining a People: Native American Religions on the Northern Plains*. Tucson: University of Arizona Press.

Hoffman, L. L., Jackson, A. P., & Smith, S.A. (2005). Career Barriers among Native American Students Living on Reservations. *Journal of Career Development*, 32(1), 31–45.

Holm, T. (1995). PTSD in Native American Vietnam Veterans: A Reassessment. *Wicazo Sa Review*, 11(2), 83–86.

Hooks, G., and Smith, C. L. (2004). The Treadmill of Destruction: National Sacrifice Areas and Native Americans. *American Sociological Review*, 69(4), 558–75.

Irwin, Lee. (1994). Walking the Sky: Visionary Traditions of the Great Plains. *The Great Plains Quarterly*, 14(4), 257–71.

Kelton, E. (1993). Visions of a Lost World. *American History Illustrated*, 27(6), 50–59.

Kracht, B. R. (1994). Kiowa Powwows: Continuity in Ritual Practice. *American Indian Quarterly*, 18(3), 321–48.

Manataka American Indian Council. (2008). "Manataka American Indian council proudly presents the National Native American Veterans Association." Accessed February 22, 2008, from: http://www.manataka.org/page830.html

National Native American Veterans Association. (2008). "Our Adopted POW/MIA." Accessed February 22, 2008, from: http://www.nnava.org/powmia.html

Powers, W. (1990). *War Dance: Plains Indian Musical Performance*. Tucson: University of Arizona Press.

Roberts, K. G. (2003). Emotivism and Pseudocultural Identities. *Howard Journal of Communications*, 14(4), 295–308.

Roberts, K. G. (2007). *Alterity & Narrative: Stories and the Negotiation of Western Identities*. Albany: State University of New York Press.

Ruml, M. F. (2000). The De-sacralization of the Powwow? Some Initial Observations. *Papers of the Algonquian Conference*, 31, 333–38.

Shoyo, Harrison. (2005). Public Oratory at the Eastern Shoshone Indian Days Powwow. June 25, Fort Washakie, Wyoming.

Silko, Leslie Marmon. (1977). *Ceremony*. New York: Penguin.

Turner, S. L., & Lapan, R. T. (2003). Native American Adolescent Career Development. *Journal of Career Development*, 30(2), 159–72.

Walker, W. (1983). More on the Cryptographic Use of Native American Languages in Tactical Operations by United States Armed Forces. *International Journal of American Linguistics*, 49(1), 93–97.

Williard, W. (1991). The First Amendment, Anglo-Conformity, and American Indian Religious Freedom. *Wicazo Sa Review*, 7(1), 25–41.

7

Representing Aboriginal Masculinity in Howard's Australia

SHINO KONISHI

Introducing Howard's Aboriginal Policy

On November 24, 2007, Australia's conservative Coalition government was voted out after eleven years in office. Its loss was so decisive that the prime minister, John Howard, suffered the ignominy of being only the second prime minister in Australian history to lose his electoral seat. A contributing factor to his downfall was his determined march towards the neoliberal Right through his economic and industrial policies. For good or ill, he will be remembered for his attempts to return the nation to the ostensibly halcyon days of the 1950s, arguably, a time when the hegemony of white patriarchy was untroubled by the clamor of political correctness (Bonnell & Crotty, 2008). In eulogizing Howard's government, his supporters celebrated his economic management and strong stance against political correctness and minority rights, continuing the Australian "culture wars" that raged throughout his term. In an essay for the conservative magazine *Quadrant*, John Stone applauded Howard, claiming that his second-greatest impact on national debate was to remain "immovable" against the charges of "black armband" historians who lamented the "alleged atrocities" committed against Aboriginal and Torres Strait Islander people (Stone, 2008, p. 48).

Stone's emphasis on Howard's Indigenous policy is not surprising. Aboriginal and Torres Strait Islander people, who have a long history of exploitation and exclusion from mainstream Australia, only represent 2.5 percent of the population, so were an easy target for Howard's divisive politics. Within his first year of government, the Human Rights and Equal Opportunity Commission (HREOC) released *Bringing Them Home: Report of the National Enquiry into the Separation of Aboriginal and Torres Strait Islander Children from Their Families* (1997). This was an investigation into the decades' old government practice of removing thousands of Indigenous children from their parents and placing them in government institutions or with non-Indigenous adoptive and foster parents. The report charted a litany of physical and emotional traumas suffered by the "Stolen Generations": one in every ten experienced sexual abuse, and 28 percent were subjected to severe "physical brutality" (HREOC, 1997, pp. 163–64, 194). The head of the inquiry, Sir Ronald Wilson, labeled the removal of children over several generations "genocide"; drawing on Article 2[e] of the 1948 United Nations Convention on Genocide, he claimed that the outcome, intended or otherwise, was to eradicate the children's connection to their culture and their Aboriginal identity (pp. 266–73).

Howard's refusal to either countenance this charge or offer an apology or compensation as a form of redress was a stark demonstration that he had little sympathy for the suffering inflicted on Indigenous Australians by past governments in the pursuit of creating a white Australia. Indeed, he failed to see Aboriginal and Torres Strait Islander people as anything more than colonial subordinates, eternally subject to the whims of government. He systematically dismantled the programs and mechanisms that preceding governments had implemented with the aim of achieving Indigenous self-determination and guaranteeing collective rights to Aboriginal lands. His government disbanded the Aboriginal and Torres Strait Islander Commission (ATSIC), a democratically elected Indigenous representative and governing body (Cunningham & Baeza, 2005). While ATSIC had a troubled history, its demise, according to Aboriginal academic Boni Robertson, meant that Indigenous Australians no longer had a role in "controlling [their] own destiny" (cited in Rintoul, 2006). Howard's government also diluted Native Title rights, amended the Commonwealth Aboriginal Land Rights (Northern Territory) Act of 1976, introduced Indigenous policies that contravened the Australian Racial Discrimination Act (1975), and refused to bow to the global shift towards decolonization and recognition of Indigenous rights by failing to ratify the United Nations Declaration on the Rights of Indigenous Peoples (Sanders, 2006; Stringer, 2007; Dodson, 2007).

Howard and his constituents abhorred the so-called special treatment that Indigenous Australians had received under previous governments in measures aimed at righting past wrongs, and elevating their socio-economic status to the same level enjoyed by non-Indigenous Australians. By employing wedge politics, Howard's government mobilized middle-Australia's economic anxieties and envy of perceived minority privilege by fostering resentment towards Indigenous Australians, even though they represent the most marginal and impoverished sector of the Australian population (Bonnell & Crotty, 2008, pp. 149–50).

Perhaps the most instrumental factor in the Howard government's campaign to wind back Indigenous self-determination and collective rights was an unwavering campaign to undermine and demonize Aboriginal masculinity. In their administrative attacks on ATSIC and Aboriginal Lands Councils, the Coalition government, supported by the conservative media, portrayed Indigenous organizations as male-run despotic regimes, rife with ineptitude, corruption, and tribal nepotism, and therefore, desperately in need of a strong guiding hand. Tony Abbott, Howard's then minister for health and current leader of the parliamentary Opposition, claimed that Indigenous communities were governed by "local 'big men' often in conflict with one another, and as a result a new form of [government] paternalism . . . [was] really unavoidable" (Abbott, 2006). As we shall see, the most effective weapon in the Howard government's political arsenal against Aboriginal sovereignty was the revival of colonial tropes of Aboriginal masculinity as destructively dysfunctional and sexually violent.

From the period of first settlement in 1788, British colonists had largely portrayed Aboriginal masculinity as the antithesis of white civilized manliness: primitive, irrational, childlike, treacherous, and barbaric towards women (Hogg, 2006). Such a portrayal was not unique to Aboriginal Australian men, however, but was typical of Western representations of nonwhite men in various imperial and colonial contexts around the world (Jordan, 1968; Fanon, 1967; Sinha, 1995; Delgado & Stefancic, 1995; Hokowhitu, 2008). Conservative commentators sympathetic to Howard's vision luridly evoked this specter of black masculinity by portraying traditional Aboriginal culture as uncivilized and misogynistic, recasting Australia's violent frontier history as a process of benign settlement and a Western civilizing endeavor still in need of completion. In August 2007, in his government's final foray into Indigenous policy, Howard replicated these ideas legislatively with the launch of his government's Northern Territory Emergency Response, or the Intervention.

Ostensibly a reaction to the *Ampe Akelyernemane Meke Mekarle: "Little Children Are Sacred"* report (Board of Inquiry into the Protection of Aboriginal Children from Sexual Abuse [BIPACSA], 2007), which found that high levels of sexual abuse existed in the Northern Territory's remote Aboriginal communities, the Intervention was presented as a means of saving Aboriginal women and children from the depredations of dysfunctional Aboriginal men.

Under the Intervention, all Aboriginal people in the prescribed areas had their welfare payments subject to "income management." Half their income was quarantined to be spent on goods deemed appropriate by the government. Further, Aboriginal people within the targeted communities were governed by appointed administrators, banned from purchasing alcohol and pornography, and subject to a host of other measures concerning Aboriginal land tenure that legal scholar Desmond Manderson argues possessed an "at best tenuous relationship to the prevention of child abuse" (Marr, 2007; Hinkson, 2007; Manderson, 2008, p. 241). The Intervention marked the nadir in Howard's strategic demonization of Aboriginal masculinity, and his most decisive assertion of the superiority of white civilizing manliness.

This chapter will examine the way in which the Howard government and its supporters revitalized colonial tropes about Aboriginal masculinity in order to progressively dismantle and undermine Indigenous rights and sovereignty, culminating in the quasi-military Intervention into supposedly dysfunctional Aboriginal communities towards the end of Howard's fourth term. I will critique and historicize a range of demeaning representations that assume Aboriginal men are violent and misogynistic. These representations, still ubiquitous today, can be traced back to initial encounters between European and Indigenous men. My aim is to bring academic, media, and governmental discourses about Aboriginal masculinity into conversation with masculinity studies, which means contextualizing notions of Aboriginal masculinity in ways that avoid unreflective colonial conceptions. Finally, this chapter will examine the public response of Aboriginal men to this demonization, and how they negotiate their own masculine identities in the face of a colonial culture that disparages them for their race and gender.

Aboriginal Male Dysfunction in the "History Wars"

When Howard came to power in 1996 he systematically set out to change the Australian culture that had emerged under his predecessor, Paul Keating. A particular concern of his was Keating's adoption of the so-called black armband view of Australian history, an interpretation that had surfaced in the 1970s after the tumultuous civil rights era, which saw Aboriginal people finally receive constitutional recognition, and the end of the discriminatory Aboriginal Protection Acts. The black armband view was exemplified in Prime Minister Keating's famous Redfern Speech of 1992, in which he addressed the need to acknowledge past wrongs: "The starting point might be to recognise that the problem starts with us non-Aboriginal Australians. It begins, I think, with the act of recognition. Recognition that it was we who did the dispossessing. We took the traditional lands and smashed the traditional way of life. We brought the diseases. The alcohol. We committed the murders. We took the children from their mothers. We practiced discrimination and exclusion. It was our ignorance and our prejudice. And our failure to imagine these things being done to us" (Keating, 1992, p. 228, cited in Crotty & Bonnell, 2008, p. 151).

Keating's speech reflected a vast body of scholarship charting the violent treatment and exploitation of Aboriginal people that had marked the Australian colonial experience, including twentieth-century massacres and the removal of children. Howard had little tolerance for this view of Aboriginal history. Shortly after winning the election he decried this interpretation of the past: "This 'black armband' view of our past reflects a belief that most Australian history since 1788 has been little more than a disgraceful story of imperialism, exploitation, racism, sexism and other forms of discrimination. I take a very different view. I believe that the balance sheet of our history is one of heroic achievement and that we have achieved much more as a nation of which we can be proud than of which we should be ashamed" (cited in Crotty & Bonnell, 2008, p. 152). Howard's push for the nation to embrace a history of which it could be proud was echoed by a number of conservative scholars who were keen to reinstate the glorious history of empire. The most successful "history warrior" was Keith Windschuttle, who released his self-published tome *The Fabrication of Aboriginal History: Volume 1: Van Diemen's Land, 1803–1847* (2002), a blatant attack on the "black armband" view of the history of the colony that is now the state of Tasmania. Tasmania's violent history has long been accepted; it was a brutal penal colony, and in the nineteenth century and for most of the twentieth century, it was widely accepted that upon the death of Trugannini, the Indigenous Tasmanians had been eradicated in a series of conflicts and removals (Curthoys, 2008).[1]

Despite the century-old belief that the Tasmanian Aborigines were extinct, Windschuttle opposes historians who use "terms such as 'genocide,' 'extermination,' and 'extirpation.'" He denies that they were almost eliminated by British colonizers, and instead argues that "the British colonization of this continent was the least violent of all Europe's encounters with the New World," for the British aimed to "trade useful products and to demonstrate by example the benefits of the civil and polite customs of Europe" (pp. 3, 32). However, in asserting the benevolence of the British, Windschuttle still had to explain the root causes of the violence that marked the Tasmanian frontier, and the Tasmanian Aborigines' near destruction. He blames Aboriginal men.

Firstly, Windschuttle opposes the argument that interracial conflict was catalyzed by European expansion into Aboriginal territory. He denies that tensions were caused by colonists appropriating Indigenous food sources and Aboriginal people defending their land. He claims that the British had their own "reliable supplies of traditional British food" and refutes the post-Mabo orthodoxy, by arguing that Aboriginal Tasmanians lacked any notions of territory or ownership (pp. 88–89, 103–11). Instead of blaming the frontier violence and near extirpation of the Aboriginal people on colonial expansion, Windschuttle argues that the so-called Black War was little more than an "outbreak of robbery and violence," and "revenge and plunder." He claims that Aborigines had acquired a taste for European goods, so they simply stole them, "kill[ing] any whites they found in their way." Thus, according to Windschuttle, the "actions of the Aborigines were not noble," and, contrary to the black armband view, the only "tragedy" was that "the Aborigines adopted such senseless violence" (p. 130).

Windschuttle's most egregious demonization of Aboriginal men, however, is his depiction of how they treated their women. Previously, feminist historians had explored the history of relations between European sealers and Aboriginal women in Tasmania, claiming that itinerant workers had kidnapped women, taking them to offshore islands, where some exploited the women sexually and also for their labor, while others treated them like wives (Ryan, 1981). Windschuttle counters this thesis that Aboriginal women were the victims of European men, and portrays Aboriginal men as harsher oppressors. Firstly, he reiterates nineteenth-century opinion that "the Tasmanians were the most primitive human society ever discovered" (p. 377). He backs American anthropologist Robert Edgerton's claim that Tasmanian Aborigines had become a "profoundly maladapted society," ostensibly because in the course of their isolation they "failed to devise social and cultural mechanisms to control their destructive tendencies" (cited in Windschuttle, 2002, p. 382).

The Aboriginal men's "destructive tendencies," according to Windschuttle, were to abduct, rape, and murder women, and to wage war on one another over access to women. It was this "internecine warfare" that contributed to the decimation of the Tasmanians, and not the impact of British colonization (p. 382). Windschuttle also restates the nineteenth-century view that it was "the absence of births even more than the frequency of deaths [that] completed the destruction of the people" (Bonwick, 1870, cited in Windschuttle, 2002, p. 376). He claims that the Tasmanian population was decimated by an increase in female sterility, a symptom of venereal disease. For this he also blames Aboriginal men, claiming that they forced their women into prostitution by "barter[ing] women for dogs and supplies" (p. 383). Windschuttle determines that "we should see [Aboriginal Tasmanians] as active agents in their own demise because their men hired out and sold off their women without contemplating the results." He contends that "Only men who held their women cheaply would allow such a thing to happen" (386). Thus he concludes: "The real tragedy of the Aborigines was not British colonization *per se* but that their society was, on the one hand, so internally dysfunctional and, on the other hand, so incompatible with the looming presence of the rest of the world" (p. 386).

Like Howard, Windschuttle wants to redeem the nation's colonial past and for Australians to be proud of their British origins. *The Fabrication of Aboriginal History* aided Howard's cultural shift to the right, for Windschuttle's views were eagerly embraced by the conservative national newspaper *The Australian,* which published extracts and ran many supportive editorials.

The book sparked one of the bloodiest battles in the Australian "history wars." Shortly after its release, its arguments were refuted by historians, most notably in a book of essays by leading academics edited by Robert Manne. *Whitewash: On Keith Windschuttle's Fabrication of Aboriginal History* (2003) comprised seventeen detailed rejoinders to the different arguments Windschuttle posed.[2] Windschuttle's critics attacked his arguments in forensic detail, without paying equal consideration to how Windschuttle's spurious claim that Aboriginal culture was inherently dysfunctional would impact on Aboriginal men and women. Tim Murray and Christine Williamson came the closest in critiquing Windschuttle's contention that the Aboriginal Tasmanians were a "profoundly maladapted population," arguing that he failed to use any archaeological evidence, thus did not grasp their 35,000 year-old history. Instead, they accuse him of selectively drawing on biased European accounts of the Aboriginal men's ill treatment of women that span only a few decades (Murray & Williamson, 2003, pp. 311–14). However, any distress caused to Aboriginal people by Windschuttle's attack on their past culture was nothing compared to the demonization of contemporary Aboriginal men in the media during the Howard era.

Aboriginal Male Dysfunction in the Media

Howard's antipathy towards both minority rights and political correctness was echoed by the Australian conservative media, and Indigenous Australian people were amongst their favored targets, alongside asylum seekers ("illegal refugees" or "queue jumpers") and Muslim Australians ("terrorists" and "rapists"). Just as key events such as the attack on the World Trade Center, the Tampa Crisis, and the Bali bombing hardened Australian attitudes toward Muslim people, the rape allegations against the former chairperson of ATSIC, Geoff Clark, and the exposé on Indigenous violence by Nannette Rogers mobilized popular support for the Howard government's intervention into Aboriginal politics. The Australian people's support was largely due to the way in which the conservative media maligned Aboriginal men in general through their representation of these particular events.[3] Indeed, the *Little Children Are Sacred Report* found that the Australian media was a key proponent in persuading mainstream Australia that Aboriginal men are inherently violent and misogynistic (BIPACSA, 2007, p. 58).

Geoff Clark was the first chairperson of ATSIC to be popularly elected by an Indigenous Australian constituency, but will be most remembered for bringing the organization into disrepute and contributing to its demise under Howard. Since the Hawke Labor government's establishment of ATSIC in 1990, this role had been an appointed position, but a push for democratic representation led to the inaugural ATSIC election in 1999. As chairperson, Clark faced the difficult task of representing Indigenous issues and agitating for increased Indigenous "rights" during the turbulence of the early Howard government, which instead pushed a "responsibilities" agenda (Heinritz & Josephi, 2006). For example, upon his election the prime minister immediately "slash[ed] $400 million from ATSIC'S budget and implement[ed] an extensive audit of Indigenous community organisations that was later found to be illegal and misplaced" (Dodson, 2007, p. 27). Clark faced his greatest challenge, however, when rape allegations against him surfaced.

In 2000 he was charged by the police after four women alleged that he had raped them two decades earlier, but the charges were soon dropped when a magistrate found that "the evidence was too weak for a jury to reach a verdict" (Rule, 2001). However, this did not prevent journalist Andrew Rule from publishing the allegations as though they were fact in a lengthy and salaciously detailed exposé, "Geoff Clark: Power and Rape" (Rule, 2001), for the newspaper, *The Age*. Clark maintained his innocence, claiming that the allegations were "false" and part of a "continued campaign" against him (Dunn & Krester, 2001; see also Schwarz, 2008, pp. 164–75). Around the same time, Clark was also involved in a "pub brawl" in his hometown, which in tandem with the rape allegations led the government to eventually suspend him on August 13, 2003 (Heinritz & Josephi, 2006, p. 32). In August 2004 the Federal Court ruled that Clark's "dismissal was unlawful and racially discriminatory" (Schwarz, 2008, p. 28); however by then it was too late for Clark and ATSIC. A Victorian court had already decided in February 2004 that his female accusers were eligible to sue Clark for damages in a civil court.

This ruling was timely fodder for the government. In a climate in which the media continued its campaign against Aboriginal self-governance and its male leaders, Howard maintained his ideological opposition to ATSIC and on April 15, 2004, announced that it would be abolished. He claimed that the "experiment in elected representation for Indigenous people has been a failure." Howard asserted that ATSIC would not be replaced, but that his government would instead "appoint a group of distinguished indigenous people to advise the government on a purely advisory basis" ("Howard Axes Aboriginal Body," 2004; see Heinritz & Josephi, 2006, p. 21). With the endorsement of a mere handful of Indigenous leaders, Howard replaced ATSIC with the National Indigenous Council, which was maligned by Indigenous leaders and media because the members were appointed by the government and their role was to be merely advisory (Behrendt, 2005; Graham, 2010).

Rule's exposé, which eventually won him the 2001 Gold Walkley, Australia's highest journalistic award, sparked a media tirade against Clark. Unfortunately, this quickly escalated into a condemnation of Aboriginal men in general, as commentators turned their attention to the prevalence of domestic violence in Aboriginal communities. For example, the *Sydney Morning Herald* columnist Paul Sheehan, a determined skeptic of the idea of a stolen generation of Aboriginal children, claimed "that domestic violence has always been endemic in Aboriginal culture, which accounted for the past and present removal of Aboriginal children from their families" (Matchett, 2001, p. 29). As the journalist and media reviewer Stephen Matchett laments, "*The Age* allegations generated so much anger and so many accusations reaching far beyond the [original] claims made against Mr. Clark" (Matchett, 2001, p. 32). The sensational coverage of the Clark case entangled the notion of Aboriginal male dysfunction with Indigenous political dysfunction in the public imagination. This association would be both strengthened and amplified in another key scandal: Nannette Rogers's 2006 exposé on the ABC's evening current affairs television program *Lateline*.

Rogers is a non-Indigenous lawyer who had moved to the Northern Territory's Alice Springs in 1980, and worked firstly as a defense lawyer for the Central Australian Aboriginal Legal Service, and then as a Crown Prosecutor. On both sides of the bench she saw many cases concerning Aboriginal domestic violence and child abuse, often fueled by alcohol and substance abuse such as petrol sniffing. In 2005 she was shown the Alice Springs Hospital's files concerning domestic violence cases, and was appalled by the extent of the problem. She was also concerned by the fact that unlike other Australian states, the Northern Territory did not have mandatory reporting of such cases to the police. This was her catalyst for speaking out about the issue to the media (Nowra, 2007, pp. 34–35).

On May 15, 2006, Rogers appeared on the ABC's *Lateline* program, exposing the horrific rape cases she had witnessed in meticulous detail. The most shocking instance concerned an "18 year old petrol sniffer" who raped and drowned a four-year-old girl (Jones, 2006a). This tragic case was widely reported by the media, and even repeated by the current leader of the Liberal party, Brendan Nelson, during his response in parliament to the new prime minister, Kevin Rudd's formal apology to the Stolen Generation on February 13, 2008 (Nelson, 2008). Rogers blamed Aboriginal culture for this epidemic of abuse, especially its influence on men's attitudes: "Men's business is a predominant aspect of life in remote communities, and young men who are initiated are given certain status in the community and feel they are not responsible for their actions. . . . In other words, they can do whatever they like" (cited in Kearney & Wilson, 2006). Rogers also claimed that Aboriginal culture is "punitive," and blamed a legal "emphasis . . . on customary law in terms of placing the offender in the best light," and the tradition of silence that "closed off the voices of the Aboriginal women" (Jones, 2006a). Rogers declared that life on the remote communities is "beyond the range of normal comprehension," where the "child grows up seeing violence all around him or her and having violence done to him or her and then becomes an adult and . . . become violent themselves" (Jones, 2006a).

The media pounced on Rogers's exposé, with headlines declaring "Men Prey on Customary Law" (Carney, 2006), "Male Rape Rife among Aborigines" (McKenna, 2006), "Spare the Victims—Remove the Violent Men" (Skelton, 2006), and "Raping Children Part of 'Men's Business'" (Kearney & Wilson, 2006). The then Indigenous Affairs minister Mal Brough entered the debate, amplifying Rogers's assertions on *Lateline* with his own spurious claim that Aboriginal communities housed organized "paedophile rings": "Everybody in those communities knows who runs the paedophile rings. They know who brings the petrol in and they know who sells the ganja. They need to be taken out of the community and dealt with, not by tribal law, but by the judicial system that operates throughout Australia. We're equal in this country and we should all be treated in the same way" (Jones, 2006b). While Rogers's legal examples were included in the *Little Children Are Sacred Report* and the Inquiry found that there were genuine problems with child sexual abuse and domestic violence in remote Aboriginal communities, her explanatory arguments were directly challenged in the report. In section 4.2, the Inquiry confronted a range of "myths." Firstly, they maintain that, "Aboriginal men have been targeted as though they were the only perpetrators of child sexual abuse in communities. This is inaccurate and has resulted in unfair shaming, and consequent further disempowerment of Aboriginal men as a whole" (BIPACSA, 2007, p. 57). In fact, in an interview on the ABC's *Stateline,* one of the report's authors, Rex Wild QC, claimed that the "worst examples of abuse of aboriginal children is [*sic*] from non-aboriginal men" (*Stateline Northern Territory* Transcripts, 2007). The *Little Children Are Sacred* report also rejects the argument that Aboriginal law is to be blamed, arguing that it "is a dangerous myth [which] reinforces prejudice and ignorance," and that the "Inquiry was unable to find any case where Aboriginal law has been used and accepted as a defence" (BIPACSA, 2007, p. 58). The Inquiry also refuted the Minister's claims, stating: "While the Inquiry found no evidence of any 'paedophile rings' operating in the Northern Territory, there was enough evidence to conclude that a number of individual non-Aboriginal 'paedophiles' had been infiltrating Aboriginal communities and offending against children" (p. 61). Finally, they condemned the role of the media in perpetuating these myths, acknowledging that such reports do little to help the situation (p. 58). Unfortunately, these aspects of the Inquiry's findings were largely unreported by the media.[4] The prominence of these exposés in the Australian media add weight to Aboriginal journalist Stan Grant's contention that journalists have "devoted endless column inches to portraying black men universally as violent sexual predators. All this is supposedly out of a fear for the safety of black women" (Grant, 2001). His skepticism regarding the "white man's concern for Aborigines" is not unfounded, given that the Aboriginal men's "trial by media" was the precursor to the Howard government's aforementioned upheaval of Aboriginal governance. Grant's assertions were echoed by Patrick Dodson, formerly the Chairman of the Council for Aboriginal Reconciliation and the Commissioner into Aboriginal Deaths in Custody, who argued that Aboriginal men "have been reduced by the media and government ideologues to sexual deviants and sociopathic automatons" (2007, p. 22), and Vince Forrester, a Traditional Owner from the Mutijulu community, who declared that "Every Aboriginal man is now tainted with a brush, they have emasculated us, they have said we are all woman bashers, we are all alcoholics, we are all child abusers" ("Aboriginals Threaten," 2008).

These testaments from Aboriginal commentators and leaders are supported by empirical studies of the media. Communications researcher Kerry McCallum found in her study of news reporting between 2000 and 2006 that most journalists reported sensationalist stories of Indigenous violence, conflict, and dysfunction. She observed that over the period there was a "shutting down of public discussion of Indigenous reconciliation, of Indigenous disadvantage, social justice or non-Indigenous racism," and that increasingly Indigenous issues were framed "through a prism of individual responsibility." Consequently, Aboriginal men were "framed [in the news media] as dangerous others, reinforcing conceptions of them as a societal risk and a threat to the existing order" (McCallum, 2007, p. 12).

I would contend that contributing to this widespread demonization of Aboriginal men is the reluctance of these colonial discourses to problematize masculinity in general. Instead, Aboriginal male violence is seen purely as a problem of ethnicity, for Aboriginal men are almost exclusively discussed in the context of Indigenous society and culture, and not in relation to other men. The rich scholarship on masculinity, both Indigenous and non-Indigenous, can provide a useful lens through which to both interpret mainstream representations of Aboriginal men, and to understand the destructive behaviors of some Aboriginal men.

Reconsidering Aboriginal Male Dysfunction through Masculinity Studies

A crucial, although unacknowledged, factor in these discussions of Aboriginal men's dysfunction is that the behavior of Aboriginal men is measured against an ostensibly normative masculinity that protects and provides for women and children. Within the Australian settler-colonial context this normative masculinity is essentially a "white" masculinity. According to Maori scholar Brendan Hokowhitu, "Indigenous and First Nations men have come to define themselves, or rather have come to be defined through an allegorical relationship to the white man" (2007, p. 331). It is this "white" masculinity that is the foundation of Australian hegemonic masculinity. Martin Crotty adapts R. W. Connell's influential definition of hegemonic masculinity and delineates it as "the ideal of manliness prevalent amongst those with the power to formulate the ideal and disseminate it" (2001, p. 4). Further, hegemonic masculinity "is the ideal that, through various social, cultural and legal practices, oppresses all those whom it excludes" (Crotty, 2001, p. 5). Crotty concludes that "heterosexual, white, middle-class hegemonic ideals oppress and marginalise all that is homosexual, black or working-class."

The concept of white hegemonic masculinity is crucial to critiquing these representations of Aboriginal male dysfunction. Firstly, it represents an "ideal," and is not representative of the majority of men, not even white men. For instance, male violence in general has been completely omitted from these discourses on Aboriginal male dysfunction. Numerous studies have long shown that male violence is a significant problem in Australian society. Sandra Eggers found that the "relationship between masculinity and violence is striking" for almost all "violent offenses" are committed by men (1995, p. xxxiii; Rayar, 1996). Moreover, there is widespread physical and sexual abuse of Australian women: a 2004 study found 48 percent of Australian women experience physical violence and 34 percent sexual assault (Sneddon, 2007). The frequency of violence and abuse is also linked to socio-economic disadvantages, such as poverty, "high unemployment, and high proportions of single parent families" (Eggers, 1995, p. xxxi), conditions that are accentuated in remote Aboriginal communities (BIPACSA, 2007, p. 224; Atkinson, 1990, p. 22). Thus, the prevalence of violence in Aboriginal communities is not a problem of Aboriginality and Indigenous culture, but rather, is one of masculinity and socio-economic disadvantage, a fact stubbornly ignored by Howard and his supporters.

The most blatant example of this tendency was perpetrated by Howard himself in an interview for *Marie Claire Australia,* a national women's magazine. The then prime minister was told that "one in three" Australian women are "affected by [domestic violence]," and asked "What practical solutions can you offer these women?" His only response was to applaud his government's Northern Territory Intervention: "Well, I think we're offering a wonderful practical demonstration in the Northern Territory at the moment because the most egregious examples of violence against women are to be found mostly in indigenous communities" (Frank, 2007, pp. 107–10). By focusing exclusively on the remote Aboriginal communities of the Northern Territory, which represent only 0.3 percent of the nation's population, Howard both ignored the "one in three" Australian women who face domestic violence and reinforced the hegemonic myth of "white civilized manliness."

The concept of white hegemonic masculinity is also important in the critique of Aboriginal male dysfunction, because as Gail Bederman and Brendan Hokowhitu have demonstrated, masculinity is intricately entangled with ideas of race, civilization, and colonialism. Bederman argues that within imperial discourses, "Civilised white men were the most manly ever evolved—firm of character; self-controlled protectors of women and children" (1995, p. 25). This self-concept was defined and bolstered by the construction of Indigenous and black men as its antithesis: "Savage men were emotional and lacked a man's ability to restrain their passions. Savage men were creatures of whim who raped women instead of protecting them" (1995, p. 25). Hokowhitu adds another crucial component to the stereotype: Indigenous men were also "in need of civilised enlightenment" (2007, p. 332), no matter how barbarically this was implemented. As stated earlier, many studies have found that this stereotype of Indigenous men was applied throughout the colonized world. Hokowhitu contends that this was because the "object of colonial discourse is to construe the colonised as a population of degenerate types on the basis of racial origin, in order to justify conquest and to establish systems of administration and instruction" (2007, p. 333). Yet, as the various case studies have shown, discussions of Aboriginal men's dysfunction fail to acknowledge this discursive legacy of colonization. Instead they singularly blame Indigenous cultural attributes such as pre-colonial gender relations, and the persistence of "customary law." They also fail to acknowledge the continuing material impact of colonization.

It is not my contention that Aboriginal male violence towards women and children is purely a figment of the discursive demonization of Aboriginal men; many legitimate studies have found that there is a genuine crisis within Indigenous Australian communities (Robertson, 2000; HREOC, 2006; NSW Aboriginal Child Sexual Assault Taskforce, 2006). Masculinity studies suggest that this problem is partly a consequence of the violence of colonization and its ensuing race relations, which produced "marginalized masculinities" that display behaviors deemed to be dysfunctional and self-destructive. When considering "black masculinity," Connell follows Robert Staples's thesis that the "level of violence among black men" must be understood in relation to the violence inflicted upon them in order to control them. Thus black masculinities were formed by "institutional oppression and physical terror" sustained by white hegemonic masculinity (Connell, 1995, p. 80).

This oppression and terror originated in the earliest days of colonization, which, despite British declarations that they would treat the natives honorably and humanely, was marked by both *de jure* and *ad hoc* violence against Aborigines in the form of collective punishment intended to "infuse a universal terror" (Governor Arthur Phillip, cited in Konishi, 2007, p. 66), and "rough bush justice" (Moore, 1998b, p. 44). Even as late as 1897, on the eve of Australia's Federation, the Queensland Police Commissioner, W. E. Parry Okeden, could still declare that some outback stations house "scoundrels" who thought it "equal good fun to shoot a nigger at sight or to ravish a gin [an Aboriginal woman]" (cited in Reynolds, 1996, p. 74). The colonization of Australia and expropriation of Aboriginal land cost Indigenous men greatly, not only because of the violence they endured, but also through the loss of their male authority.

While it is extremely difficult to reconstruct an accurate picture of pre-colonial gender relations due to the paucity of sources, it is widely held that

Aboriginal men and women participated in separate economic and ritual spheres, with women exercising a relative degree of independence (Williams & Jolly, 1992; Atkinson, 1990). The highest authority in the clans was generally the male elders, who maintained and disseminated knowledge about the Dreaming, sacred sites, and laws, but as a consequence of colonization their "power relations altered considerably" (Atkinson, 1990, p. 22). According to Atkinson, "Men in their dispossession [from their ancestral lands], struggled to hold their positions as husbands, fathers, sons, teachers, and elder statesmen of authority and status. Rape of the body proved to be not as devastating as rape of the soul." The state governments' Aboriginal protection acts, implemented from the 1860s until the 1960s, further undermined Aboriginal men's patriarchal authority. These race-based laws declared that most Aboriginal people were wards of the Chief Protector, who was vested with the power to make decisions regarding Aborigines' labor, freedom of movement, education, and familial relationships, including the removal of their children. In accordance with the states' assimilationist endeavors, Aboriginal culture was denigrated and marginalized: Indigenous languages and cultural practices were mostly barred on government reserves. This colonial legacy, which was certainly not unique to Australia, has contributed to the current crisis in Aboriginal communities, and the dysfunctional behavior of some men. Hokowhitu contends that: "The alienation of Indigenous and First Nations men from their culture, while also limiting the right to be self-determining in the wider colonial societies, led many Indigenous men to assert themselves dysfunctionally. A recourse to violence and abuse against themselves and others has been one way in which some Indigenous and First Nations men have confronted their powerlessness" (2007, p. 333).

Violence and dysfunction are not just a consequence of colonized men's powerlessness, however, but was also perhaps modeled on the aggression enacted by the colonizers. The impact of colonial belligerence on Indigenous Australians has also been forgotten by Howard and his supporters in their discourses on dysfunctional Aboriginal masculinity. Colonialism's disruption of Indigenous gender orders, according to Connell, "made it more feasible for indigenous men to be drawn into the masculinising practices and hierarchies of colonial society" (Connell, 2005, p. 75). One of these practices was the abhorrent maltreatment of Indigenous women, who suffered much physical and sexual abuse at the hands of the colonists. Larissa Behrendt contends that it "is the legacy of colonialism . . . that the women of the conquered are assumed to become the property of the conquering" (Behrendt, 2000, p. 353). She illustrates this point with an extract from the nineteenth-century diary of Emily Creaghe: "The usual method here of bringing in a new wild gin is to put a rope around her neck and drag her along from horseback, the gin on foot" (cited in Behrendt, 2000). Aboriginal women were known as "Black Velvet" and frequently regarded as "'low-class" prostitutes and raped, with the men beaten if they refused to hand women over. Behrendt contends that the women had little recourse to the law, "as allegations against white men were usually dismissed" (p. 354).[5]

While it is no excuse for the current abuse in communities, perhaps the colonizers' rape and maltreatment of Indigenous women impacted on Aboriginal men's attitude towards them? Michael Hardin's study of Mexican *machismo* is particularly suggestive on this matter. Latin American historiography generally constructs *machismo* as an assemblage of negative traits, for instance: "aggressive, oppressive, narcissistic, insecure, loud-mouthed, womanizers, massive drinkers, [and] persons who have uncontrollable sexual prowess" (Ramirez, cited in Hardin, 2002, p. 3). Many of these characteristics typify the behavior of some Aboriginal men in Australia, which is not surprising given that Hardin primarily defines *machismo* "as a product of the Conquest" (Hardin, 2002, p. 3). He argues that colonization "redefined masculinity: for the Spaniards, masculinity meant permission to rape and abuse, something that was not permitted in Spain or with Spanish women, and for the Indigenous men, it was the 'Christian' model" (Hardin, 2002, p. 16). This thesis suggests that colonized men might have emulated the colonizers' violent model, and adopted the "swagger of conquest" (p. 17) in an attempt to emulate the colonizers' power, or at least as a sign to attest that they were not emasculated by colonization.

Colonial abuse was not just limited to Aboriginal men and women, however, but also inflicted upon Indigenous children. As stated earlier, the *Bringing Them Home* report found that almost one in three removed children suffered physical abuse and one in ten sexual abuse. One of the Inquiry's informants admitted that "There was tampering with boys" in the orphanage to which he was taken, but that this "was seen to be the white man's way of lookin' after you" (cited in HREOC, 1997, p. 163). In the absence of functional parents, it was not uncommon for the Stolen Generations to be abused, which in turn provided a tragic model for their own parenting skills. A study found that "approximately one-third of child victims of abuse grow up to have significant difficulties parenting, or becoming abusive of their own children. One-third do not have these outcomes, but the other third remain vulnerable, and, in the face of social stress there is an increased likelihood of them becoming abusive" (cited in HREOC, 1997, p. 195).

Like Connell, Hokowhitu argues that the "consumption of Western masculinity by Indigenous men served to assimilate them into the patriarchal and hypermasculine world of the coloniser" (2007, p. 333). Thus, when considering the contemporary problem of Aboriginal male violence and abuse, we have to consider the past colonial treatment of Aboriginal people, and how, with the loss of their own traditional male roles and role models, their abject treatment at the hands of the colonizers provided a new model for how Aboriginal men should treat women and children.

However, the colonial past is not the only cause of some Aboriginal men's destructive tendencies towards others and themselves, for masculinity studies suggest that this is also a product of Aboriginal men's continuing marginalization from the hegemonic ideal of masculinity. Connell examines the impact of class on gender roles and notes that the power of hegemonic masculinity subordinates the men whom it excludes, leaving them feeling powerless and insecure, yet determined to compensate for this by accentuating their masculinity. He finds that, in a "tense, freaky façade, [they make] a claim to power where there are no real resources for power" (1995, p. 111, cited in Walker, 2006, p. 7). "Protest masculinity" then, is "a masculinity that rejects and/or challenges hegemonic masculinity" (Walker, 2006, p. 7), and is best exemplified by working-class macho behavior that plays on aggression, sexism, and racism. Connell sees that protest masculinity can be divisive because it separates its proponents from their subordinated compatriots; for example, it splinters working-class men from working-class women, and white working-class men from black working-class men. As such, it is "a possible cause and consequence of . . . alienation" (Walker, 2006, p. 7).

In his analysis of working-class masculinity, Walker finds Connell's concept too narrow, so divides "protest masculinity" into two types: "anomic protest masculinity" and "disciplined protest masculinity." He uses Durkheim's concept of anomie: typically a consequence of industrialization, it is a condition where social norms are either confused, unclear, or absent, which leads to deviant behaviour. This state was preventable in cases where people are "sufficiently in contact and . . . have an active and permanent feeling of mutual dependence" (Durkheim, 1972, p. 184). Thus anomic protest masculinity arises when men are unable to live up to the expectations of hegemonic masculinity, or feel alienated by it, and the result, according to Walker, is "more than loneliness, it is an actual loss of self coupled with sensations of depressions and anxiety at some points and sensations of narcissism at others" (2006, p. 8). Walker explains that "in compensation for stigmatised work and low economic position, men will emphasise their masculinity (as through sexual prowess) as a cultural resource" (2006, p. 5), and that this can manifest in destructive ways. "Disciplined protest masculinity," on the other hand, is a "masculine identity strongly regulated by a masculine peer group," for instance, within unions or amongst blue-collar co-workers, and it helps to not only resist and protest hegemonic masculinity, but also to censure and avert anomic protest masculinity (p. 9). Walker contends that "disciplined protest masculinity can emerge among any group of men who have the need for solidarity in the face of anomic conditions" (p. 21).

The destructive posturing and conduct of Aboriginal men is evidently an example of anomic protest masculinity. Indigenous men have played no part in creating the normative roles for how Australian men should behave, so some have instead adopted deviant behaviors because their own masculine norms have been confused or obliterated by colonization. David Ross, the director of the Central Land Council (CLC), acknowledged this state of Indigenous anomie: "There are a large number of Aboriginal men from remote areas who have never had an education, never had a job and find it difficult to reconcile their role as traditional men in a modern society. They feel powerless and deeply alienated from the rest of the population" (CLC, 2006a).

Therefore, a consideration of Aboriginal masculinity in structural terms rather than cultural and ethnic terms points to constructive ways to address the dysfunctional behavior of some Aboriginal men. Walker's thesis suggests how Aboriginal men might communally develop a disciplined masculine identity that regulates anomic tendencies, without having to submit to the dominance of hegemonic masculinity, which in Australia is saturated with colonial discourses, and gives rise to hypocrisy and paternalism. Rather than being forced to adopt Western ways, Aboriginal leaders contend that upholding traditional cultural practices such as men's initiation ceremonies and reinforcing male roles is the key. CLC chairman Lindsay Bookie posits that "Maintaining these ceremonial traditions is healthy. They help to preserve order and protocols in Aboriginal society, provide young Aboriginal people with their place within their own society and enrich Aboriginal people's lives. They are important to maintaining identity and contribute to a functional society" (CLC, 2006b).

Outside of continuing traditional cultural practices, Aboriginal men might emulate disciplined protest masculinity by "stand[ing] up and speak[ing] out" against anomic tendencies such as "drunkenness and domestic violence" (CLC, 2006a), or highlighting Indigenous male roles that counter the prevailing stereotypes of dysfunction. In early 2008, Indigenous curator Djon Mundine developed a photographic exhibition by Aboriginal men called

More Than My Skin. He argued that "Aboriginal men are sick of being stereo-typed as paedophiles, wife abusers or alcoholics," and wanted to prove that "contrary to common perceptions, they hold down jobs, pay taxes, bring up families and own homes" ("Go Beyond," 2008). Masculinity studies provides a useful lens to analyze both the demeaning representations of Aboriginal men and also the anomic and dysfunctional behaviors of some Aboriginal men. Through discussions of masculinity as a whole and comparisons with other marginalized masculinities, the structural factors that contribute to the problems both faced and caused by some Aboriginal men can be better understood.

Conclusion

Looking back at the Howard government's time in office, we can see that the image of a universal dysfunctional Aboriginal masculinity was frequently mobilized in order to justify the government's efforts to dismantle the cov-enant rights of Indigenous people and resist the global tide of decolonization. The apogee of this endeavor was the Emergency Response Northern Territory Intervention, which enabled the government to take control over the income and land of Indigenous Northern Territorians within the prescribed area and to implement race-based bans and controls over that entire population. This was apparently introduced in order to eradicate the violence and sexual abuse that had ravaged remote communities and introduce order and normality. Tragically, the sense of anomic powerlessness that contributed to causing the abuse through some men and male youths harnessing their masculinity in dysfunctional ways can only be exacerbated by such harsh controls. A study conducted in March 2008 found that 90 percent of respondents have had serious problems with the Intervention's income management scheme, and 74 percent said this caused "problems within families." Moreover, the vast majority said they had experienced increased racism, and 85 percent were opposed to the Intervention (Ravens, 2008).

It is ironic to remember that one of the first Indigenous issues the How-ard government had to address was the *Bringing Them Home* report, which outlined the long-term suffering of Aboriginal children who were removed from their parents by government agents and placed in the hands of non-Indigenous caregivers and institutions, resulting in one in three reporting that they had suffered physical abuse and one in ten sexual abuse. Over his eleven years as prime minister, Howard had effectively erased these particular details from national memory, and mobilized support for his interventionist

Aboriginal policy, which asserted the neoliberal ethos of individual responsibility over collective rights. The handmaidens to this cultural shift to the Right were the conservative media and academics who sparked the "history wars" and also invoked the specter of a predatory black masculinity in their rewriting of Australia's violent colonial history as one of benign settlement and civilized enlightenment.

With Howard now gone, it is difficult to predict what the future for Indigenous Australians will be and whether or not Aboriginal men will again be demonized for political ends. So far the Labor government has shown its support by offering a formal apology to the Stolen Generations, establishing a new Indigenous representative body, the National Congress of Australia's First Peoples, and ratifying the UN Declaration on the Rights of Indigenous People. Further, its new Closing the Gap on Indigenous Disadvantage policy has refrained from blaming poor health, employment, and education outcomes on Indigenous individuals or cultural dysfunction. However, the government has also refused to offer any compensation to the Stolen Generations, and ignored the recommendations of the Northern Territory Emergency Response Review it launched in 2008 by maintaining some of Howard's measures, including the income management scheme, which it now hopes to extend to all welfare recipients, both Indigenous and non-Indigenous. We can only hope that the government might be able to work with Aboriginal communities and together solve the structural problems of poverty and alienation that have marginalized Aboriginal men.

Notes

1. Today's indigenous Tasmanians, largely descended from the women who had been taken to offshore islands by European sealers, had to fight for recognition, which has only been conceded in recent decades.

2. *Whitewash* in turn incited its own critical response, *Washout: On the Academic Response to the Fabrication of Aboriginal History* (Dawson, 2004), by Windschuttle acolyte John Dawson, and published by Windschuttle's own press.

3. Kerry McCallum found in her study of media stories between 2000 and 2006 that "there was a pattern of sharp 'spikes' in reporting [of Indigenous violence], followed by very limited interest in Indigenous issues" (McCallum, 2007, p. 7).

4. Rogers's interview on *Lateline* was just one in a series of reports ostensibly exposing the problem of domestic violence in remote Aboriginal communities. One month earlier the program's host Tony Jones interviewed an anonymous ex-youth worker who had alleged that sexual abuse was rife amongst the community leaders at Mutitjulu, who are the traditional owners of Australia's iconic monolith Uluru (formerly known as Ayer's Rock). Whilst the ABC is often regarded as a Left-wing institution,

under the Howard government it was constantly investigated for its political bias. Yet, *Lateline*'s stories on Aboriginal male violence illustrate that the ABC was capable of sharing the government's sympathies and perhaps inadvertently serving its interests. It was later found, although barely reported, that its key source, the aforementioned anonymous ex-youth worker, was in fact one of Indigenous Affairs minister "Mal Brough's personal staffers," and that their interview which denigrated the community leaders as sexual predators coincided with the government's attempt to take control of the Mutitjulu Community Aboriginal Corporation (MCAC) (Stringer, 2007, para. 17). According to Jennifer Martiniello, "the content of the interview was laden with myths and mistruths," and the "staffer in question failed to appear when summoned before a Senate inquiry to explain" (cited in Stringer, 2007). However, by the time the courts were able to review MCAC's case, the Howard government had already seized control of all communities under its Emergency Response Northern Territory Intervention (Stringer, 2007). Ironically, the Intervention's separate racially based laws contradicted Brough's and Howards's claims that all Australians "should all be treated in the same way." While the cited cases of abuse are utterly appalling, it must be remembered that they are still relatively few in a community of more than 60,000 people, yet the Intervention punishes all equally, regardless of their culpability.

5. Unfortunately, Aboriginal women still face this kind of abuse. In an extreme example, three government inquiries in the 1990s found that Aboriginal women had been subject to "assault, sexual assault, or sexual harassment" by police officers (Kimm, 2004, p. 29).

References

Abbott, T. (2006, June 21). Few Aboriginal Communities Can Govern Themselves. *The Age.*

"Aboriginals Threaten to Ban Tourists from Uluru." (2008, June 21). *Brisbane Times.*

Atkinson, J. (1990). Violence in Aboriginal Australia: Colonization and Its Impact on Gender. *Refractory Girl, 36,* 21–24.

Bederman, G. (1995). *Manliness and Civilization: A Cultural History of Gender and Race in the United States, 1880–1917.* Chicago: University of Chicago Press.

Behrendt, L. (2000). Consent in a (Neo)Colonial Society: Aboriginal Women as Sexual and Legal "Other." *Australian Feminist Studies, 15*(33), 353–67.

Behrendt. L. (2005, March). Back to the Future: The Shift Back to Failed Policies of "Mainstreaming" Indigenous Affairs Is Irresponsible. *Arena Magazine.*

Board of Inquiry into the Protection of Aboriginal Children from Sexual Abuse. (2007). *Ampe Akelyernemane Meke Mekarle "Little Children Are Sacred": Report of the Northern Territory Board of Inquiry into the Protection of Aboriginal Children from Sexual Abuse.* Darwin: Northern Territory Government.

Bonnell, A., & Crotty, M. (2008). Australia's History under Howard, 1996–2007. *ANNALS of the American Academy of Political and Social Science, 617,* 149–65.

Carney, J. (2006, July 21). Men Prey on Customary Law. *Australian.*

Central Land Council (CLC). (2006a, May 16). "CLC Speaks Out on Violence" *CLC Media Release*. Retrieved April 22, 2008 from: http://www.clc.org.au/media/releases/2006/violence.asp

Central Land Council (CLC). (2006b, September 8). "Aboriginal Culture, Sexual Abuse, the Media . . ." *CLC Media Release*. Retrieved April 22, 2008, from: http://www.clc.org.au/media/releases/2006/sex_abuse.asp

Connell, R. W. (1995). *Masculinities*. St. Leonards, Australia: Allen & Unwin.

Connell, R. W. (2005). Globalization, Imperialism, and Masculinities. In M. S. Kimmel, J. Hearn, & R. W. Connell (Eds). *Handbook of Studies on Men and Masculinities* (pp. 71–89). Thousand Oaks, Calif.: Sage.

Crotty, M. (2001). *Making the Australian Male: Middle-Class Masculinity, 1870–1920*. Carlton, Australia: Melbourne University Press.

Cunningham, J., & Baeza, J. I. (2005). An "Experiment" in Indigenous Social Policy: The Rise and Fall of Australia's Aboriginal and Torres Strait Islander Commission (ATSIC). *Policy & Politics, 33*(3), 461–73.

Curthoys, A. (2008). Genocide in Tasmania: The History of an Idea. In Dirk Moses (Ed.), *Empire, Colony, Genocide: Conquest, Occupation, and Subaltern Resistance in World History* (pp. 229–52). New York: Berghahn Books.

Dawson, J. (2004). *Washout: On the Academic Response to the Fabrication of Aboriginal History*. Sydney: Macleay Press.

Delgado, R., & Stefancic, J. (1995). Minority Men, Misery, and the Marketplace of Ideas. In M. Berger, B. Wallis, & S. Watson (Eds.), *Constructing Masculinity* (pp. 211–20). New York: Routledge.

Dodson, P. (2007). "Whatever Happened to Reconciliation?" In J. Altman and M. Hinkson (Eds.), *Coercive Reconciliation: Stabilise, Normalise, Exit Aboriginal Australia* (pp. 21–30). North Carlton, Australia: Arena Publications Association.

Dunn, M., & de Krester, L. (2001, June 15). Rape Claims an Outrage—Clark. *Herald-Sun*.

Durkheim, E. (1972). *The Division of Labor in Society*. In A. Giddens (Ed.), *Emile Durkheim: Selected Writings* (pp. 141–54). London: Cambridge University Press.

Eggers, S. (1995). Preface: An Overview of Violence in Australia. In D. Chappell & S. Egger (Eds.), *Australian Violence: Contemporary Perspectives II* (pp. xl–1). Canberra: Australian Institute of Criminology.

Fanon, F. (1967). *Black Skin, White Masks*. New York: Grove.

Frank, J. (2007). Rudd vs. Howard: Jackie Frank Puts Our Pollies to the Test. *Marie Claire Australia, 146*, 104–10.

"Go Beyond to Find Real Aboriginal Male." (2008, February 4). *West Australian*.

Graham, C. (2010, February 5). At Large: Heroes: The Great Divide. *National Indigenous Times*, 194.

Grant, S. (2001, June 26). Spare Us the White Man's "Concern" for Aborigines. *Sydney Morning Herald*, 14.

Hardin, M. (2002). Altering Masculinities: The Spanish Conquest and the Evolution of the Latin American Machismo. *International Journal of Sexuality and Gender Studies*, 7(1), 1–21.

Heinritz, L., & Josephi, B. (2006). The Framing of ATSIC Chairman Geoff Clark in the *Australian*. *Australian Studies in Journalism*, 17, 17–40.

Hinkson, M. (2007). Introduction: In the Name of the Child. In J. Altman & M. Hinkson (Eds.), *Coercive Reconciliation: Stabilise, Normalise, Exit Aboriginal Australia* (pp. 1–12). North Carlton, Australia: Arena Publications Association.

Hogg, R. (2006). The Unmanly Savage: "Aboriginalism" and Subordinate Masculinities on the Queensland Frontier. *Crossings* [online], 11(2). Retrieved March 22, 2011, from: http://www.inasa.org/crossings/11_1/index.php?apply=hogg

Hokowhitu, B. (2007). Indigenous and First Nations Masculinities. In M. Flood, J. Kegan, B. Pease, & K. Pringle (Eds). *International Encyclopedia of Men and Masculinities* (pp. 331–35). New York: Routledge.

Hokowhitu, B. (2008). The Death of Koro Paka: "Traditional" Maori Patriarchy. *Contemporary Pacific*, 20(1), 115–41.

"Howard Axes Aboriginal Body." (2004, April 15). *BBC News: Asia Pacific*.

Human Rights and Equal Opportunity Commission (HREOC). (1997). *Bringing Them Home: Report of the National Inquiry into the Separation of Aboriginal and Torres Strait Islander Children from Their Families*. Sydney: Human Rights and Equal Opportunity Commission.

Human Rights and Equal Opportunity Commission (HREOC). (2006). *Ending Family Violence and Abuse in Aboriginal and Torres Strait Islander Communities—Key Issues: An Overview Paper of Research and Findings by the Human Rights and Equal Opportunity Commission, 2001–2006*. Sydney: Human Rights and Equal Opportunity Commission.

Jones, T. (2006a, May 15). Culture of Violence Revealed in Central Australia. *Lateline*. Australian Broadcasting Corporation Transcripts.

Jones, T. (2006b, May 15). Paedophile Rings Operate in Remote Communities: Brough. *Lateline*. Australian Broadcasting Corporation Transcripts.

Jordan, W. (1968) *White Over Black: American Attitudes Toward the Negro, 1550–1812*. Chapel Hill, N.C.: University of North Carolina Press.

Kearney, S., & Wilson, A. (2006, May 16). Raping Children Part of "Men's Business." *Australian*.

Kimm, J. (2004). *A Fatal Conjunction: Two Laws Two Cultures*. Annandale: Federation Press.

Konishi, S. (2007). The Father Governor: The British Administration of Aboriginal People at Port Jackson, 1788–1792. In M. McCormack (Ed.), *Public Men: Masculinity and Politics in Modern Britain* (pp. 54–72). New York: Palgrave Macmillan.

Manderson, D. (2008). Not Yet: Aboriginal People and the Deferral of the Rule of Law. *Arena Journal*, 2(30), 219–72.

Manne, R. (Ed.). *Whitewash: On Keith Windschuttle's Fabrication of Aboriginal History*. Melbourne: Black Inc.

Marr, D. (2007, August 11). Entering Dangerous Territory. *Sydney Morning Herald*.

Matchett, S. (2001). Trial by Media or Freedom of the Press? *Sydney Institute Quarterly*, 15(5), nos. 3&4, 28–32.

McCallum, K. (2007). Indigenous Violence as a "Mediated Public Crisis." Communication, Civics, Industry, ANZCA and La Trobe University, Conference Proceedings, 1–15.

McKenna, M. (2006, May 10). Male Rape Rife among Aborigines. *Weekend Australian*, 20–22.

Moore, C. (1998a). Guest Editorial: Australian Masculinities. *Journal of Australian Studies*, 56, 1–16.

Moore, C. (1998b). Colonial Manhood and Masculinities. *Journal of Australian Studies*, 56, 35–50.

Murray, T., & Williamson, C. (2003). Archaeology and History. In R. Manne (Ed.), *Whitewash: On Keith Windschuttle's Fabrication of Aboriginal History* (pp. 311–33). Melbourne: Black Inc.

Nelson, B. (2008, February 13). Apology to Australia's Indigenous People. Retrieved May 1, 2008, from: http://www.aph.gov.au/house/Nelson_speech.pdf

New South Wales Aboriginal Child Sexual Assault Taskforce (NSW). (2006). *Breaking the Silence: Creating the Future, Addressing Child Sexual Assault in Aboriginal Communities in NSW*. Sydney: NSW Attorney General's Department.

Nowra, L. (2007). *Bad Dreaming: Aboriginal Men's Violence against Women and Children*. North Melbourne: Pluto Press.

Ravens, T. (2008, June 5). NT Intervention Has Led to Racism, Senators Told. *Canberra Times*.

Rayar, J. C. (1996). A Cross-Cultural Perspective on Violence: The View from Down Under. *University of Queensland Law Journal*, 19(1), 1–25.

Reynolds, H. (1996). *Frontier: Aborigines, Settlers, and Land*. St. Leonards, Australia: Allen & Unwin.

Rintoul, S. (2006, July 3). Aborigines Fear "New Paternalism." *The Australian*.

Robertson, B. (2000). *The Aboriginal and Torres Strait Islander Women's Task Force on Violence Report*. Queensland: Department of Aboriginal and Torres Strait Islander Policy and Development.

Rule, A. (2001, June 14). Geoff Clark: Power and Rape. *The Age*.

Ryan, L. (1981). *The Aboriginal Tasmanians*. St. Lucia: University of Queensland Press.

Sanders, W. G. (2006). Indigenous Affairs after the Howard Decade: Administrative Revolution While Defying Decolonization. *Centre for Aboriginal Economic Policy Research, Topical Issue* 3. Retrieved March 4, 2008, from: http://www.anu.edu.au/caepr

Schwarz, M. (2008). *A Question of Power: The Geoff Clark Case*. Melbourne: Black Inc.

Sinha, M. (1995). *Colonial Masculinity: The "Manly Englishman" and the "Effeminate Bengali" in the Late Nineteenth Century*. London: Manchester University Press.

Skelton, R. (2006, May 24). Spare the Victims—Remove the Violent Men. *Sydney Morning Herald*.

Sneddon, C. (2007). *Scoping Violence against Women in Australia*. New South Wales: Australian Domestic and Family Violence Clearinghouse.

Stateline Northern Territory Transcripts. (2007). Coordination Needed to Combat Sex Abuse. Retrieved April 11, 2008, from: http://www.abc.net.au/stateline/nt/content/2006/s1953014.htm

Stone, J. (2008, April). Time to Stop the Dreaming. *Quadrant*, 48–54.

Stringer, R. (2007). A Nightmare of the Neocolonial Kind: Politics of Suffering in Howard's Northern Territory Intervention. *Borderlands e-journal*, 6(2). Retrieved April 11, 2008, from: http://www.borderlands.net.au/vol6no2_2007/stringer_intervention.htm

Walker, G. W. (2006). Disciplining Protest Masculinity. *Men and Masculinities*, 9(5), 5–22.

Williams, N. M., & Jolly, L. (1992). From Time Immemorial? Gender Relations in Aboriginal Societies before "White Contact." In K. Saunders and R. Evans (Eds.), *Gender Relations in Australia: Domination and Negotiation* (pp. 9–19). Sydney: Harcourt Brace Jovanovich.

Windschuttle, K. (2002). *The Fabrication of Aboriginal History: Volume 1: Van Diemen's Land, 1803–1847*. Sydney: Macleay Press.

8

Beyond Jackie Chan

MURALI BALAJI

In recent years, cultural theorists and other media scholars have noted the impact that globalization has had on media representations. For scholars such as Fiske (1997), globalization has had an empowering impact on audiences. He argues that "global capitalism has no choice but to recognize that it has to deal with multiple markets," and as a result, the cultural industries "will have to stop claiming the national as their local and will have to be explicitly localized or denationalized" (Fiske, 1997, pp. 58, 64). But Fiske's celebration of the new global audience and the "eroding" power of the cultural industries overlooks an important point. The control over images is *not* in the hands of consumers, but tightly bound to the media producers. The production of images is controlled by multinational cultural industries whose primary task is to make money for their shareholders. While the production of these images might be shaped by various stages of cultural work, they are ultimately tied to the resources of the corporation (Ryan, 1992; Banks, 2007; Hesmondhalgh, 2007). Valuable cultural texts, as scholars such as Hesmondhalgh (2007) note, are produced, but they are of secondary importance to the corporations' bottom-line imperative in the cultural production process. In an age of global media, cultural texts are being exchanged at increasingly rapid rates, yet the production of culture remains in the hands of a handful of corporate conglomerates (Bettig, 1996; McChesney, 2004).

But cultural production is not just an economic process; it also an ideological one that is grounded in Western control of the cultural industries. Despite the fact that countries such as India and China produce thousands of cultural products that generate millions in revenues for local producers, their distribution remains in the hands of Western conglomerates such as Disney, News Corp., and Universal. As a result, representations of Asia and Asian identities continue to be controlled by a Western filter. More importantly, despite the globalization of media and the supposed celebration of multiculturalism, representations of Asian masculinity in film and television have, for the most part, remained Othered. While the West continues to be fascinated with Asia and the growing numbers of Asian women on screen, ranging from Gong Li, Lucy Liu, and Frieda Pinto in the movies and Padma Lakshmi and Ming Na on television, representations of Asian masculinity— shaped largely by both Orientalist constructs and the bottom-line considerations of Anglo-dominated media companies—are few and far between.

The depictions of Asian men, particularly their masculine identities, are products of both ideology and economics. While postcolonial scholars such as Bhabha (1994) and Said (2003) argue that Asian masculinity in the media is a product of the former, an I-Other discourse, I believe that these representations are equally informed by economic considerations. As I have argued in my works on South Asian representations in the media, media companies seek to benefit from those images that are financially beneficial. In this chapter, I seek to show how and why presenting alternative and diverse images of Asian men in Western media run contrary to the interests of the media institutions charged with producing cultural texts.

Negus (1998, 2004) argues that culture produces industry and industry produces culture. I would argue, however, that industry produces *caricature*. These caricatures not only benefit the corporations that produce them, but they serve to uphold a white patriarchal worldview, one where Asian men are either marginalized, vilified, or made into comic objects that serve as visual contrasts to hegemonic maleness. Moreover, in an age of market consolidation, these representations are more impactful than ever before. Using the *Rush Hour* trilogy as a case study, I sketch out how Asian[1] masculinity is Othered in order to conform to ideologies *and* the corporations' pursuit of profit.

The Political Economy of Identity

Numerous studies on the media portrayals of Asian and Asian American masculinity have emphasized the marginalization and emasculation of Asian men in film and television. For example, Shek (2006) argues that Asian and Asian American masculinity "has been externally defined" and as a result, they "are then subordinated, as are other forms of masculinity, such as those among men of color, gay men and bisexual men" (p. 383). But Chan (2000) adds that the Asian masculinity advanced by Bruce Lee became "co-opted by the media industry into another stereotype of Asian men: the chop-socky, kung-fu fighting Asian American male" (p. 372). As a result, Asian masculinity has been primarily depicted on opposite ends of one-dimensionality: either as effeminate and wimpy or as hypersexual. Nakayama (1994) adds to this notion by arguing that depictions of Asian and Asian American masculinity serve to "re-center" white masculinity by creating a normative/Other paradigm. Nakayama argues that these images are popular in films such as *Showdown in Little Tokyo*, which help to depict Asian masculinity as marginal and in opposition to heroic white masculinity.

The aforementioned scholars' assessment of mediated Asian masculinity overlooks an important aspect of understanding these representations. This is because critical race theory and postcolonial theory might explain the ideologies behind images of Asians in Western media, but they fail to account for how these depictions are, in effect, industrialized. This is why political economy is a valuable tool. As scholars such as Bettig (1996), Ryan (1992), McChesney (2004), and Hesmondhalgh (2007) have argued, understanding the role that media oligopolies play in the shaping of the cultural industries is critical to how texts are constructed. Meehan (2005) notes that because of media consolidation and the exertion of control by the culture industries, "we may need to rethink assumptions about program content and popular culture" (p. 122). Similarly, I argue for postcolonial scholars to examine the political economy of identity, which examines how cultural production of mediated identities is shaped by economic processes (Balaji, 2008, 2009). The representations of Asian masculinity, particularly in American television shows and films, are grounded in stereotypes and presented as the opposite of the hegemonic (white) masculinity that has been constructed as the ideal (Connell, 2001).

Corporations have little interest in producing diverse images of Asian men because there is simply little economic benefit. As media companies consolidated at an alarming rate in the 1990s and 2000s, images of racial and ethnic minorities became more narrowly cast and relied upon stereotypical tropes. Media producers chose to either make Asian men invisible or represent them as villains, buffoons, sidekicks, or irreconcilable Others (Nakayama, 1994; Shu, 2003; Shek, 2006). For example, in films such as *The Fast and the Furious* (2000) and *The Fast and the Furious III: Tokyo Drift* (2006), *Die Another Day* (2002), *Rambo* (2008), and *The Mummy III* (2008), Asian male characters are presented as evil and as obstacles to the white male protagonist. This theme is also evident in the remake of *The Karate Kid* (2010), in which an African

American teen must "conquer" his Chinese rivals in a Kung-Fu competition. In films such as *The Guru* (2001), *How High* (2001), *Van Wilder* (2002), and the *Harold & Kumar* series (2004, 2008), Asian men are presented as buffoons or as sidekicks for the main characters.[2] These caricatures of Asian men and the trivialization of masculinity are important in not only upholding hegemonic masculine ideologies but also the capitalist system that profits from them (hooks, 2003; Chan, 2000). Moreover, Towbin et al. (2003) note that in conflicts between whites and Asians, white men win and are portrayed as both stronger and more intelligent than their Asian counterparts.

While scholars such as hooks (1994; 2003) and Collins (2005) have blamed an abstract "white patriarchal capitalism," the production of Asian masculinity is a far more complex process. Corporations are motivated to produce for profits, but the representations of cultural identity—specifically of cultural Others—are often grounded in what studio executives believe is an accurate representation of cultural identities. These representations are not malicious in intent, but devastating in their ideological impact (Uchida, 1998; Paek & Shah, 2003). To understand why corporations stick to these formatted representations of cultural identity despite the changing demography of Western society and the makeup of audiences who consumer these images, one must understand the political economy of culture through the cultural industries approach.

Jhally (1989) argues that cultural industries cannot be looked at as merely content producers, but corporations whose desire to cater to public interest must intersect with profit demands. As he notes, "the media here are literally an industry which attempts to produce a form of consciousness in the audience that benefits the class that controls the media and industry in general. . . . They are owned and controlled by the corporations who have concentrated wealth and power in their hands. They thus reflect the needs of their owners" (p. 68). Jhally's argument lends credibility to the idea that representations of Others—in this case, Asian men—are controlled by multinational corporations with little incentive to change what has been profitable: the (re)production of images that lampoon or typecast Asian masculinity while upholding the white hegemonic masculine ideal. Shu (2003) affirms this notion, arguing that depictions in kung-fu movies, including Jackie Chan films, cater to the consumption styles of middle-class consumers. Notions of culture and identity, Shu concludes, come second to making money.

But while profits are the primary consideration, the cultural products produced by the cultural industries must also warrant examination, as more nuanced works in political economy show. The cultural industries, as scholars such as Ryan (1992), Hesmondhalgh (2007), and Banks (2007) argue, are complex institutions governed by both their economic imperatives and, to a lesser extent, the culture they are tasked with producing. Hesmondhalgh (2007) argues that the "cultural industries have a dual role—as economic systems of production and cultural producers of texts"—and that "we need to take account of both the politics of redistribution, focused on issues of political economy, and the politics of recognition, focused on questions of cultural identity" (p. 47). Taking Hesmondhalgh's approach into consideration, it must also be noted that representations of Otherness have been reproduced through formats that allow corporations to manage the creative processes of cultural production. Ryan (1992) argues that "formats have played a crucial role in consolidating the conditions of creative (as opposed to artistic) work and sedimenting professional cultural practice" (p. 138). By formatting cultural production, Ryan argues, "corporations can administer the creative stage in a manner which systematically supplies them with the originals they need to expand in an unpredictable and competitive market" (p. 184). These production formats often lead to on-screen identity "molds." In television, Asian American men appear more often as gay friends, servers, or mere background props. As I noted earlier, the rise of Asian and Asian American women in television and films has been matched by the conspicuous absence or marginalization of Asian and Asian American men. Though there are exceptions, the most prevalent depictions of Asian men and their masculinity in popular media continue to play upon stereotypes. Without the pressure of having to change on-screen portrayals of Asian men, media producers continue to re-create, recycle, and repackage representations of Asian masculinity (Meehan, 2005). The cultural industries' willingness to go with formatted representations rather than take perceived risks by diversifying them has, in effect, kept Asian maleness and notions of their masculinity restricted to the confines of Otherness.

But cultural industries approaches must be grounded within a larger political economic framework. Critical race theory and postcolonial scholarship often dwell on the politics of representation without taking into consideration the economic function of the cultural industries. As Sayer (2001) argues, producing culture must not be conflated with the economic systems of production and distribution that govern the cultural industries, for they are, after all corporations. Sayer and other scholars of political economy have argued that notions of cultural production have too often focused on cultural and not enough on the economics of production and distribution. Indeed, if representing cultural identities were deemed unprofitable for private corporations, then they would have no incentive to represent diversity in the marketplace of consumption.

This is why films such as *Rush Hour*, masked under the guise of multiculturalism, are so effective in wedding ideologies with economic considerations. As the next section will show, the box office sales of the film went hand in hand with the Orientalist constructions of Asian masculinity and the neo-minstrelsy the film sought to project.

Case Study: Asian Masculinity as Neo-Minstrelsy in *Rush Hour*

No media product has been as exemplary in highlighting both the political economy of identity and the ideologies of Otherness than the *Rush Hour* trilogy. The film franchise, which features an African American cop played by Chris Tucker and his Hong Kong "sidekick" played by Jackie Chan, has grossed nearly $850 million in international sales by exploiting hackneyed jokes about Chinese male sexuality and the stereotype that Asians are predisposed to martial arts. As Banerjee (2006) notes, the *Rush Hour* films are reflective of a new type of minstrelsy in which Asian male characters have to don another type of blackface—signified by caricatured representations of their behaviors—in order to have on-screen legitimacy. The *Rush Hour* films copy popular buddy action flicks, reproducing a format that has yielded Hollywood billions in revenues through earlier movies such as *48 Hours, Lethal Weapon, Bad Company,* and *Running Scared*. The interracial aspect of these films, often with a white main character and an African American comedic sidekick, are played up, usually as a source of comedic tension. As Ryan (1992) notes, *Rush Hour* follows a format of cultural production that corporations use to minimize risk and maximize return on investment. However, such "safe" bets also rely on archaic notions of Asian masculinity, drawing upon decades-old stereotypes that continue to resonate among Western consumers (Ling, 1997). Though Asian Americans have made strides in representation, and films such as *Harold & Kumar, The Namesake,* and *Better Luck Tomorrow* have presented Asian men in multiple forms, it has been much easier—and profitable—to keep Asian men Othered and "foreign."

The genius of *Rush Hour*, at least from its producers' point of view, is that it made economic sense to create, recycle, and reproduce the same stereotypes about Asian men while representing the expanse of Chinese culture as an easily consumable Other. The film's producer, New Line, a subsidiary of Warner Bros., was able to make the three films into a single "thread" without altering the plotline. This, as Meehan (2005) notes, is tantamount to re-versioning, which allows the producer to "sell" the movie franchise without having to make significant alterations. Though Jackie Chan plays a Hong Kong detective in the series, the primary aim of *Rush Hour* is to universalize Asian masculinity and somehow make its expansiveness and diversity into a consumable commodity for the Western audience. This universalization of Asian masculinity is in line with Jhally's (1989) argument that culture becomes industrialized for the purpose of mass reproduction. In this case, Chan's character fits with the trope of Asian masculinity that has been produced and distributed to Western audiences for decades. To better understand how Chan's character in these films conforms to a widely reproduced stereotype of Asian masculinity, one must understand the plot of the *Rush Hour* films. The *Rush Hour* trilogy essentially follows the same plot as most action-comedy "buddy" movies, but as Meehan (2005) notes, the product is cleverly "re-versioned" so that it retains the façade of originality. The popularity of co-stars Chan and Chris Tucker, even before the film, also served to allow the film's distributor, New Line, to focus marketing efforts on them without needing to "give away" the story. In other words, this was an action flick that did not need any extra marketing campaigns—due to the stars' name recognition and the promise of a slapstick martial arts plot, the film largely marketed itself.

To showcase the replication of Asian male Otherness in these films, I watched the *Rush Hour* trilogy, keeping in mind Condit's (1989) idea of making informed interpretations of texts. This section will highlight some key scenes from the movies, linking them with larger themes of Asian masculinity and how these representations factor into the economics and ideologies of Otherness. The interpretation of these scenes was aided by frameworks by Bailey (1988) and Condit (1989), who argue that analysis of visual texts must be referenced with the cultural histories of such images. Watching *Rush Hour* involved reading the texts using the historical contexts of images, particularly how these images have evolved in Western popular culture.

In the first *Rush Hour,* Detective James Carter (Tucker) is forced to "babysit" Hong Kong cop Lee (Chan) during an investigation into the kidnapping of a Chinese diplomat's daughter. When the two first meet at the Los Angeles Airport, Carter starts speaking to Lee, only to find Lee staring at him with a smile. Exasperated, Carter asks Lee, "Do you understand the words that are coming out of my mouth?" While this line was meant to draw laughs and play upon the culture clash between an African American and his Chinese counterpart, it also reinforces the Otherness of Asian men. The language jokes continue in the first film, and at the end credits, there are numerous outtakes highlighting Chan's failure to grasp the English language. In addition to mock-ing Lee's command of the English language, Carter also makes fun of Lee's sexuality, a common theme that emerges in the two sequels of the film. The punch line, which is either explicitly stated or implied, is that Asian men do not have sexual prowess. This has echoed popular representations of Asian men as either emasculated or having very small penises. As Ling (1997) notes, "the West's willful 'feminization' of Asian men . . . is premised on its aware-ness of its power relationship with the East, as well as the tacit assumption that powerless Asians will not challenge the established West-East hierarchy and are therefore harmless" (p. 315). Similarly, as Espiritu (1997) and Shek (2006) argue, constructions of Asian masculinity in film can make Asian men hyper-masculine and render them effeminate *simultaneously*. Carter's belittling of Lee throughout the trilogy does exactly that.

The Asian men's sexuality jokes did not hinder *Rush Hour*'s box office sales. In fact, judging from the sales of the sequels, they were good for business and cemented the film's brand. The minimizing of Asian men's sexual potency cre-ates the impression that they are unable to achieve the hegemonic male status of (hetero) hypersexuality, a position that Tucker's character occupies by virtue of his charms. Paradoxically, the film portrays every Chinese man in the film as being able to fight martial arts, another trope of Asian masculinity that has yielded millions in box office and video sales. The economics of martial arts and its connection to Asian men made Chan—who was a megastar in Hong Kong before making his U.S. debut in the 1995 film *Rumble in the Bronx*—a natural fit. More importantly, the mystification of Chinese masculinity in the West allowed U.S. media companies to import films by Chan and another Chinese martial arts star, Jet Li, to a large Western audience.

In *Rush Hour*, Lee and most of the Chinese men in the film are adept at some form of martial arts. However, Carter is ultimately able to defeat them using his own superior martial arts skills, despite having no training to speak of. Carter, as the representation of the hegemonic Western masculine ideal, symbolically conquers the East—the Other—through his impressive martial arts performance. Though Carter is African American, he assumes the role of the white male protagonist who asserts his domination over his Asian counterparts, similar to Tom Cruise's domination of his Japanese male coun-terparts in *The Last Samurai,* Seann William Scott's role as the chosen one in *Bulletproof Monk,* and Uma Thurman—who, like Tucker, is symbolically thrust into the white male protagonist role—defeating an army of Yakuza gangsters with her sword in *Kill Bill, Vol. 1* (Tierney, 2006). As Tierney (2006) argues, the cultural appropriation of the Other upholds the "right" of whiteness to take over other cultures while vilifying those who stand in the way of that right. In each of the aforementioned films, Asian male (and female) characters symbolically and physically stand in the way of such appropriation, and in doing so, they are destroyed by the protagonist. Though Tucker is the "stand-in," he shows how he can appropriate martial arts and, with the help of Chan, defeat any opposition presented by Chinese men.

In *Rush Hour 2,* the appropriation of Chinese culture becomes a punch line, as Tucker's character confronts a character played by Don Cheadle. In the scenes, Carter upbraids Cheadle's character for taking on Chinese culture—in this case, by wearing traditional Chinese clothes, running a Chinese wing store, and marrying a Chinese woman—and not "keeping it real" by being "true" to his African American identity. The inference in this scene is that Cheadle somehow lowered himself by "becoming" a Chinese man, who in the hierarchy of Western constructed masculinity, is somehow less of a man. As Eng (2001) also notes, the racial castration of Asian men places them symbolically in the bottom of masculine hierarchies, making it unacceptable for Westerners to aspire to their place. However, Cheadle's character in *Rush Hour,* as well as Cruise's character in *The Last Samurai,* takes the place of Asian men by seemingly conquering the culture. In other words, they continue to assert their superiority within these substitution roles (Tierney, 2006). While Cheadle's "yellowface" is meant to draw laughs, it reaffirms the hierarchies of race and masculinity, and by doing so, continues to reify Asian men's Otherness.

Another theme of the *Rush Hour* films is the idea of sameness, more specifically, the sameness of the Other. In other words, Asian men—regardless of their ethnic or national backgrounds—can somehow be lumped in together as a homogenous and emasculated whole. Chinese men become props in the film's action sequences, and in fight scenes Carter and Lee use them as punching bags that continually absorb the heroes' blows—much to the audience's delight. Moreover, their interchangeability as the objects of Lee and Carter's punches and kicks highlight the notion of sameness. For example, in a fight scene in the second *Rush Hour,* Carter accidentally hits Lee. When Lee asks why Carter him, he responds, "Y'all look alike to me." This blending of Asian masculinity into nondistinctive Otherness is even more apparent—and troubling—in the third installment. The movie starts with an attempted assassination of a Chinese diplomat, which causes Lee to pursue the assassin across the city. When he finally catches up to the assassin, it is learned that the villain is Lee's Japanese adopted brother Kenji, who somehow becomes a leader in the Chinese Triad gang. At several times in the film, Kenji speaks to Lee in Japanese, to which Lee responds by speaking in Chinese. Beyond the utter implausibility of such an exchange, the deeper implication of this scene is that Japan and China's complex history—which included the Japanese takeover of China prior to World War II—must be ignored because Japanese and Chinese men are basically the same. By ignoring the complexities of Chinese and Japanese masculinity, as well as the tensions that exist between cultures, the film's producers are asking viewers to buy in to the idea of Asia as a homogeneous and interchangeable Other. Holtzman (2000) and Towbin et al. (2003) note that Asian cultural identities are "collapsed" into one in order to make the notion of a homogeneous Asian identity consumable for white audiences.

This sameness is shown in other significant ways. The fight scenes and the cultural clashes, which might have appeared humorous in the first film, become downright cartoonish in the third movie. By the third installment, Lee's masculinity is defined by repeated allusions to his sexual impotency and his loyalty to his job, both stereotypical traits attributed to Asian men (Eng, 2001; Tierney, 2006). The conflation between Asian male Otherness as the opposite of normative (Western) masculinity is expressed throughout the film series, but in *Rush Hour 3*, the Asian jokes and allusions to the impotency and Otherness of Asian men become hyperbolic, reaching a point of going beyond humor. In one scene that mocks Chinese names, Carter begins an Abbott and Costello dialogue with the leader of a martial arts studio, an older bald man with a long Fu Manchu moustache. Carter asks, "Who are you?" to which the man responds "Yu." The scene continues, including an interjection from one of the elder's assistants who says, "I am Mi." The confusion over "Yu" and "Mi" ends with Carter threatening to beat up the elder, prompting Lee to haplessly plead for Carter to end the conversation. While the sequence becomes more and more outrageous, particularly through the use of Chinese male names as pronouns, it also indicates the producers' level of comfort in enacting the scene with little regard for issues of cultural sensitivity.

In another scene that highlights this hyperbole, when Carter and Lee go to Paris to pursue the Triads, who are behind the attempted assassination of the Chinese consul, they get into a long fight scene with Triad assassins. One of the vanquished assassins speaks to Carter in French, to which Carter asks Lee, "What kind of Chinamen speaks French?" The assumption in this sequence is that Chinese men can only speak English or Chinese, and that if they speak another language they are immediately out-of-place. The man is subsequently tortured by Carter and Lee—with the blessing of a French nun who acts as a translator—until he gives in. The torture of the Triad mirrors scenes in movies such as *Donnie Brasco* and Jet Li's *Kiss of the Dragon,* where Asian men are brutally beaten until they are killed. While *Rush Hour*'s torture scene does not result in the death of the Triad member, there is an implicit claim in the sequence that Chinese men are allowed to be tortured and brutalized as a consequence of their Otherness.

Analysis: The Economics of Othering Asian Masculinity

The *Rush Hour* trilogy's success at the box office reaffirmed two assumptions for movie executives: re-treaded action plot lines and stereotypical notions of Asian manhood often lead to a return on investment. At a time when media mergers are leading to fewer investments in innovative and original ideas in film and television, more studios and production houses are relying on the tried-and-true tropes, especially if they generate little backlash. While the films played to the stereotypes of Asian men and exaggerated their Otherness, there were no public objections raised by Asian American groups.

The implicit *acceptance* of these caricatured representations by Asian American media watchdog groups is troubling, especially since it gives media companies little incentive—financial or social—to change the way they produce depictions of Asian masculinity. While representations of Asian femininity do continue to draw from stereotypes drawn from Orientalist fetishes, Asian and Asian American women have become increasingly integrated—and assimilated—into the cultural industries (Paek & Shah, 2003). However, as noted in the previous section, portrayals of Asian masculinity have stayed remarkably consistent in their Otherness. While television shows such as *Heroes, House,* and *Law & Order: SVU* have shown diversity and multi-dimensionality in their Asian male characters, representations in film have been far less progressive. Perhaps, as scholars such as Hesmondhalgh (2007) note, the film industry is under more pressure to meet returns on their investments, and as a result, they must be risk-averse when it comes to diverse representations. Images that threaten the hegemonic male ideal might not be good for overall sales, and as a result, are shelved in favor of those that recycle stereotypes and exploited tropes (Ling, 1997; Balaji, 2008).

In postcolonial discourse, representations of Asian masculinity are grounded in power relations and an inescapable Western gaze (Bhabha, 1994; Chan, 2000; Said, 2003). Similarly, in poststructural approaches to the cultural industries, scholars argue that the values of executives play a significant role in the cultural production process. Negus (2004) argues that the backgrounds of executives tasked with overseeing cultural production can make ideologies—particularly notions of Otherness—a factor in how texts are created and how identities are represented. But in the cultural industries, ideologies must be tied in with the bottom line: corporate profit imperatives. If Asian masculinity had been merely Othered for the sake of power relations, it would hold little merit to the corporations tasked with producing culture. However, if the marginalizing, vilifying, and lampooning of Asian masculinity are financially fruitful for corporate producers of culture, then—in the absence of any financially viable alternatives—Othering becomes a wise business decision.

As Jhally (1989) notes, ideologies must often take a backseat to the profit imperatives of large corporations, but a cultural product is most effective when it merges ideology with profitability. In the case of *Rush Hour*, Othering of Asian masculinity was an ideal marriage of both economics and ideologies. The films grossed hundreds of millions of dollars, while the images in the film upheld Orientalist notions of Asian manhood. The representations of Asian men in *Rush Hour* are part of a cultural production formula based in part in consumers' familiarity with the stereotypes of Asian masculinity: their lack of sexuality, their clumsiness. Moreover, the binary of hero-Other that has manifested itself in so many Western films becomes an important aspect of *Rush Hour* that has helped its commercial success. In the production of films, particularly the action genre, the Other is often unsympathetic and made to be a monotonous evil, such as the Borg in *Star Trek* or the Nazis in the *Indiana Jones films*. The hero-Other binary is one of the most successful formats used by Hollywood and other Western filmmakers because it gives the audience few complexities in terms of character development and plot, and it is easily reproduced (Meehan, 2005). By reproducing and re-versioning Asian masculinity over the years, it has become apparent that Asian men have become an easy Other, subject to being lampooned or destroyed by the protagonists—even if, in the case of *Rush Hour*, an Asian male is complicit in their destruction.

Conclusion: Getting beyond Jackie Chan?

Because of the Orientalist constructs that have shaped Western media, films such as the *Rush Hour* trilogy, *Big Trouble in Little China*, *The Last Dragon*, and *Shanghai Knights* (and its sequel, *Shanghai Noon*) continue to be produced and to draw mass audiences. In addition, films such as *The Guru*, *The Love Guru*, and *Bride and Prejudice* also continue to have some mass appeal by exploiting notions of Asian Otherness. The saturation of these films in the media marketplace and the lack of images that challenge the West-East hierarchies make these films especially problematic. When taken alone, a movie such as *Rush Hour* and its representations of Asian masculinity can seem innocuously comedic. However, the pervasiveness of these representations of Asian men as the Other in popular media make *Rush Hour* a force in cultivating and reifying this Otherness. While scholars such as Rotundo (1994) and Connell (2001) argue that one way to change the perceptions of masculinity is to diversify representations of men in Western popular culture, it can be argued that diverse representations of masculinity in Western media exist—for white men. As Ling (1997) notes, it has been very difficult for cultural producers to move past West-East hierarchies in the shaping of Asian male representations, even if those representations are archaic and inaccurate.

Part of changing representations of Asian masculinity is to change how we consume cultural texts. While black men continue to face issues of Otherness in popular culture, most producers of culture have shifted away from representing black masculinity in ways that African Americans find offensive, in part due to the potential for economic backlash. Still, as Hurt (2006) notes, representations of black men continue to be "in a box," due to African American consumption of images that categorize them as violent and hypersexual. Similarly, the "in-the-box" depictions of Asian masculinity, grounded in both historical and cultural constructions of Otherness, continue to be upheld because not enough consumers turn away from them. In the global marketplace of consumption, films such as *Rush Hour* draw significant audiences and have even higher demand in DVD (legal or pirated) sales, making it even more difficult to justify any financial incentive to stop the marginalizing and stereotyping of Asian masculinity. Part of Chan's popularity in the Asian film market is that he plays the comedic protagonist, which is in stark contrast to more stoic protagonists such as Chow Yun Fat and Jet Li. While consumers in countries such as China, Taiwan, Japan, and Singapore might be offended by some of *Rush Hour*'s depictions of Asian masculinity, particularly when it comes to the universalizing of East Asian cultural identities, there are enough cultural products in those countries that offset the negative stereotypes in a "foreign" film. On the other hand, martial arts, mysticism, vilification, and buffoonery have been the most common images of Asian men in the Western markets, making *Rush Hour* a reaffirmation of what is already familiar to the Western media consumer. In the absence of any significant demand for more diverse representation or any other financial incentives, Jackie Chan and his tropes of Asian masculinity will continue to be the norm in Western-produced films. To return to Negus's idea, the cultural industries might have some investment in producing and distributing culture, but when caricatures have saturated the market for decades, the need for accurate and culturally sensitive portrayals of Asian masculinity becomes obsolete. Bottom-line considerations trump accuracy, particularly when cultural industries have become more risk averse in the production and distribution of images as commodities (Ryan, 1992; Shu, 2003; Meehan, 2005; Hesmondhalgh, 2007; Balaji, 2008).

As a result, the discourse of Asian masculinity and its representations in Western media will continue to be predicated upon the stereotypical images seen in popular films and television shows. Until these representations no longer become economically beneficial to the corporations that produce them, they will continue to be replicated and (re)distributed to a global audience, reinforcing the hegemonic masculine ideal that has served to keep Asian masculinity as the constant Other.

Notes

1. Though the term "Asian" includes people from diverse countries in the Middle East, South Asia, and Southeast Asia, this chapter focuses on depictions of Chinese and, to a lesser extent, Japanese masculinities.

2. It should be noted that Asian and Asian American men are conflated, since, as Eng (2001) points out, they are equally disempowered and marginalized in popular culture representations.

References

Bailey, C. (1988). N***er/Lover: The Thin Sheen of Race in "Something Wild." *Screen*, 29(4), 28–40.

Balaji, M. (2008). Bollyville, U.S.A: The Commodification of the Other and MTV's Construction of the "Ideal Type" Desi. *Democratic Communique*, 22(1), 23–40.

Balaji, M. (2009). Owning Black Masculinity: The Intersection of Cultural Commodification and Self-Construction in Music Videos. *Communication, Culture & Critique*, 2, 21–38.

Banerjee, M. (2006). The *Rush Hour* of Black/Asian Coalitions? Jackie Chan and Blackface Minstrelsy. In H. Raphael-Hernandez & S. Steen (Eds.), *AfroAsian Encounters: Culture, History, Politics* (pp. 204–21). New York: New York University Press.

Banks, M. A. (2007). *The Politics of Cultural Work*. New York: Palgrave Macmillan.

Bettig, R. V. (1996). *Copyrighting Culture: The Political Economy of Intellectual Property*. Boulder, Colo.: Westview Press.

Bhabha, H. K. (1994). *The Location of Culture*. New York: Routledge.

Chan, J. W. (2000). Bruce Lee's Fictional Models of Masculinity. *Men and Masculinities*, 2, 371–87.

Collins, P. H. (2005). *Black Sexual Politics: African Americans, Gender, and the New Racism.* New York: Routledge.

Condit, C. (1989). The Rhetorical Limits of Polysemy. *Critical Studies in Mass Communication*, 6, 103–22.

Connell, R. W. (2001). The Social Organization of Masculinity. In S. M. Whitehead & F. J. Barrett (Eds.), *The Masculinities Reader* (pp. 30–49). Cambridge, U.K.: Polity.

Eng, D. L. (2001). *Racial Castration: Managing Masculinity in Asian America.* Durham, N.C.: Duke University Press.

Espiritu, Y. L. (1997). *Asian American Woman and Men: Labor, Laws, and Love.* Thousand Oaks, Calif.: Sage.

Fiske, J. (1997). National, Local? Some Problems of Culture in a Postmodern Word. *Velvet Light Trap*, 40, 56–66.

Hesmondhalgh, D. (2007). *The Cultural Industries.* London: Sage.

Holtzman, L. (2000). *Media Messages: What Film, Television and Popular Music Teach Us about Race, Class, Gender, and Sexual Orientation.* Armonk, N.Y.: M.E. Sharpe.

hooks, b. (1994). *Black Looks: Race and Representation.* Boston: South End Press.

hooks, b. (2003). *We Real Cool: Black Men and Masculinity.* New York: Routledge.

Hurt, B. (2006). *Hip-hop: Beyond Beats and Rhymes* (Video Recording). Northampton, Mass.: Media Education Foundation.

Jhally, S. (1989). The Political Economy of Culture. In S. Jhally and I. Angus (Eds.), *Cultural Politics in Contemporary America* (pp. 217–29). New York: Routledge.

Ling, J. (1997). Identity Crisis and Gender Politics: Reappropriating Asian American Masculinity. In K. Cheung (Ed.), *An Interethnic Companion to Asian American Literature* (pp. 312–37). New York: Cambridge University Press.

McChesney, R. W. (2004). *The Problem of the Media: U.S. Communication Politics in the 21st Century.* New York: Monthly Review Press.

Meehan, E. (2005). *Why TV Is Not Our Fault: Television Programming, Viewers, and Who's Really in Control.* Lanham, Md.: Rowman & Littlefield.

Nakayama, T. K. (1994). Show/down Time: "Race," Gender, Sexuality, and Popular Culture. *Critical Studies in Mass Communication*, 11, 162–79.

Negus, K. (1998). Cultural Production and the Corporation: Musical Genres and the Strategic Management of Creativity in the US Recording Industry. *Media, Culture & Society*, 20, 359–79.

Negus, K. (2004). The Business of Rap: Between the Street and the Executive Suite. In M. Forman and M. A. Neal (Eds.), *That's the Joint: The Hip-Hop Studies Reader* (pp. 525–40). New York: Routledge.

Paek, H. J., & Shah, H. (2003). Racial Ideology, Model Minorities, and the "Not-So-Silent Partner": Stereotyping of Asian-Americans in U.S. Magazine Advertising. *Howard Journal of Communication*, 14, 225–43.

Rotundo, E. A. (1994). *American Manhood.* New York: Basic Books.

Ryan, B. (1992). *Making Capital from Culture: The Corporate Form of Capitalist Cultural Production*. Berlin: Walter de Gruyter.

Said, E. (2003). *Orientalism*. New York: Vintage.

Sayer, A. (2001). For a Critical Cultural Political Economy. *Antipode, 33*(4), 687–708.

Shek, Y. L. (2006). Asian American Masculinity: A Review of the Literature. *Journal of Men's Studies,* 14, 379–91.

Shu, Y. (2003). Reading the Kung-Fu Film in an American Context: From Bruce Lee to Jackie Chan. *Journal of Popular Film and Television,* 31, 50–59.

Tierney, S. M. (2006). Themes of Whiteness in *Bulletproof Monk, Kill Bill,* and *The Last Samurai. Journal of Communication,* 56, 607–24.

Towbin, M., Haddock, S. A., Zimmerman, T. S., Lund, L. K., & Tanner, L. R. (2003). Images of Gender, Race, and Sexual Orientation in Disney Feature-Length Animated Films. *Journal of Feminist Family Therapy,* 15, 19–42.

Uchida, A. (1998). The Orientalization of Asian Women in America. *Women's Studies International Forum,* 21, 161–74.

9

Body Politics
Masculinities in Sport

KATH WOODWARD

Introduction

This chapter explores some of the processes through which embodied masculinities are reproduced and experienced in sport. These processes inextricably bring together the materiality of bodies and the social and cultural practices through which identifications in particular versions of masculinity are made. Sport has strong and long-lasting associations with both masculinity and embodiment and I seek to explore some of the interconnections between the two by looking at the centrality of bodies and body practices in sport and the histories of embodied masculinity that have such powerful resonance in sporting narratives, especially those of social exclusion and the struggles against inequalities. I have chosen to focus upon a sport where corporeality is pivotal, a contact sport that might seem to be both the most physically dangerous (although it is not actually top of the league table for injuries) and the most dramatic, with its one-on-one contact and pugilistic associations, namely boxing. Boxing highlights the physicality of sport, through the routine rigorous training regimes, which also characterize all sports and, especially, in its own practices; no other sport actually awards points or an outright victory to the person who renders the opponent unconscious, deliberately. Because bodies are so central to boxing, the sport offers an excellent site for theorizing gendered embodiment, especially in a sport that is also marked by histories of racism and social exclusion. A focus upon bodies in sport can present problems; even more so with boxing, which is beset by inequalities of class, race, ethnicity, impairment, generation, and location, which might entail the risk of reducing the self to the body by dwelling on the embodied aspects of selfhood at the expense of other dimensions, notably the intellectual and affective. These different dimensions of inequality are interconnected and demonstrate the social implications and situations of embodiment. My aim is to explore the possibilities of rethinking embodiment without such reductionism, but within a framework that retains the materiality of corporeality in the configuration of embodied identifications and acknowledges the importance of bodies themselves as situations through which gendered identities are forged.

Unequal Bodies: Differentiation

Sports such as boxing have been seen as an appropriate route for black and minority ethnic young men to gain self-respect and escape poverty (Sammons, 1988). Narratives of escape from poverty and the ghetto have leant enormous weight to the cultural capital of boxing (Berkowitz & Ungar, 2007; Boddy, 2008). Boxing embodies and performs anxieties about class, gender, race, ethnicity, and sexuality. However, such a path may also include the reinstatement of inequalities and assume a reductionist view of embodied identifications.

Sporting masculinities present problems for theories of embodied identification, for example, through the possibility of devaluing the body in relation to the mind. For black athletes, the celebration of body practices in sport may be at the expense of success in intellectual practices. For example, the long tradition of boxing as a route out of poverty for migrant young men, in particular, can mean that it is the only escape and physical capital the sole investment, overriding other forms of cultural capital, which could, for example, be accessed through education and intellectual activity. Phenomenological accounts of the often contradictory experiences of lived bodies in sport have challenged the mind-body binary (Bourdieu, 1990; Crossley, 2000; Merleau-Ponty, 1962; Wacquant, 1995a; Young, 2005). Other versions of the thinking body engage with the psychosocial dimensions of the self, such as Jefferson (1996), allowing the possibility of seeing the self as an assemblage of inner and outer worlds. This chapter sets out the issues relating to taking an embodied understanding of gendered identification in the case of masculinities in sport and suggests some solutions to the limitations through an approach that encompasses material bodies as situations and as situated, drawing upon the feminist work of Simone de Beauvoir as developed by Iris Marion Young.

Masculinities

Global sport remains largely dominated by the "men's game" in so many fields (Messner, 2002). However, the "men's game" does not necessarily invoke an unproblematic, hegemonic masculinity (Connell, 1995, 2002, 2005). The centrality of bodies and the measures of embodiment are part of the culture of sport which offers such primacy to masculinities, but sporting masculinities are ambivalent and ambiguous, too, and are subject to the cultural transformations of other gendered identifications (Woodward, 2009b, 2007).

Men's boxing holds out the promise of a more stable trajectory; the sport retains a high degree of cultural dominance and its genealogy is strongly configured around its associations with traditional masculinity. Joyce Carol Oates expresses this powerfully: "Boxing is for men and is about men, and is men" (1987, p. 72). Her comment is more than an empirical observation about the people who take part; it is also an expression of the powerfully gendered metaphors of the sport. Women have been prize fighters (Hargreaves, 2002) and women's boxing has a long history. The sport has achieved considerable popularity among women, especially in the United States in recent years (WBAN, 2010). Despite the popularity of other, less mainstream, forms of boxing, like mixed martial arts (MMA) and cage fighting, in which women have also participated, men's boxing in particular reconstitutes the culture of boxing legends and constructs the myths of masculinity in which practitioners and followers make attachments. Boxing is not just about men; it is about masculinity and the processes through which particular versions of masculinity are re-created.

Boxing has contributed to the genealogy of cultural masculinities, although these might have passed unstated, as taken for granted. However, as Robert A. Nye notes in his review of literature on masculinity: "Men are no longer the invisible, unmarked gender, the Archimedean point from which all norms, laws and rights flow; men are themselves the objects of the gaze of women, of other men and of a new critical scholarship that is deeply informed by the feminist insights . . . and scholarship of pioneers in the study of masculinity" (2005, p. 1,938).

Some of the detailed work that has been conducted on masculinities has pointed to the complicity or collusion that takes place at particular sites, of which sport is a good example (Connell, 2005). Connell's concept of hegemonic masculinity (1995) remains useful for exploring some of the ways in which masculinities are constituted in historically specific contexts, because it incorporates a social constructionist approach with an acknowledgment of the importance of the material body and its body-reflexive practices. It includes the systems of race, class, and ethnicity through which hegemonic masculinity is forged and reinstated and the networks of organizers, spectators, and reporters, as well as the embodied practitioners. Much of the engagement of recent work on masculinity has been in dialogue with Connell's conceptualization (McKay, Messner, & Sabo, 2000: Whitehead, 2002). Sport is a social world that remains dominated by strong configurations of traditional masculinities (Messner, 2002), although this is changing and many women are challenging these attachments through their participation in a wide range of sports. Messner maps peer collaboration in the performance of violent masculinity, which is most frequent in the revenue-producing contact sports. Status is accorded to conformity with a particular code of heterosexual masculinity, which resonates with Connell's hegemonic masculinity. Messner's "manhood formula" (2002, p. 123), which he bases upon evidence of U.S. media coverage, describes a script that is rehearsed and replayed by gendered performances.

Boxing draws on stories of its heroes and anti-heroes, from a history marked by traditional masculinities (Boddy, 2008; Woodward, 2007) that have been associated with physical strength and force and courage, and is thus a place where one might expect to find the entrenchment of tradition through the iteration of hegemonic masculinity and its articulation as a "manhood formula," as well as some resistance to the emerging "new masculinities." It is those who have experienced marginalization, racism, and exclusion who have often sought some security within the culture and practice of boxing, and often the white middle-class men who have occupied its peripheries through boxing's cultural networks. Hegemonic masculinity is an idealized concept premised upon men's supposed superiority over both women and other men who do not comply with its requirements. Although many, if not all men, do not achieve the apparent mental and physical status of hegemonic masculinity, many men and women behave as if it represented actuality. Hegemonic masculinity involves the configuration of gender practices that guarantee (or are taken to guarantee) the dominant position of men and the subordination of women and of those men who do not conform to its racialized, ethnicized, sexualized, and heterosexualized standard. More recent reworkings of the concept of hegemonic masculinity have used a geographical framework of levels and have highlighted the ambiguity of boundaries between the masculinity that is manifest in one context, at one level and in another (Connell & Messerschmidt, 2005), thus allowing for the complexities of experiences of masculinity.

Boxing masculinities have also been most powerfully made within the politics of race. Boxing has provided a significant site for the fight against racism and the assertion of a heroic black masculinity. Muhammad Ali is an important figure in this tradition (Marqusee, 2000; Hauser, 1991) that is particularly resonant in the history of the sport in the United States dating back to the struggles of black boxers, such as Jack Johnson's against white supremacy and Joe Louis's great comeback to defeat Hitler's champion, the white Max Schmeling in 1938 (Sammons, 1988). Mike Tyson has occupied a more ambiguous position, combining, at different moments hero and more frequently anti-hero (O'Connor, 2002). Black boxers are at some moments included in heroic masculinity, but at others they are subject to the othering and exclusion of the hegemony of white racism in the cultural narratives of boxing and its representation (Grieveson, 1998). Boxing heroes have been at the forefront of challenging the dominance of whiteness as well as being subjected to its exploitation. Joe Louis's defeat of Schmeling has been described as "a test of freedom and democracy versus Nazi philosophy and totalitarianism. It was the clearest symbolic confrontation between good and evil in the history of sport" (Hauser, 2007). Here boxing is incorporated into U.S. democracy and the discourse of freedom, with hegemonic masculinity offering a space in which heroic status is accorded through intersections of racialization, class, and gender for men in boxing.

Connell's concept of hegemonic masculinity remains useful, not so much because of the actual dominance of men, but the normalization of attachments to this version of masculinity and its focus upon the social, cultural, and embodied processes through which this masculinity is reconstituted. Gendered attachments can override others and provide a space within this social world in which some socially excluded "outsiders" have been able to negotiate their own identities to some extent.

Bodies are gendered and carry different status. In boxing, masculinity has higher value than femininity, economically, culturally, and as material bodies, because traditional masculinities have dominated the sport of boxing and its heroes and its body practices. The concept of hegemonic masculinity provides a useful concept for exploring how gendered identifications are made because it brings in all those who identify with boxing masculinities and not just the people who actually box, and it shows how material bodies and culture are inextricably linked. Individuals live the masculinity that has the highest cultural capital and social value, as shown by films, legends, and the media (Boddy, 2008; Woodward, 2007).

Cultured Bodies: Embodiment

The sexing of bodies as female or male can itself be seen as a social process (Butler, 1990). Rather than the material body determining the sex it is accorded, it is the social and cultural meanings given to that body that create it as female or male; sex itself is an inscription upon the body that comes to be taken for granted as natural. Butler draws upon the work of Michel Foucault (1977), who used the notion of inscription to argue that bodies do not exist in some unmediated natural realm that is unaffected by social and political relations. Gender relations and inequalities are part of the political field that Butler identifies and these gender divisions dominate sport, which abounds with regulatory practices through which bodies and what we do with them are disciplined and configured. Similarly in the case of race, the categories that organize people in sport are not just the result of the sort of body they have, but also of the social and historical circumstances, which means that bodies are the *effect* and not the *cause* of the particular categories that are used (Foucault, 1977). What also matters is what people do with their bodies, that is the practices, routines, and technologies with which they engage. It is through these practices that attachments and possible transformations are made. Bodies are not just the passive recipients of the social world that constructs them; social bodies can act as well as be acted upon. As Foucault notes, practices "permit individuals to effect by their own means or with the help of others a certain number of operations in their own bodies and some thoughts, conduct and way of being, so as to transform themselves" (Foucault, 1988, p. 18). Boxing requires dedicated training regimes, and boxers' bodies are not only subjected to grueling fitness programs but also to injury, whether in the ring, in a sport that necessarily involves being hit and hitting your opponent, or in the gym, for example, in the hand injuries that are so often incurred in this most contact of sports. Boxers *are* their bodies in a most powerful sense through the routine practices of the sport.

Social bodies have been seen as the product of historical and social processes. In more extreme social constructionist views, it might seem that the body is only a social construct and hardly a material body at all. An overemphasis upon social bodies might marginalize the material bodies and their practices and experiences, which constitute some of the techniques through which selves might be transformed. Foucault suggested that bodies were inscribed with power relations, but that individuals participate in the regulation of their own bodies and selves through disciplinary practices in an approach that might be too disembodied for an analysis of boxing masculinities; cultured embodiment redresses this imbalance.

Cultured Embodiment

The experience of the material body is most dramatically represented and experienced in boxing through the risks to which boxers subject themselves. Boxers are constantly reminded of the frailty as well as the strength of the flesh, and have been throughout the sport's history (Early, 1994; Gorn, 1986; Sammons, 1988). The dangers of the sport suggest that explanations of the processes of attachment have to encompass material bodies that feel pain, bleed and suffer, and go beyond the processes of regulation and inscription. Boxers are not simply shaped by external forces; they are their bodies too. How are these bodies implicated in the exercise of control? How are bodies *situations* as well as *situated* by social and cultural forces?

The perceived risks of the sport and the very real threat of physical pain and possibly damage in the ring might suggest that boxers need to exercise enormous control, which could be expressed as "mind over matter" in commonsense parlance. The relationship between mind and body is one that has concerned not only work that has been done on sport, but also has been expressed in the wider field of academic study on the status of "the body" and bodies. In thinking about how attachments are formed and, especially, why boxers take part in their sport, the particular routine practices of the social world are important. What is happening when people subject themselves to such punishing regimes and expose themselves to possible pain and injury? Are they exercising "mind over matter" and consciously forcing their bodies to go on? How useful is a distinction between "mind" and "body"? The phenomenological notion of the term "embodiment" overcomes the problem of either having to separate mind from body or of marginalizing the physical dimensions of gendered identifications. Material bodies become part of the equation and make up identities rather than being "mere" flesh that has to be controlled and disciplined.

Body Practices: Minds and Bodies

Boxing offers an important site for the development of understanding about how "we are our bodies" in a form of "direct embodiment" (Wacquant, 2004, p. 60) where there is no distinction made between mind and body. Sociologists have drawn upon phenomenological accounts to theorize "the body" and to address problems about the status of bodies in the making of selves (Crossley, 2004, 2005).

Loïc Wacquant adopts a practice-based approach that is strongly influenced by Maurice Merleau-Ponty's phenomenological account, in order to address not only the question of how boxers engage in their sport but why. Wacquant deploys this approach, through which Merleau-Ponty sought to overcome mind-body dualism, in order to understand boxers' "willing embrace and submission to the pain and rigour of their chosen sport" (Wacquant, 1995a, p. 88). Wacquant acknowledges the social and economic context of boxing and the argument that boxers are likely to have only physical capital to invest in their attachment to this social world. However, he seeks to find an explanation of the processes through which boxers become part of this social world and transform themselves within it, which is not only dependent upon economic disadvantage. He claims that for the boxer, "There is an *unconscious fit between his (pugilistic) habitus and the very field which has produced it. . . .* The boxer's desire to fight flows from a practical *belief* constituted in and by the immediate co-presence of, and mutual understanding between, his (re) socialized body and the game" (1995a, p. 88; emphases in original).

In his work, Wacquant draws upon Pierre Bourdieu's concept of *habitus* as the system of dispositions and set of ways of doing things and thinking about them that belongs to specific societies (Bourdieu, 1977). Bourdieu's conceptualization has parallels with the phenomenological account of lived bodies and of situated bodies in Simone de Beauvoir's work. The relationship between habitus and the individual is materialized through these practical beliefs. "Practical belief" is not a state of mind but rather a "state of body" (Bourdieu, 1990, p. 68).

> The boxer wilfully perseveres into this potentially self-destructive trade because, in a very real sense, he is inhabited by the game he inhabits. A veteran middleweight who has "rumbled" on three continents for over a decade and who reported breaking his hands twice and his foot once, persistent problems with his knuckles (because of calcium deposits forming around them) as well as a punctured ear drum and several facial cuts necessitating stitches, reveals his . . . acceptance, made body of the states of pugilism when he fails to find cause for alarm in his string of injuries: "Sure you do think about it, but then you regroup yourself, start thinkin', you can't, *it's in your blood so much,* you can't, you been doin' it so long, you can't give it up." (Wacquant, 1995a, p. 88)

Mind and body are one through "the shared belief in, and collectively manufactured illusion of the value of the games (real) men play [which] becomes progressively instilled and inscribed in a particular biological in-dividual" (Wacquant, 1995c, p. 173). Wacquant's understanding of inscription goes further than a purely social process in order to produce an understand-ing of embodied attachment, which permits agency, through which body and mind are one. His approach is one that adopts a methodology of *observing participation*. It is worth noting that this is materialized through Wacquant himself becoming an active participant in boxing (Wacquant, 2004). It is thus through corporeal engagement that the attachment becomes "natural" and "in the blood." That which seems "natural" in the attraction of boxing to black and ethnic minority men especially, is not the result of having particular physical characteristics, but through routine practices, which are cultural, social, and driven by economic factors.

Wacquant's account is persuasive in describing the processes of embodied attachment that take place, for example, in training regimes and the commit-ment of boxers to their sport. Boxers *are* their bodies and only become boxers through practice and physical engagement. It is not possible to differentiate between mind and body or body and self. Such ethnographic accounts, which draw upon Merleau-Ponty's notion of embodiment, give high priority to body practices in the making of attachments and demonstrate how engagement in the pugilistic activity of boxing works. This could, of course, apply to any activity in which practice is so effective that actions are carried out without reflection. This is not to suggest that great athletes do not think or make judgments. Judgments are only possible through a synchrony of mind and body made possible through the naturalness of routines; training involves practice and a repeated iteration of acts that ultimately eliminate the need for reflection. This version of lived experience also demonstrates the body as situation and provides a route into understanding the naturalization of gendered identities as well as sporting practices. Not only are the actions of the pugilist "in the blood" to the extent that they are both normalized and naturalized, the framework can also be used to explain how cultured mascu-linities "work." Wacquant's account is particularly useful in its focus on the practices of the material body and on demonstrating how mind and body are one, although it is based on the assumption that there are no disruptions or conflicts and the synchrony of mind and body always works.

Wacquant's account also assumes rather than explores associations with masculinity as constituted and experienced in the social world of boxing and suggests a universal embodiment that fails to accommodate the specificities of gender (Woodward, 2007, 2009a). A generic and universal mind-body elision is assumed. I suggest that a more useful application of the approach is to deploy it to explain the processes of naturalization whereby gendered and racialized identities are assumed to be biological. The absence of gender difference is, however, one of the criticisms of Merleau-Ponty's approach as taken up by Wacquant, which has been more directly addressed within the tradition of phenomenology through Young's development of the feminist work of Simone de Beauvoir, and in the analyses of masculinities and body-reflexive practices in the work of Connell, which also challenges the determinism of accounts based on body practices and suggests more differentiated and complex embodied identifications than are implied in accounts such as Wacquant's.

The phenomenological concept of embodiment provides a useful means of combining mind and body in an analysis of some of the processes of attachment. Powerful links are made between individuals and social worlds through an embodied self. Individuals are actively implicated in their relationships with their bodies where mind and body operate in symbiosis, rather than passively. Mind and body come together in practical belief, which provides a means of explaining why boxers become attached to a masculinity that involves such apparently risky practices through a merging of the social world and the material body. Accounts such as Wacquant's are effective in challenging the mind/body binary, but less so in explaining the gendered embodied practices that constitute the body as situation, that is the material body that acts as well as being acted upon.

Lived Bodies: Bodies as Situations

The body clearly matters. For example, boxers are haunted by the risk of physical damage; having to negotiate a body that is impaired creates a completely different experience of the world and of the self than having the previously experienced athletic, powerful body. The world reacts in different ways to the impaired than to the fit strong body and boxing bodies do break down and are damaged in many different ways, ranging from the routine injuries incurred in training to severe damage from which they may never recover, as in the case of Gerald McClellan in his fight against Nigel Benn in 1995, or what was described as mental breakdown in the ring in the case of Oliver McCall in 1997. Boxers have died in the ring; the first woman to do so in modern times was Becky Zerlentes, in 2005.

The meanings of this body are not written on its surface; boxing bodies are not only not "mere inscriptions" or even the product of training regimes. Following de Beauvoir's use of the work of Merleau-Ponty, the human body can be seen as ambiguous, subject to natural laws and to the human production of meaning. According to de Beauvoir, "It is not merely as a body, but rather as a body subject to taboos, to laws, that the subject becomes conscious of himself and attains fulfilment—it is with reference to certain values that he valorizes himself. To repeat once more: physiology cannot ground any values; rather, the facts of biology take on the values that the existent bestows upon them" (1989, p. 76).

Bodies are weighed, measured, and trained for the sport and become situations because it is through experience and practices as well as corporeality that masculinity becomes lived. As Toril Moi argues "lived experience is, as it were, sedimented over time through my interactions with the world and thus itself becomes part of my situatedness" (Moi, 1999, p. 63). Bodies are crucial to an understanding of selfhood and the processes through which people position themselves and are positioned within the social world. For many black ethnic minority or migrant people, especially men, physical capital is their only investment and boxing is the route to realizing some return on that investment as is manifest in the histories of diverse black, African, African Caribbean, Jewish, Irish, gypsy, traveler boxers (Boddy, 2008; Sugden, 1996). As de Beauvoir notes, "The body is not a thing, it is a situation: it is the instrument of our grasp upon the world, a limiting factor for projects" (de Beauvoir, 1989, p. 66).

De Beauvoir's approach, which has significant parallels with Merleau-Ponty's, informs many such critiques and focuses upon having a specific kind of body and the meaning that body has for the situated individual. However, de Beauvoir foregrounds the gendered dimensions of the situation *and* the situated body, unlike Merleau-Ponty, which means including the body as object, as situation, lived experience, gendered myths and embodied sex/gender, rather than "simple" sex/gender or mind/body binaries (de Beauvoir, 1989). This approach provides a way of bringing together the enfleshed, material body and the situation that re-creates the lived body. Bodies are not "just" in a situation, nor just objects of empirical or scientific inquiry, although, of course, science can both describe and treat bodies and sport is a key site where this happens, but it is not enough; bodies are more than this. De Beauvoir's analysis of the "lived body" provides a means of enabling, what Rosi Braidotti has called "a situated way of seeing the subject based on the understanding that the most important location or situation is the roots of the subject in the spatial frame of the body" (Braidotti, 1994, p. 161).

The idea of the lived body offers an explanation of how, in everyday life, people think of themselves as "this body" that sets the boundaries of who they are, where one's self is distinguished from another by the body they inhabit. Boxing masculinities are practiced and lived in the gym and in the ring through actions and experiences that constitute a masculinity that is configured around control, regulation, physical strength and skill, and a language of tempered aggression, which is coded male (Woodward, 2007, 2009b; Oates, 1987). De Beauvoir's emphasis on situated lived bodies can contribute most usefully to an analysis of body practices if it is developed to focus upon the modalities, meanings, and implications of actual, moving bodies, although her account does not accommodate such specific exploration (Young, 2005; Moi, 1999). Young argues that the specificities of experience and practice should be the focus of analyses of gender, setting up a framework in which other embodied attachments can be understood. In order to do this, Young draws upon de Beauvoir's feminist existentialist approach, in which being-in-the-world consists of projecting purposes and goals that structure "being situated" through the opposing forces of transcendence, which involves going beyond the body and immanence. Young demonstrates how bodies operate in space, and in her work she describes how this works specifically for women by explicitly examining the comportment of girls.

Young makes a strong case for the gender differentiation that takes place through bodily comportment and motility, and, unlike Wacquant, focuses not only upon women's experience but on gender as a dimension of experience. Her analysis is influenced by de Beauvoir's critique of the lived body, which for Young is most importantly set in particular social and cultural situations that frequently privilege masculinity, and she reflects upon the processes of objectification that shape women's bodily experiences. These processes clearly have relevance for embodied masculinity, which similarly can be located within the wider situation. This wider situation is also one in which gender identities are not homogenous. While de Beauvoir was arguing that gender privilege operates as if there were only one category of masculinity, boxing offers a site at which those who develop attachments to the gender identities that are available are far from privileged, for example in relation to class, ethnicity, and race. Those who have experienced racialization and ethnicization have used boxing as a form of resistance (Boddy, 2008). Men who box are also likely to suffer the limitations of intentionality to which Young refers in the other social worlds of which they are part. Even those who achieve enormous success and have exceptionally high degrees of competence, like Mike Tyson, are still constrained by racialized cultural regimes and the contradictions of their own biographies (Boddy, 2008; Oates, 1987; O'Connor, 2002).

Young's approach, which deploys the phenomenological concept of embodiment, attempts to redress the imbalance in Merleau-Ponty's work by focusing on gender and, in particular, the specificities of women's embodiment. Young challenges the universal account of the gender-neutral body implied by Merleau-Ponty and claims that the female body is not simply experienced as a direct communication with the active self, but is also experienced as an object. She suggests that there are distinctive manners of comportment and movement that are associated with women (hence "Throwing Like a Girl" as the title of her original essay on the subject). Young attributes these different modalities, firstly, to the social spaces in which women learn to comport themselves. In terms of sport this involves constraints of space and learning to act in less assertive and aggressive ways than men. Conversely, from this it might be deduced that men acquire those embodied practices, as in boxing, that are aggressive. Boxing is about throwing punches "like a man." Secondly, Young suggests women are encouraged to see themselves through the gaze of others, including the "male gaze" (Mulvey, 1975) and to become more aware of themselves as objects of the scrutiny of others. Similarly, men who box view themselves through the gaze of heroic masculinity as enacted in the sport and by its public heroes (Boddy, 2008; Woodward, 2007), and often embody the possibilities of resistance achieved in the sport by its heroic figures, the greatest of which must be Muhammad Ali (Ali & Durham, 1975; Hauser, 1991; Marqusee, 2000).

Masculinities are gendered identifications made through bodily comportment and dispositions involving the constitutive ways in which bodies move in different spaces. These dispositions are gender specific and not the property of biological bodies, but manifest through the "lived body." Embodied gendered identifications, too, are made under intentional limitations that are situated. These situations, like the embodied individual that operates within them, are gendered.

Body-Reflexive Practices

Connell's approach foregrounds gender by addressing masculinity rather than femininity, developing the concept of hegemonic masculinity discussed above. Connell's conceptualization of body-reflexive practices provides a means of challenging the notion of the body as entirely socially constructed and determined by its social location and inscriptions. For boxing, this would mean sharing Wacquant's skepticism about economic and social factors being the main determinant for boxers, but suggesting more agency than his account seems to include. Connell retains an understanding of the body as having social dimensions. He uses the concept of body-reflexive practices to put the body back into its social context, while retaining the importance of the body in order to accommodate an understanding of bodies as having some agency. Thus, the body is both agent and object of practice and it is through these bodily practices that the structures within which bodies are formed and made meaningful and embodied identities are forged, defined, and organized. Through body-reflexive practices "more than individual lives are formed: a social world is formed" (Connell, 1995, p. 64). The idea of body-reflexive practices permits an understanding of the body as implicated in and addressed by social, temporal processes, without ceasing to be material bodies. Bodies are the world and are part of what makes social relations meaningful. Thus, masculinities are not only made up by body practices, they *are* body practices.

The pugilistic bodily activities that constitute boxing are made meaningful and create a social order aligned with a particular version of masculinity through a set of practices; routines in Wacquant's account (1995b, 2004). Boxing might appear to be a limited space, albeit one that includes the most traditional and expected of practices associated with masculinity, including those that involve strength, aggression, and the ability to inflict pain upon one's fellow combatant. However, these activities still operate within the wider social field and relate to other masculinities and other dimensions of masculinity. For example, hegemonic masculinity is associated with heterosexual assertiveness (Connell, 1995). Even if boxing may offer a homoerotic spectacle (Boddy, 2008; James, 1996) this is rarely if ever acknowledged in any ways in the sport by practitioners (Woodward, 2007). Heterosexuality is often expressed in sport through the visible presence of a female partner, for example as an anxious spectator, ringside in boxing films (Woodward, 2007). Boxers, like most competitive sportsmen, are discouraged from engaging in sexual activity in the period before competition (Sugden, 1996). This abstinence can be accommodated within hegemonic masculinity through the bodily practice of abstinence along with the explanation that the aggression of the libido is then translated into aggression against the opponent in the ring, thus configuring a particular masculine body as situation. The heterosexuality of this masculinity is uncompromised; its force unrestrained and even reconfirmed, just rechanneled. The punches directed at the targeted areas of the opponent's body are body practices that are part of the repertoire of the boxer and are situated within a framework both of understandings of masculinity and the regulatory apparatuses of the sport, which, for example, permits hits on the head and upper body but not below the belt.

Reflexive body practices mean that, "with bodies both objects and agents of practice and the practice itself forming the structures within which bodies are appropriated and defined" (Connell, 1995, p. 61), it is necessary to look in more detail at the spatial and temporal dimensions of these practices. The practices and the identities produced within and through them are subject to ambivalences and contradictions and to historical disruption. Connell proposes a three-fold model of the structure of gender that can be illustrated by Lafferty and McKay's study of the interactions between women and men in a boxing gym. Connell's three-fold model brings in the interplay between the different elements implicated in body-reflexive practices. Firstly, power relations incorporate the structure identified as patriarchy, albeit somewhat simplistically. Sometimes in boxing this is expressed simply, for example, in the explicit exaltation of men as "warriors, thereby 'proving' their biological superiority over women" (Lafferty & McKay, 2005, p. 256), although there is slippage between biological and embodied capacities. Second, Connell uses the structure of production relations, which includes the division of labor. In the gym, labor is illustrated by the lack of resources that women boxers are able to access in order to improve their competence and, especially, the association of women with "soft boxing" and men with the transformation of the body into a weapon (Lafferty & McKay, 2005, p. 256). "Soft boxing" is resonant of Young's description above of the specific dispositions and bodily comportment of women and the modalities of their embodiment. Cathexis, or emotional attachment, is Connell's third structure, which Lafferty and McKay use to locate the highly sexualized status of women in the sport, as card girls for example. In a mixed gym, they argue, women are presented as sexually tempting to men (Lafferty & McKay, 2005), which accords with much of the literature on boxing of women being excluded from gyms (Sammons, 1988; Sugden, 1996; Woodward, 1997, 2004). In this instance, women are permitted to participate but are still subject to the same regime of marginalization and sexualization. Lafferty and McKay include representation, which relates to the glorification of male boxers (in the gym as well as in the wider world outside) as an additional structure that informs their analysis. This is a useful way of demonstrating how boxing is a gender regime, especially in showing how sport can accommodate "difference" while not making any changes to its hyper-masculine structure (Lafferty & McKay, 2005, p. 274).

However, the universalism of claims about the gender binaries of boxing is also challenged by the incremental changes that are taking place. On revisiting the U.K. gym where I undertook my first fieldwork (Woodward, 2004), a gym from which women had been excluded, I found that there were, in 2008, a small number of women joining in training sessions (Woodward, 2009a). This demonstrates the accommodation of transformation and the possibilities of change that are afforded by using the framework of lived bodies and, especially, bodies as situations. Women's exclusion is not based on biological difference, although everyday, commonsense justifications of their marginalization are largely framed within a discourse of anatomy. Cultural shifts are made through the reconfiguration of selves through situations and body practices.

Bodies in the gym are the sites of these exclusionary practices of a gendered regime. However, the structures through which the regime is constituted also have to accommodate the cultural terrain that informs the body practices of the gym. If it is not the physical body that prevents wider and more successful participation in the sport, then the continuance of hegemonic masculinity has to be attributed to the gender regime and primarily to its cultural and social hold (Woodward, 2007, 2009). Particular masculinities do persist, in spite of multiple challenges and points at which they have been disrupted. Boxing is a site that offers evidence of strong attachments to traditional masculinities and regimes of gender exclusion, although, as some research has indicated, even in boxing gyms there are men who are also performing different masculinities in the rest of their lives (de Garis, 2000).

A fight includes the bodies of those in the ring and those of the spectators who perceive some greater authenticity in being physically present rather than being television viewers of a disembodied, sanitized event (Oates, 1987), but who are not engaged in the actual, physical conflict itself. The corporeal techniques that are practiced in the gym and in sparring and form the public presentation of boxing in the ring and in its representation constitute meanings about gender that extend far beyond the ring itself. The physical regime of training, with all its privations and routines, involves external factors, such as the advice of the trainer, the competitive spirit, including the encouragement to think and act antagonistically towards the opponent, even to hate him, and, finally and most importantly, the self-control (Woodward, 2007). These often involve the ability to control the pain and discipline that operate not only internally but are part of what constitutes this masculinity temporally and spatially. Pain is a large part of the experience of the boxer, especially in the training regime, largely because of the pressure under which athletes are put when they seek to achieve success in their sport. Boxers have to discipline themselves in order to achieve self-esteem and the respect of others as part of the traditional masculinity that involves standing up for yourself (Woodward, 2004). Bodily reflexive practices are not only internal to the individual boxer; they include social relations and institutions such as the regulatory bodies of the sport, as well as its whole culture and tradition.

Connell's idea of body-reflexive practices provides a means of redressing the problem of the "over-social" body, which is the body that is entirely socially constructed at the expense of any recognition of the material, living body. These body-reflexive practices incorporate power relations as experienced through the body and the social world, including its regulations and representations. Body-reflexive practices are located within the different spaces that constitute the social world of boxing—in the gym and the wider cultural terrain through the experiences of lived bodies.

Conclusion

Boxing offers a very particular social world, even within the field of the sports world, because of its strong associations with traditional, enfleshed masculinities and challenges to the inequalities of social relations. I suggest that it is also a particularly useful site at which to explore the ways in which identities are made and remade through body practices and through the idea of bodies as situations, a view that has application to an understanding of cultured subjectivities in the wider terrain. By deploying the concepts of body-reflexive practices and feminist phenomenological accounts of bodies as situations, albeit which have been developed in spaces far removed from sport and to explain women's experiences, I have endeavored to demonstrate some of the ways in which masculinities are formed and re-formed within racialized regimes. Boxing is not predominantly a sport associated with men and masculinity with so powerful a genealogy of heroic masculinity solely because men have bigger, stronger bodies than women or are more aggressive, but because its masculinities are configured through a range of body practices and social, cultural, and economic situations with which people engage and in which they are situated. The racialization of boxing is experienced and resisted by embodied selves, bodies as situations, but is not caused by embodiment. Body practices are situated within social and cultural processes and forces of exclusion and inclusion and there is not a simple narrative of progress. It is necessary to be attentive to bodies as situations within a context of intersecting social, cultural, and corporeal systems. Neither are boxing masculinities only part of a cultural narrative in which the main protagonists are male; bodies and their practices are inextricably part of the process. The familiarity of boxing as a sport enjoyed as a spectacle linked to traditional masculinities is also part of the situation through which gendered identifications are experienced. These masculinities are not simply learned; those who engage in the sport and who follow it become complicit in its strongly gendered practices, in the ring and in the gym.

References

Ali, M., and Durham, R. (1975). *The Greatest: My Own Story*. New York: Random House.

Berkowitz, M., & Ungar, R. (Eds). (2007). *Fighting Back? Jewish and Black Boxers in Britain*. London: UCL.

Boddy, K. (2008). *Boxing: A Cultural History*. London: Reaktion Books.

Bourdieu, P. (1977). *Outline of a Theory of Practice*. Cambridge: Cambridge University Press.

Bourdieu, P. (1990). *In Other Words*. Cambridge: Polity.

Braidotti, R. (1994). *Nomadic Subjects: Embodiment and Sexual Difference in Contemporary Feminist Theory*. New York: Columbia University Press.

Butler, J. (1990). *Gender Trouble: Feminism and the Subversion of Identity*. New York: Routledge.

Chandler, D. (Ed.). (1996). *Boxer: An Anthology of Writing on Boxing and Visual Culture*. London: Institute of Visual Arts.

Connell, R. W. (1995). *Masculinities*. Cambridge: Polity.

Connell, R. W. (2002). *Gender*. Cambridge: Polity.

Connell, R. W. (2005). Change among the Gatekeepers: Men, Masculinities, and Gender Equality in the Global Arena. *Signs*, 30(3), 1802–25.

Connell, R. W., & Messerschmidt, J. W. (2005). Hegemonic Masculinity: Rethinking the Concept. *Gender and Society*, 19(6), 829–59.

Crossley, N. (2001) *The Social Body: Habit, Identity, Desire*. London: Sage.

Crossley, N. (2004). The Circuit Trainer's Habitus: Reflexive Body Techniques and the Sociality of the Workout. *Body and Society*, 10, 37–69.

Crossley, N. (2005). Mapping Body Reflexive Techniques: On Body Modification and Maintenance. *Body and Society*, 11, 1–35.

de Beauvoir, S. (1989). *The Second Sex*. London: Vintage Books.

de Garis, L. (2000) "Be a Buddy to Your Buddy": Male Identity, Aggression, and Intimacy in a Boxing Gym. In J. McKay, M. Messner, & D. Sabo (Eds.), *Masculinities, Gender Relations, and Sport* (pp. 87–107). London: Sage.

Early, G. (1994). *The Culture of Bruising: Essays on Prizefighting, Literature, and Modern American Culture*. Hopewell, N.J.: Ecco.

Foucault, M. (1977). *Discipline and Punish: The Birth of the Prison*. Harmondsworth, U.K.: Penguin.

Foucault, M. (1988). Technologies of the Self. In L. Martin, H. Gutman, & P. Hutton (Eds.), *Technologies of the Self: A Seminar with Michel Foucault* (pp. 16–49). Amherst: University of Massachusetts Press.

Gorn, E. J. (1986). *The Manly Art: The Lives and Times of the Great Bare-Knuckle Champions.* London: Robson Books.

Grieveson, L. (1998). Fighting Films. *Cinema Journal,* 38(1), 40–72.

Hargreaves, J. (1994). *Sporting Females: Critical Issues in the History and Sociology of Women's Sports.* London: Routledge.

Hargreaves, J. (1996). Bruising Peg to Boxerobics: Gendered Boxing—Images and Meanings. In D. Chandler (Ed.), *Boxer: An Anthology of Writing on Boxing and Visual Culture* (pp. 121–31). Boston: MIT Press.

Hargreaves, J. (2002). *Heroines of Sport: The Politics of Difference and Identity.* London: Routledge.

Hauser, T. (1991). *Muhammad Ali: His Life and Times.* New York: Simon & Schuster.

Hauser, T. (2007). The Brown Bomber is Destroyed in His Last Ever Fight. *Observer Sport Monthly,* 53.

James, N. (1996). Raging Bulls: Sexuality and the Boxing Movie. In D. Chandler (Ed.), *Boxer: An Anthology of Writing on Boxing and Visual Culture* (pp. 113–19). Boston: MIT Press.

Jefferson, T. (1996). From "Little Fairy Boy" to "Complete Destroyer": Subjectivity and Transformation in the Biography of Mike Tyson. In M. Mac an Ghaill (Ed.), *Understanding Masculinities: Social Relations and Cultural Arenas* (pp.157–67). Buckingham, U.K.: Open University Press.

Lafferty, Y., and McKay, J. (2005). "Suffragettes in Satin Shorts?" Gender and Competitive Boxing. *Qualitative Sociology,* 27(3), 249–76.

Marqusee, M. (2000). *Redemption Song.* London: Verso.

McKay, J., Messner, M., & Sabo, D. (Eds.). (2000). *Masculinities, Gender Relations, and Sport.* London: Sage.

Merleau-Ponty, M. (1962). *Phenomenology of Perception.* New York: Routledge.

Messner, M. (2002). *Taking the Field: Women, Men, and Sports.* Minneapolis: University of Minnesota Press.

Moi, T. (1999). *What Is a Woman?* Oxford: Oxford University Press.

Mulvey, L. (1975). Visual Pleasure and Narrative Cinema. *Screen,* 16(3), 6–18.

Nye, R. A. (2005). Locating Masculinity: Some Recent Work on Men. *Signs,* 30(31), 1937–62.

Oates, J. C. (1987). *On Boxing.* London: Bloomsbury.

O'Connor, D. (Ed) (2002). *Iron Mike: A Mike Tyson Reader.* New York: Thunder's Mouth Press.

Sammons, J. (1988). *Beyond the Ring: The Role of Boxing in American Society.* Urbana: University of Illinois Press.

Sugden, J. (1996). *Boxing and Society: An International Analysis.* Manchester: Manchester University Press.

Wacquant, L. (1995a). Pugs at Work: Bodily Capital and Bodily Labour among Professional Boxers. *Body and Society,* 1(1), 65–93.

Wacquant, L. (1995b). The Pugilistic Point of View: How Boxers Think about Their Trade. *Theory and Society,* 24(4), 489–535.

Wacquant, L. (1995c). Review Article, "Why Men Desire Muscles." *Body and Society,* 1, 163–79.

Wacquant, L. (2001). Whores, Slaves, and Stallions: Languages of Exploitation and Accommodation among Professional Fighters. *Body and Society,* 7, 181–94.

Wacquant, L. (2004). *Body and Soul: Notebooks of an Apprentice Boxer.* Oxford: Oxford University Press.

Whitehead, S. M. (2002). *Men and Masculinities.* Cambridge, U.K.: Polity.

Women's Boxing Archive Network (WBAN). Accessed March 23, 2010, from: http://www.womenboxing.com

Woodward, K. (2004). Rumbles in the Jungle: Boxing, Racialization, and the Performance of Masculinity. *Leisure Studies,* 23(1), 1–13.

Woodward, K. (2007). *Boxing, Masculinity, and Identity: The "I" of the Tiger.* London: Routledge.

Woodward, K. (2009). Hanging Out and Hanging About: Insider/Outsider Research in the Sport of Boxing. *Ethnography,* 9(4), 536–60.

Woodward, K. (2009a). Bodies on the Margins: Regulating Bodies, Regulatory Bodies. *Leisure Studies,* 28(2), 143–56.

Woodward, K. (2009b). *Embodied Sporting Practices: Regulating and Regulatory Bodies.* Basingstoke, U.K.: Palgrave MacMillan.

Young, I. M. (2005). *On Female Body Experience: "Throwing Like a Girl" and Other Essays.* Oxford: Oxford University Press.

Contributors

BRYANT KEITH ALEXANDER, author of *Performing Black Masculinity: Race, Culture, and Queer Identity* (Alta Mira Press), is professor of communication and associate dean of the College of Arts & Letters at California State University, Los Angeles. His scholarship is interdisciplinary, contributing to the fields of communication and cultural studies, gender and queer studies, African American Studies, performance and pedagogical studies.

MOLEFI K. ASANTE is a professor of African American Studies at Temple University and one of the foremost scholars in Black Studies. He is formerly chair of communication at SUNY–Buffalo and is the author of more than sixty-five books, including most recently *Race, Rhetoric, and Identity: The Architecton of Soul.*

MURALI BALAJI is the Director of Education and Curriculum Reform at the Hindu American Foundation in Washington, D.C. He is the author of two books, including *The Professor and the Pupil: The Politics and Friendship of W. E. B. Du Bois and Paul Robeson*, and his research focuses on cultural production, political economy, and mediated representations of identity.

MAURICE HALL is associate professor of communication at Villanova University. The span of his research includes issues ranging from diversity training and strategic diversity management, to conflict management, team building, cross-cultural communication and leadership training for national and international clients. His most recent work explores the postcolonial culture of Jamaica.

RONALD L. JACKSON II, author of *Scripting the Black Masculine Identity in Popular Culture*, is dean of McMicken College of Arts & Sciences at the University of Cincinnati. His published works explore intersections and ne-gotiations of race, cultural identity, and gender.

SHINO KONISHI is an Indigenous Research Fellow at the National Museum of Australia, Canberra. She received an Australian Institute of Aboriginal and Torres Strait Islander Studies Research Grant with Leah Lui-Chivizhe, of the Koori Centre, to work on the project *Laying the Tracks: Torres Strait Islander Labour in Northern Australia*. Her research investigates the histories of Indigenous Australians in the nineteenth and twentieth centuries.

NIL MUTLUER, a doctoral student in the Department of Gender Studies at the Central European University in Budapest, is editor of the book *States of Gender: The Intersectional Borders of Gender in Turkey*. Her work examines how cultural, social, political, and economic institutions play a role in the formation of masculinities in various power-based contexts. She specifically explores gender, ethnicity, and nationalism among internally displaced Kurd-ish men in Tarlabaşı, Istanbul.

MICH NYAWALO is a doctoral student in the Department of Comparative Literature at Penn State University. His research interests include the politics of language in African literature, in addition to the social construction of masculinities in Kenya.

KATHLEEN GLENISTER ROBERTS, author of *Alterity and Narrative: Stories and the Negotiation of Western Identities*, is associate professor of communi-cation at Duquesne University. Her research focuses primarily on identities in conflict and interrogates narrative constructions of Western biases toward non-Western Others.

MARGARITA SAONA is associate professor of Spanish, French, Italian, and Portuguese at the University of Illinois at Chicago. Her work explores the impact of postcoloniality and historical trauma on the way masculinity is depicted in Peru and how, in turn, the image of a wounded manhood illus-trates how the equation of manhood and power has resulted in not only a pessimistic image of Peru, but also a sense of inadequacy regarding the ideal, unattainable, hegemonic masculinity.

KATH WOODWARD is professor and head of sociology at The Open University. She has published extensively in the areas of gender theory and identity studies and is the author of *Embodied Sporting Practices: Regulating and Regulatory Bodies*, among other works.

Index

The University of Illinois Press
is a founding member of the
Association of American University Presses.

University of Illinois Press
1325 South Oak Street
Champaign, IL 61820-6903
www.press.uillinois.edu